The sporting ground for our people has been a ground of truth and reconciliation, a proving ground for young men and women where black and white meet and play on equal terms and agreed rules. Black Pearls shares the proud history of First Nations sportspeople in shaping the sporting history of Australia. It is a story that can be told and retold.
Senator Patrick Dodson

This is a wonderfully insightful book on a very important issue.
Peter FitzSimons, AM

It is a national tragedy that a sporting nation like ours remains mostly unaware of these incredible feats by so many Aboriginal and Torres Strait Islander athletes. In Black Pearls Colin and Paul Tatz hold up a mirror reflecting the stories of champions that walk amongst us yet so few of us see. Like an archaeologist on a dig this book reveals discovery after discovery. How thrilling, and yet, how disturbing that these stories have not been part of our sporting conversations till now.
Tracey Holmes

It is a truism that some of the damage and disregard white society inflicted on first nations people has been remedied in part by the style, grace, intelligence and talent many Aboriginal and Torres Strait Islander athletes have brought to that great focus of Australian attention, the sporting arena. The triumphs of many Black Pearls, triumphs not always allowed to emerge without accompanying derision and tragedy, have asserted the dignity of Aboriginal and Torres Strait Islander people in the most palpable and accessible way, and this history tells their fascinating and unforgettable tales, each one of them rich in drama.
Tom Keneally, AO

Black Pearls *is an incredible follow up to* Black Diamonds *(1996) and* Black Gold *(2000), capturing the immense contribution and achievements of Aboriginal and Torres Strait Islander people in sport from the colonial period to modern times. In sport, Aboriginal people have demonstrated excellence, determination and courage, often overcoming poverty, disadvantage, segregation and bigotry. Sporting success requires skill, discipline and strength of mind. If we can achieve in sport we can achieve in anything.*
Nyunggai Warren Mundine, AO

How our First Nations great sports people achieved so much in the face of such challenges is probably not considered by many Australians. Black Pearls *tells the stories of how these athletes overcame so much to achieve international and national sporting success. It is an important part of our history which should now be celebrated.*
Fiona Stanley, AC

To
edward joseph (ted) egan
administrator, folk musician, historian,
public servant, sportsman, and friend —

for his unique contribution to Aboriginal and Islander history,
to their music and cultural traditions, their sport and,
above all, for his subtle and distinctive approach to educating
his audiences and readers about race relations in Australia.

BLACK PEARLS

THE ABORIGINAL AND ISLANDER SPORTS HALL OF FAME

COLIN TATZ & PAUL TATZ

ABORIGINAL
STUDIES PRESS

First published in 2018
by Aboriginal Studies Press

© Colin Tatz and Paul Tatz, 2018

All rights reserved. No part of this book may be reproduced or transmitted in any form or by any means, electronic or mechanical, including photocopying, recording or by any information storage and retrieval system, without prior permission in writing from the publisher. The Australian *Copyright Act 1968* (the Act) allows a maximum of one chapter or 10 per cent of this book, whichever is the greater, to be photocopied by any educational institution for its education purposes provided that the educational institution (or body that administers it) has given a remuneration notice to Copyright Agency Limited (CAL) under the Act.

Aboriginal Studies Press is the publishing arm of the
Australian Institute of Aboriginal and Torres Strait Islander Studies.
GPO Box 553, Canberra, ACT 2601

Phone: (61 2) 6246 1183
Fax: (61 2) 6261 4288
Email: asp@aiatsis.gov.au
Web: www.aiatsis.gov.au/asp/about.html

The opinions expressed in this book are the authors' own and do not necessarily reflect the view of AIATSIS or ASP.

Aboriginal and Torres Strait Islander people are respectfully advised that this publication contains names and images of deceased persons, and culturally sensitive information.

The images in *Obstacle Race: Aborigines in Sport* (1995), *Black Diamonds* (1996), *Black Gold* (2000) and *Black Pearls* (2018) have been provided by individual sportspeople, their family members and sports and media organisations. They have been licensed to us on the understanding that these books (and subsequent articles) are intended to illustrate Aboriginal and Islander achievement and to broaden public awareness of their history.

National Library of Australia Cataloguing-In-Publication data is available at www.trove.nla.gov.au

ISBN: 9781925302950 (pb)
ISBN: 9781925302882 (epub)
ISBN: 9781925302899 (Kindle)
ISBN: 9781925302974 (ebook PDF)

Printed in Australia by Ligare

Front cover: Catherine (Cathy) Freeman (courtesy of John Fairfax Holdings) and Peter Matera (News Limited).
Back cover: Tony Mundine (John Fairfax Group).

Cover design by Amity Raymont, Australia
Typeset in Garamond by Amity Raymont, Australia

CONTENTS

Foreword: Craig Ritchie, Chief Executive Officer, AIATSIS		vi
Thanks		vii
1	The Hall of Fame	1
2	Singular Sports	21
3	Athletics	41
4	Australian Football	61
5	Badminton	122
6	Basketball	125
7	Boxing	139
8	Cricket	175
9	Darts	195
10	Disabled Sports	202
11	Hockey	213
12	Horse Sports	223
13	Netball	244
14	Powerlifting	250
15	Rugby League	253
16	Rugby Union	308
17	Soccer	321
18	Softball	334
19	Squash	341
20	Tennis	344
21	Touch Football/Oztag	347
22	Volleyball	350
23	Water Polo	354
24	Woodchopping	357
25	Wrestling	360
Addendum I: Olympic and Commonwealth Games Representatives		363
Addendum II: Hall of Fame Members		367
Addendum III: The Eras of Achievement		371
General Index		375
Index of Aboriginal and Islander Sportspeople		378

FOREWORD

To coincide with the Sydney 2000 Olympics, AIATSIS published *Black Gold: The Aboriginal and Islander Sports Hall of Fame.* The book showcased the stories of Aboriginal and Islander sporting champions, featuring such legends as Pastor Doug Nicholls, Evonne Goolagong-Cawley, Cathy Freeman, Artie Beetson, Polly Farmer, Lionel Rose and the Ella brothers, among many others.

Now we are delighted to publish *Black Pearls: The Aboriginal and Islander Sports Hall of Fame,* a significant update and expansion of the previous book. This volume features stars from a wide variety of sporting fields — including the all-Aboriginal side of 1868 (the first Australian cricket team to tour England), the Redfern All Blacks rugby league team, AFL footy legend Adam Goodes, Paralympic swimmer and cyclist Amanda Reid, the world-ranking tennis player Ashleigh Barty, Olympic water polo captain Nathan Thomas, and Olympic 'Hockeyroo' Brooke Peris.

Craig Ritchie
CEO, AIATSIS

Sport and sporting achievements have played an important part in our history as the First Australian people. For me, sport is important in many ways. First, it has provided one of the primary vehicles through which we have been able to exercise our own agency and pursue our own goals and objectives. Second, sport has been and continues to be an arena of Aboriginal and Torres Strait Islander excellence. Third, the sporting field has been a place where Aboriginal and Torres Strait Islander people experience inclusion and acceptance. Fourth, sport has had a liberating effect for many people, providing a pathway out of poverty for both individuals and their families. Fifth, sport represents a location for contemporary embodiment of deeply-held ancient cultural values and places where we affirm our relationships and our identities in powerful and meaningful ways. Given the role that sport has played in Aboriginal and Islander life and in Australia as a nation, this is an important and timely publication.

Our story, as Aboriginal, Torres Strait Islander and South Sea Islander people, is the story of strength, resilience and achievement. I am excited to see this story being lived out in an ever-growing number of Aboriginal and Islander people who are achieving outstanding results at all levels of sporting endeavour. From the dusty AFL grounds in remote communities to the Super Bowl arena of American football, from Centralian darts competitions in pubs to title fights in Tokyo and Buenos Aires, our sporting talent and achievement is truly a global phenomenon. This Hall of Fame is a museum and a tribute not only to individual achievement but to the power and strength of Aboriginal, Torres Strait Islander and South Sea Islander peoples. We have done more than simply survive — we have achieved and we continue to make our mark even in the face of colonisation, its ongoing impacts, and the enduring obstacles still in our way.

Whether it be winning a medal or beating a personal best time, being named in any Hall of Fame is something of which to be proud. At AIATSIS, we understand how hard our sports people have worked to go above and beyond in their sporting careers and I am delighted that the accomplishments of our First Australians are now illustrated and honoured in this revised edition.

THANKS

Richard Aggiss, Jemma Caon, John Sanders and Ben Somerford of Hockey Australia; Douglas Booth; Richard Broome; Shane Cantelmi of Softball Australia; Peter Carey and Lisa Hasker of Basketball Australia; John Davis; Gary Ella, selector; Katrina Fanning, selector; Fairfaxmedia Photo Sales (Anastasia Symeonides); Anna Haebich, Darryl Kickett and Yumba Kickett; Jeff and Ann Hardy; Roy Hay and Trevor Ruddell; Jenny Hicks; Barbara Holloway; Colin Hutchinson, AFL statistician; Rachel Ippoliti, Marie Ferris, Frances Glavimans and Stephanie Bloxsome from Aboriginal Studies Press; Mary Anne Jebb; Nick and Julie Landy-Ariel; Bennie Lew Fatt; Christine May of the Australian Institute of Sport; Maryna Mews and Susan Pierotti for their indexes; David Masel, Stockman's Hall of Fame; John Maynard, selector; Gilbert McAdam, selector; Kym McMahon, Swimming Australia; David Middleton, rugby league statistician and selector; Sarah Morton, AFL Media; Nova Peris, selector; Robin Poke; Amity Raymont for her cover and book design; Craig Ritchie; Lauren Robertson and the Paralympic Committee; Matthew Stephen; Karen Tatz; Sandra Tatz for her critical editorial comments and her invaluable literary and technical help; Jamie Trew, Newspix; Grant Trouville and Matthew Long of NRL Photos.

The perception of Aboriginal people determined the ways they were to be treated — in a genocidal manner for close on a century, and in isolated segregation for another 80 years thereafter. Always regarded as 'the other', often as other than human, how could they engage in modern Western sport amid the maltreatment? This is the story of their talent, determination and resilience. It is also a pictorial tale of the slowness of change, of obstacles that had to be overcome and the many hurdles that remain.

CHAPTER 1
THE HALL OF FAME

THE DARK AGES

Soon after the British arrived in 1788 to take possession of the land in the name of King George III, appalling things happened to Aboriginal people. In 1804 the first genocidal massacre took place at Risdon Cove, near Hobart, with some 60 deaths. Historians Lyndall Ryan and Henry Reynolds have found that between 1804 and 1928 at least 150 massacres took place across the country, with a probable death toll of 30,000 people. They were killed, with intent, because of who they were rather than because of anything they had done. This is a history that is commonly ignored, denied, suppressed, sanitised, and hardly ever memorialised. How they were treated in life and death at other times is equally shameful.

The Tasmanian cricketer Shiney, or Shinal, was the first Aboriginal player we could locate in a modern Western sport. In

1835 he made three ducks in a row in Hobart Town — but he was to become renowned in quite another way. On his death, his head was severed by a local resident surgeon and sent to an Irish museum. Decades of local campaigning led to the return of his remains and their cremation in an all-Aboriginal ceremony in 1992.

Towards the end of the nineteenth century and at the start of the twentieth, authorities thought the demise of the targeted native people likely. They began isolating remnant populations in remote and often inaccessible reserves, on places called settlements and mission stations. As well as geographic isolation, draconian statutes ensured that predators couldn't get to those they wanted to kill, to kidnap or to whom they wanted to sell opium. So began the protection-segregation era in which some 70,000 to 90,000 people were incarcerated and isolated. It was to last until the 1970s.

The practice of removing children from their natural parents, always said to be 'in their best interests', began in the colony of Victoria in the late 1830s. That behaviour became systematic and continued across the continent until the closure of the last assimilation home for such children — at Bomaderry in New South Wales — in 1988. Scholars assess the figure of stolen generations at 30,000 to 35,000 children.

Amid the harsh segregation, and in a quite contradictory way, the official policy became 'assimilation' in the 1930s. It was intended that Aboriginality would be 'erased from the landscape'. Three methods were envisaged: traditional people were considered to be doomed and 'destined to die out' in remote reserves, incapable of surviving modernity and 'progress'; inter-marriage between mixed-descent people and Whites would be encouraged (to 'breed out the colour'); and forcible removal of 'half-caste' children and their fostering or placement in assimilation institutions would 'de-culturate' them. The intention was to soon reach the point where, in the words of officialdom, 'it would be possible to eventually forget that there were any Aborigines in Australia'. It was only in the 1980s that the eras of some real liberation began.

Survival was difficult enough, yet some men overcame the distances, evaded the stringent controls and arrived at the professional running tracks, the rodeos, the travelling circus boxing tents and the major stadium rings, and the early football fields. Their achievements in the face of enormous obstacles make for a dramatic tale of alienation and ambition, one that we started researching shortly before the Australian bicentenary in 1988.

When the festivities began taking shape, a number of our Aboriginal friends refused to join in, insisting they had nothing to celebrate. For most of them, 1788 was (and remains) the year of invasion, the start of much grief and a long mourning. For sport they were prepared to make an exception as at least one visible sign of success — even in the face of the dismal and drastic racist policies and practices to date. The obvious question was: where could they, let alone the rest of society, find these sporting achievements?

RECOVERING THE FEATS

We began to document sporting achievements and published the first short and rough sketch of notable deeds with *Aborigines in Sport*, published by the Australian Society for Sports History in 1987. During fieldwork in Aboriginal communities in 1989, Colin met Chris ('Honky') Clark, then manager of the Willow Bend Aboriginal Community and director of the then Aboriginal-owned and run sports complex at Condobolin in rural New South Wales. Honky had seen the

1987 book — and wanted more: 'I want pictures of all our heroes on the walls for all to admire and, perhaps, emulate.'

Research continued for a very much larger work that became *Obstacle Race: Aborigines in Sport*, published in 1995. It is wide-ranging and complex, at once a history book and a sports book, with sport used to illustrate the Aboriginal experience since White settlement. (It won the 1995 Australian Human Rights Award for Non-Fiction.) *Obstacle Race* addresses many of the obstacles confronting Aboriginal and Islander people. So do our 'daughter books' that followed: *Black Diamonds* in 1996, *Black Gold* in 2000 and this volume in 2018.

THE NATURE OF THIS BOOK

A hall of fame is usually a structure housing memorials or tributes to illustrious people. The presentation is often by way of names on honour boards or pictures on the walls of organisations. The popular song 'Hall of Fame' contains this verse:

> Standing in the hall of fame (yeah)
> And the world's gonna know your name (yeah)
> 'Cause you burn with the brightest flame (yeah)
> And the world's gonna know your name (yeah)
> And you'll be on the walls of the hall of fame …

This unusual honouring of Aboriginal and Islander achievement comes to public attention not on the walls but in book form — a tribute museum in prose and portrait form. This chapter discusses in detail the past and present policies and practices that impact on Aboriginal, Torres Strait Islander and South Sea Islander peoples. It needs to be read in order to appreciate their amazing sporting achievements. The book is not a one-theme story that needs to be read from start to finish. It is a large volume that can be dipped into, browsed, consulted. By its nature, there will be some repetition in the essays and the biographies.

Chris ('Honky') Clarke
Photo: Chris Clarke

THEMES

Several themes run through these works. The awkward and inconsistent definition of Aboriginal and Islander people is but one of them, vivid in the outlandish race classification laws from the 1850s through to the mid-1970s. Australian officials were obsessed with blood and the arithmetic of colour, going to great lengths to identify sportsmen or women as 'full blood', 'half-caste', 'quarter-caste' (quadroon), and 'eighth-caste' (octoroon) people.

The genocidal massacre era emerges through a number of sports biographies here, as does the seeming improbability of people escaping rigid physical control under the practices of protection, segregation and isolation. The later insistence on forced assimilation and the removal of 'half-caste' children to institutions influenced the lives of dozens of players.

The sports metaphor tells us much about the political, legal, geographic, economic, social and sporting discrimination across the decades from the 1850s to the present. At the end of this book Addendum III indicates which members of the Hall of Fame emerged in the different (but sometimes overlapping) periods: the 'era of freedom' — which was, in reality, the genocidal era (1804 to 1896, and even up to the 1920s); the protection-segregation period (1897 to 1975); the assimilation/child removal decades (1937 to the 1970s and 1839 to 1988 respectively) the decades of hope (1960 to 1985); the decades of (relative) liberation (1986 to the present).

The final chapter of *Obstacle Race* lists the 129 members of the *initial* Aboriginal and Islander Sports Hall of Fame, men and women not on the walls for all to see, but there, at least, recorded on paper. To fulfil Honky Clark's dream of a *wall* of fame, we set out to produce 100 sets of the 129 photographs as permanent photographic exhibitions, mainly for schools. When that project appeared too costly, the renowned historian and balladeer Ted Egan suggested that a low-priced book would reach more people, especially youth. *Black Diamonds: The Aboriginal and Islander Sports Hall of Fame* was inexpensive and produced in a way (A4 size, one image per page) that allowed communities to extract and laminate their own exhibitions of champions. An update in 2008 took the Hall membership to 224, and this edition has added another 52 inductees.

SELECTORS AND SELECTION CRITERIA

[Throughout this book, all members of the Hall of Fame are presented in bold font.]

The initial Hall membership was determined in 1995 by four renowned Aboriginal sports achievers — **Mark Ella**, **Syd Jackson**, **Faith Thomas** and **Charles Perkins** — and three non-Aboriginal historians, Ted Egan, the late Alick Jackomos and Colin Tatz. The 2000 selection panel included **Artie Beetson**, **Gary Ella**, **Evonne Goolagong-Cawley**, **Lloyd McDermott** and Ken Edwards. Seven of the 2008 selectors were Aboriginal: **Artie Beetson**, Carl Currey, **Gary Ella**, **Syd Jackson**, **Lloyd McDermott**, John Maynard and **Nova Peris**. The 2018 panel comprised **Gary Ella**, **Katrina Fanning**, **Gilbert McAdam**, Aboriginal academic John Maynard, **Nova Peris**, rugby league statistician and historian David Middleton, Colin Tatz and Paul Tatz. **George Bracken** helped select the boxers, and Col Hutchinson, the pre-eminent Australian football statistician, gave advice and materials on star players.

Membership of the Hall is restricted to those who have represented Australia or their state or territory; or who have held a national or international record or title; or who have achieved a notable 'first' or some distinguished performance; or who, in the case of Australian football, were acclaimed senior players and/or medal winners; or who had notable success as referees or umpires; or those who through their coaching, administration or organisation have helped create Aboriginal teams and a space for them in competitions. A further criterion is the person's contribution to Aboriginal or Islander identity. The criteria are tough. There are no sentimental selections and there is no talking up achievements that are simply not there. Perhaps only ten of the 276

Hall members didn't reach any of these standards. They warranted election because they were the first Aboriginal people to break colour, social and even legal barriers, or they defied the accepted conventions on race, or were way ahead of their time, or their enormous talent (or identity) was suppressed by the authorities during their heydays. This is not simply a catalogue of high-achieving sportsmen and women. It is a tribute to success in the context of having a separate (and inferior) legal status; of living in segregated reserves, missions and settlements; and of being members of a society treated all too often with disregard and disrespect. To reach the top, they also had to beat opponents who generally (though not universally) enjoyed freedom to compete and who had the facilities to match.

Inevitably, elections to halls of fame are difficult. Who gets in and who gets left out always involves tough and often emotional decisions. Almost every hall of fame is for a single sport, and very rarely, if ever, do nations have a mechanism to recognise merit across all sports. Several Australian states now have Halls of Champions which cover multiple sports. There are 276 members of this Aboriginal Hall of Fame, 267 individual men and women and nine teams — seemingly a large number, listed in Addendum II. The achievers in this book encompass *at least 36 sports activities over some 166 years*, albeit unevenly. By comparison, the Australian Sports Hall of Fame has over 500 members across 39 sports. The stadium sports — Australian football, basketball, boxing, rugby league, rugby union, and soccer — account for just on 60 per cent of the members (see discussion below). Unlike most halls of fame, there are some new members who are still playing their sport. Note that this updated Hall has given preference to older generation champions over current

Ted Egan
Photo: Bob Marchant/Ted Egan

John Maynard
Photo: John Maynard

achievers: their turn will come soon enough. The burgeoning of achievement has been so great in recent times that we may have overlooked some worthy people.

There are hundreds of achievers who haven't found a place in this Hall. Some — like the great sprinters of the nineteenth century, Combardello Billy, Fred Kingsmill and R R (Bobby) Williams — have been omitted for want of photographs or drawings

Paul Tatz
Photo: Corey Tatz

Colin Tatz
Photo: Karen Tatz

or biographical detail. We have made every effort to include people from the earlier eras. In addition, many successful current players will be recognised in due course. (Note that the Hall has virtually doubled between 1995 and 2018. Noteworthy, too, is that 29 Hall members have been awarded Imperial or Australian honours — 10.8 per cent of the individual inductees!)

It is heartening to see the growth of research in Aboriginal history. Ken Edwards has been working on biographies of **Charlie Samuels** and **Jerry Jerome**, and may find records of some of the outstanding men of those eras. Matthew Stephen has researched the history of Aboriginal sport and leisure in the Northern Territory, and has unearthed a great deal of new material on athletes like **Reuben Cooper** and **Willie Allen**. Roy Hay is finding material on early Australian footballers and athletes, with men like **Albert (Pompey) Austin** coming to light. Historian Richard Broome has given us an important profile of 'Mulga Fred', the roughrider **Fred Wilson**. He has also published the defining history of Aboriginal involvement in travelling circus shows.

EXHIBITING THE SUCCESSES

In July 1998, museum curator Marcelle Jacobs exhibited *Black Diamonds* at the Homebush Sports Centre in Sydney. The display — called 'Dark Side of the Moon: Aboriginal Achievement in Sport' — remained open till 2000. Marcelle took her theme from actor Ernie Dingo's poetic fragment quoted on the title page of *Obstacle Race*:

> Aboriginal achievement
> Is like the dark side of
> the moon,
> For it is there
> But so little is known.

From October 1997 to February 1998, the Penrith Regional Gallery and the Lewers Bequest (NSW) presented 'Tries and Tribulations: Aborigines in Sport', displaying many of the achievers in that book. The Inaugural Queensland Indigenous Sport Recognition Night was held at the Greek Club in Brisbane in June 1999 to honour **Artie Beetson**, **Mabel Campbell**, **Edna Crouch**, **Eddie Gilbert**, **Darby McCarthy**, **Lloyd McDermott** and **Ron Richards**. Wayne Coolwell, a Murri journalist and

[then] broadcaster with the ABC, presented material from *Black Diamonds*, together with some marvellous video footage of the achievers in action.

Black Gold was the vehicle for an expanded, updated and consolidated Hall of Fame. There was no physical home for the Hall at that time. For four months during the Olympic period, the Museum of Contemporary Art (MCA) in Sydney exhibited 72 enlarged and mounted portraits (800 mm x 1200 mm) under the title *Sporting Life*. There were similar exhibitions at the Adelaide Oval, in Darwin, at the Australian Institute of Sport (AIS) in Canberra, at National Aboriginal Sports Award nights, regrettably closed down in 2013 because government funding ceased. Exhibitions were also held at international sports conferences in Perth and in Copenhagen. In 2000, Sydney's Powerhouse Museum opened a new Aboriginal gallery with a simultaneous exhibition of the 43 additional Hall members presented in *Black Gold*. Global Arts Link in Ipswich (Qld) presented the initial enlarged portraits at a major exhibition (*Black Diamonds: Queensland's Indigenous Sports Heroes*) in 2001, as did the National Portrait Gallery in Canberra where a set of 72 mounted portraits was displayed in Old Parliament House for a few months.

The search for a permanent home for the enlarged portraits wasn't easy. After initial agreement and actual transfer, it was mutually agreed that the collection of both mounted and unmounted portraits would best be housed permanently at the Australian Institute of Aboriginal and Torres Strait Islander Studies (AIATSIS). On 18 November 2004, an exhibition and a ceremony in the Institute's Mabo Room concluded with then AIATSIS Chair Professor Mick Dodson and Colin Tatz signing a Deed of Gift of the portrait collection. This

An iconic image from 1993 — Nicky Winmar pointing out with pride to the Collingwood crowd the colour of his skin.
Photo: Wayne Ludby

book is a partial fulfilment of an AIATSIS and Tatz-family goal to record, archive and disseminate Aboriginal and Islander sporting achievements. (Organisations can seek permission from AIATSIS to borrow and exhibit parts of the Hall.)

WORD USAGE

We understand very well why people talk about *indigenous* rights when discussing land, sea beds, fishing and hunting rights. These are moral, human and legal rights arising out of prior occupation as a people who had forms of governance and a reign of law. But such rights — indigenous rights — should not be confused with the names by which people call themselves and wish to be known. Aboriginal people — unlike the native peoples of Canada, the United States, South Africa and New Zealand — have never been accorded their own name for themselves. In the past 40 years they have struggled fiercely for the right to call themselves Koorie or Koori in New South Wales and Victoria, Nyungar or Nyoongah in Western Australia, Nunga in South Australia, Yolgna in the top end of the Northern Territory, Anangu in Central Australia, Palawa in Tasmania, and Murri in Queensland. The people of the Torres Straits do *not* have the same history and the same grievances as mainland people and they have finally won the right to their own separate identity and their own flag. In 1994, they were given that official recognition. In 1992 the South Sea Island community was given some limited recognition from the federal government and the Queensland government — notably through its Recognition Statement in 2000 — which has done much to enhance and support the separate identity of the 60,000 to 70,000 people, many of whom live in and around Mackay and Bundaberg in Queensland. Members of this originally non-indigenous community were always treated by government authorities as Aboriginal people — and suffered the very same and all-too-real discrimination and loss of rights.

'Indigenous' is plainly not the name that the people in this book call themselves. In the six decades of our involvement in Aboriginal and Islander affairs, we have never heard the people we work with refer to themselves as indigenees or Indigenees, or as people who have an 'indigenist' viewpoint, or suffer from an 'indigineity crisis'. Given that *indigenous* generally and universally means native or locally born, no census can ask whether anyone born in Australia is 'indigenous' (or not).

Ironically, those who have made 'indigenous' fashionable in the past 25 years — mainly bureaucrats, journalists, teachers and academics — sincerely (and seriously) believe they are somehow bestowing an especial dignity and respect by using the term. It began as a convenient White term, and in our view it remains one.

The nouns by which people are defined can often become tangled — and messy. Aboriginal and Islander are our preferred terms but Black is a generally acceptable word, even an agreeable one in some contexts, an acceptable shorthand, and clearly one we have used in a respectful way for titles of these books.

'Islander' is used to identify two separate people who were treated as Aboriginal people socially and legally but who have different histories, cultures and experiences: the Torres Strait Islanders and the South Sea Islanders. The latter are descended from Pacific islanders who were 'blackbirded', that is, kidnapped, chained and brought to the colony of Queensland to work as serfs in the sugar cane fields and in the whaling industry. They call themselves 'sugar slaves' and some 70,000 people are descended from those 'blackbirded'.

WHO IS ABORIGINAL AND ISLANDER?

Who is or isn't Aboriginal or Islander is now a matter of self-identification. That moral right became accepted, in phases and stages, from 1969. It wasn't always so. Before then, identity was a matter of mainstream notions of racial biology, of ideas about 'blood' and fractions thereof, that found their way into the laws which administered Aboriginals and Islanders.

This Hall of Fame illustrates many phases of the Aboriginal experience. At times some sports administrations pressed them to deny or keep quiet about their Aboriginality. Some found the social and sports barriers so great that they claimed to be Greek or Filipino or New Zealander, anything exotic. Some only discovered their Aboriginality after their careers ended. Some were told about their adoptions but others had to fight for the right to find their origins. Some had to endure a life with surnames based on the rivers or towns or pastoral properties where they were born or raised, or to which they were 'stationed out' as unpaid labourers, a common practice.

We have sought the consent to inclusion of those Hall of Famers who are living. Over the years since 1995, only three nominees have declined inclusion and we have respected their decision. For those who are no longer alive, we have sought help, even permission, from kin. We have omitted several great achievers because we simply didn't know enough about their identity. (One uncertain case is that of John Cutts, the jockey who rode Archer to victory in the first Melbourne Cup in 1861.) In at least two cases, the jockey Peter St Albans and rugby league player George Green, there is still debate, but we have included them. Mal Meninga is in this Hall: he was asked if he could be honoured as a South Sea Islander, to which he said yes. Other organisations have asked him if he would accept honours as an Aboriginal man — which he declined.

TRIBAL AND LINGUISTIC AFFILIATION

There are many ways that Aboriginal people identify their connection to family, land or language group, and they vary according to context and era. The term 'tribe' was developed by anthropologists and often refers to language grouping and shared connection to a tract of land. Aboriginal people sometimes use these language group or 'tribe' terms to identify themselves, but not always. Anthropologists also developed the term 'clan' to refer to smaller groupings of people who make up an extended family group who share rights to land. The actual term 'clan' is not often used, but many Aboriginal people identify themselves through their small group name in their own language. It is a term we use in this book for a collectivity of people, especially the Nyungar families of

Walter Mussing was an immensely popular South Sea Islander who played 37 games for St George immediately after World War II
Photo: Ian Collis.

Kicketts and Collards or the Yolngu 'mob' of Riolis. Many people also identify themselves according to what has become known as a 'skin' name, one that refers especially to their social relationships.

Where possible, we indicate the clan, tribal, linguistic, or nation affiliation of Hall members. It is difficult to confidently identify people. For the earlier era members, we have no records that identify social groupings, languages or relationship to land or how people referred to themselves in their own language. For those forcibly removed, their origins are unknown or rarely listed in official records. For those adopted or fostered, we have no access to records. Tribal or language affiliations were occasionally used in public documents, but reference to clan or 'skin' name was rare. The younger generations are more inclined to define their origins and belonging and where possible we use those terms.

From time to time tribal/linguistic maps have been drawn, notably by the late anthropologist Norman Tindale in the 1970s. Tindale's map was further developed by David Horton (published by AIATSIS in 1994) and has become a standard representation for the approximate location of more than 300 language groups in Australia and the Torres Straits. Maps and terms like 'tribe' or language group are useful because they can indicate where Hall members may have lived or where their affiliation to country might be. They are also terms that recognise people have a connection to land beyond their Westernised names. We have provided tribe, clan or nation references where the information was reliable. It is likely that in the future more information will be known about Hall members as families and language groups reclaim and identify people whose identity may have been submerged by past policies and attitudes.

GENDER

There is clearly an imbalance between male and female achievers. Women comprise 48 or 18.6 per cent of the members (see Addendum II), up two per cent since the Hall was last updated in 2008. Most male members are in the stadium sports. Until fairly recently there was no female participation in Australian football, the two rugby codes, in boxing, wrestling or woodchopping. The percentage of women is more like 36 per cent if we exclude the essentially male-only sports. Many of the women in this Hall are multi-skilled, more so than the men: several have played four or even five sports.

Black Gold had a separate chapter on women in sport and another on Olympic and Commonwealth Games representatives. Some eighteen years later, we have integrated the women's and the Games' achievements into the various sports chapters: we chose to avoid any suggestion of special pleading or inflating their deeds. They stand tall alongside male records, and at times they are better. Addendum I lists Aboriginal and Islander sportspeople who have represented Australia at the Olympics, Paralympics and Commonwealth Games. Note how this dovetails with Addendum III, The Eras of Achievement. The first Olympians appeared in 1964, the first Commonwealth Games competitors participated in 1962 — the era we call the 'decades of hope'.

Aboriginal and Islander women face immeasurably greater difficulties than women in White society. They have less access to sport than their menfolk. They participate less. They face the highest possible hurdles — they are Black, they are women, and they endure historical, social and cultural legacies as well as clan restrictions in some domains.

In remote Australia, sporting facilities are inadequate — or there are none. Sport for women still remains on the very fringe, outside the priority given to male sport; and too often women have acquiesced in their lesser status. Many are simply not interested in sports. For women, catching up is still a long way off. Sporting activities for women, for the most part, go unrecognised, underfunded (mostly unfunded), and unpublicised. Yet, with the abolition of discriminatory legislation and liberation generally, organised competitive sport is coming slowly to remote communities.

Cultural, social and historical factors offer a perspective and an explanation. First, in many Aboriginal communities childbearing women are regarded as an economic resource. Many have their first child at as young an age as 14 or 15, followed by many more. In a great majority of rural and remote Aboriginal societies, the sole source of income derives from social service benefits. Second, women recognise that it is imperative that they take leading roles in community organisations. They exhibit greater staying power in the politics and economics of their communities and in many instances they are the backbone of these bodies, especially in health and medical units, education centres, legal aid agencies and land councils. This leaves little or no time for sport or contemplation of a full-time sporting career away from home. Purely from a sports viewpoint, this is a pity as Aboriginal women, in our view, often show more all-round talent than men, and are more at ease participating in several sports simultaneously. The evidence is there to see in the biographies of these all-rounders.

Evonne Goolagong-Cawley and **Cathy Freeman** are two of Australia's greatest sporting achievers, both listed officially as national sporting legends, both adored internationally. The new International Tennis Centre at Homebush honoured Evonne by naming the centre court the 'Evonne Goolagong Court'. (She chose her maiden name for this honour.) Cathy adorns covers of books, magazines and calendars, and is frequently seen on television news and sports program promotions and introductions. French, Swedish and German journalists have long travelled to Australia to 'examine' Cathy's life after retirement, and she remains probably the most photographed sportsperson in Australia.

Cathy may be the forerunner of a generation of young women who can make it against the barriers of racism, sexism and stereotyping. Yet her breaking through, her sprinting out, made her a convenient 'sample of one' — the attractive, sunny, world champion whose very agreeable presence on centre stage proved that Australians are not racist. She was always well aware of this tokenism and symbolism, the readiness of all to embrace her, to appropriate her as if she has single-handedly transformed the whole Aboriginal experience into the opposite of what it really is. There may well be neither malice nor ulterior motive in this taking over of Cathy, but her success was and is still portrayed, or sometimes interpreted, as proof of the (allegedly) vast improvements in Aboriginal life. Her belief 'that dreams really do come true' is, regrettably, not true for enough Aboriginal and Islander aspirants, most especially women.

Evonne and Cathy are, in effect, aberrations — that is, their careers and their chosen sports are not the norm for Aboriginal or Islander women. If tennis and athletics can give rise to such champions, it is not surprising that swimming has given the world **Samantha Riley**, winner of so many medals at the Olympics, Commonwealth Games and world championships. And while they are great role models, it is unlikely that they will be emulated by youth in the same way that men are in rugby league, rugby union, Australian football, boxing and, in recent years, hockey and soccer.

Until Aboriginal and Islander incomes rise above a minimum subsistence level, it is unlikely that women can achieve on the same scale and at the same rate as men in the stadium sports. Few Aboriginal and Islander women engage in individual sports: the majority of achievers are found in Australian football, basketball, netball, softball, volleyball, rugby, rugby sevens, and soccer teams. Women's teams in Australian football have become popular. As with men, the team is a place of togetherness, often shared to a quite remarkable degree with close relatives and kin.

In recent years, women have ventured into different or unusual sports. The late **Leigh-Anne Goodwin** achieved the almost unthinkable when she became a successful Aboriginal female jockey in senior horseracing. Softball and touch (football) have become attractive and many young women have proved themselves, including **Donna Hunter**, **Joanne Lesiputty**, **Kelly McKellar-Nathan**, **Stacey Porter** and young Vanessa Stokes in the former, and **Bo de la Cruz**, Lilly Jane Collins, Debbie Norford, Erin Vickery, Tania Sewter and Nicole Suey in the latter. **Georgina Archer** not only played hockey for Queensland but also captained the state's team in vigoro, a game similar to cricket but played and controlled solely by women. She was also an international hockey umpire. Weightlifting and powerlifting attracted **Jodi Edwards**. Karate, trampolining, lacrosse, tenpin bowling and ice skating have interested some of the young athletes. Both outdoor soccer and the indoor game — known as futsal — have appealed to Aboriginal and Islander women, more so than men perhaps: six internationals are celebrated here — **Leanne Edmundson**, **Felicity Huntington**, **Kayleen Janssen**, **Karen Menzies**, **Bridgette Starr** and **Lydia Williams**. Belinda Dawney has done much to enhance the sport.

Darts and Aboriginal people have a strong and warm relationship. Here the matter of access is well illustrated. There is no need for cream flannels, expensive equipment, especial training facilities, costly memberships and travel expenses — a flight of darts and a local pub dartboard will do. **Charmaine Barney**, **Eileen Foster (Wilson)** and **Ivy Hampton** have won national titles and played for Australia. Harena Williamson, at 17, won the girl's event at the inaugural World Youth Cup in Durban in 1999, Kathleen Logue was dual World Youth Champion in Pairs and Team in 2003, and Nancy Homer has won several major events.

Netball has been an attractive team sport, with national representatives — **Nicole Cusack**, **Marcia Ella**, **Sharon Finnan**, **Bianca Franklin** and **Andrea Mason** — as the role models. Softball is represented by international players **Kelly McKellar-Nathan** and **Stacey Porter**; basketball by **Rohanee Cox**, and **Michelle Musselwhite (Cosier)**.

In coaching and administration, Maisie Austin became a major orchestrator of sport, especially basketball, in which she represented the Northern Territory. Professor Megan Davis, a South Sea Islander, has become a Commissioner on the board of Australian Rugby League. Patsy Elarde was the first Aboriginal basketball coach at the Australian Institute of Sport (AIS). Among her many roles in sport, Helen Fejo-Frith has been the only woman coach of an Australian football team — at Bamyili in the Northern Territory. Eunice Peachy has been the mother of Aboriginal sport in the Dubbo (NSW) district.

THE HALL OF FAME

Maisie Austin
Photo: *NT News*

For several women not yet in this Hall of Fame, sport has been the springboard to other careers. Treanha Hamm began life in judo — and became a painter of significance; Leonie Dickson (Tasmania) and Andrea Collins (Queensland) were representative basketballers who went on to become state and Aboriginal team coaches; Alison Bush played cricket for New South Wales from 1972 to 1977 and went on to a senior nursing career. Mary Ball, once Queensland Champion of Champions in lawn bowls, was a major force in World War II support services.

There is a substantial list of women who have played at state level or in national age competitions: Thelma Crouch in cricket (Qld); Pauline Mullett in badminton (Vic); Marion Chalker in junior golf (WA); Clarissa Harp in lacrosse (WA). The basketball list is much longer: Priscilla West, Cilla Preece, Debbie Jose and Valerie Ahwong (Qld); Toni and Aretha Gabelish (NT); Leonie Dickson and Bobbi Dillon (Tas); Laura Agius and Michelle Ahmatt (SA). Priscilla Tucker and Melissa Bennell played hockey for Western Australia, Letitia Warlosz played for Queensland and Terry Elms represented the Northern Territory for seven years. **Katrina Fanning** has enjoyed a fine record as a player of rugby league, rugby union and soccer. Aboriginal interest in surfing has grown in the past decade, culminating in Melissa Combo coming fifth in a world longboard competition.

Despite their Cinderella status in society at large and their secondary status in male-oriented Aboriginal society, women's achievements have been remarkable.

UNEVEN DISTRIBUTION

Although membership of this Hall of Fame derives from 36 sports, at least 60 per cent come from six 'stadium sports': Australian rules, basketball, boxing, rugby league, rugby union and soccer. Some 46 per cent are from the trio of Australian football, league and boxing. Access — physical and financial — has pushed Aboriginal participation into sports that are more working class, less costly, less elitist. In this Hall there are noticeable absences or only one or two representatives in the boat sports of canoeing, rowing, kayaking, yachting; in archery, baseball, cycling, extreme sports, fencing, gymnastics, lacrosse, modern pentathlon, motor racing, polo, shooting, triathlon, and winter sports. Twelve sports in this book have only *one* representative; eight sports have but *two*.

Ice-skating now has some Aboriginal participants, as does tenpin bowling. Non-participation in some sports usually has a sociological or cultural explanation: too costly, too class-ridden, an absence of kin companionship, the lack of role models, the lack of 'cultural fit'. The last point is well illustrated by a well-intentioned but misguided project initiated by the great marathon runner Robert de Castella to organise groups of Aboriginal youth for training as marathon runners. Unlike Kenyans and Ethiopians, many of whom have lived in an animal shepherding culture, Aboriginal people traditionally conserved energy. The Aboriginal fast bowlers in this book — **Roger Brown**, **Eddie Gilbert**, **Jason Gillespie**, **Alec Henry**, **Ian King**, **Jack Marsh** and **Faith Thomas** — bowled off short or shortish runs, often asserting that this was the ideal way to conserve energy. While the marathon project had admirable goals, travel opportunities and positive social outcomes, we believe the African metaphor was misplaced.

SPORT AND KINSHIP

In 1982 Colin interviewed athletes at the Brisbane Commonwealth Games. What stood out was the answer to the question put to the women's sprint relay team from Canada, all hailing from the West Indies. Asked why this was so, the reply was simple: mothers and aunties arrived in Canada, joined local harriers and athletics clubs and the sport became the home and hub for family and kinship groups.

There is much kinship in Aboriginal and Islander sport, perhaps more so than in *any* other distinct ethnic communities. In Australian football there are over a dozen major clans: Betts, Burgoyne, Collard, James, Jetta, Johncock, Kickett, Krakouer, Lew Fatt, Lewis, Long, McAdam, Matera, Motlop, Narkle, Pickett, Rioli, Ugle and Winmar; in rugby union, we have three Ella brothers, plus brother Rodney and uncle Bruce ('Larpa') Stewart, netball sister **Marcia Ella** and rugby league cousin **Steve Ella**. League has many related families: Ambrum, Blacklock, Crouch, Currie, Johnson, Liddiard, Longbottom, and Peachey.

Athletics has had several kinsmen named Wandin, Briggs and Nicholls. Golf has **May Chalker**, her son and daughter. Australian football player **Lance Franklin** and his sister **Bianca Franklin** make for a unique double. Boxing has the renowned Sands brothers (five of them) the Roberts and Williams brothers, and the father and son **Tony** and **Anthony Mundine** pair. **Cathy Freeman** is the grand-daughter of **Frank Fisher**. **Evonne Goolagong-Cawley** is the aunt of softballer **Jeff Goolagong**. Roughriders **Alec Hayden** and **Jimmy Williams** were cousins. In darts, **Ivy Hampton** and **Eileen Foster** are sisters, and **Kyle Anderson** and Beau Anderson are brothers. In hockey, **Des Abbott** and **Joel Carroll** are cousins, as are **Nova Peris** and **Brooke Peris**. Woodchopping has two Lovell brothers. Badminton has a veritable 'tribe' of Mullett siblings.

THE OLYMPIC AND COMMONWEALTH GAMES

Australia has competed in every Olympic Games since 1896. The nation is one of few to be awarded the Games twice — Melbourne in 1956 and Sydney in 2000. Amid the excitement and hype of the 2000 Games we tended to forget that throughout the 1920s and 1930s it was the Empire (now Commonwealth) Games that held sway with sports people and sports fans. The national ideology was very much 'Empire first, Australia second'. Since the Soviet Union's entry at the 1952 Helsinki Olympics, Australian sports priorities have been reversed. The Olympic Games are heralded as the greatest show on earth and the Commonwealth Games have been relegated to a lesser event in which Australia always triumphs over its major opponents — Canada, Britain and New Zealand — and the sporting minnow nations of Jamaica, St Kitts, Malaysia, Uganda, Nigeria and Singapore. This doesn't diminish any person's selection for Commonwealth competition — simply, there is so much more kudos in gaining selection for the very much bigger, tougher global event.

A list of Aboriginal representatives at these two sets of Games appears in Addendum I: 31 in the Commonwealth Games and 69 in the Olympic Games to the end of 2016. In analysing Aboriginal and Islander participation across the decades, it is plain that they were excluded from many sports and had no access to many others. In the era before World War II, their only possible national representation was in boxing. There was certainly Aboriginal talent in those years: Jack Bowden, **Tommy Chapman**, **Rollo Hinton**, Peter ('Cocoa') Jackson, **Ron Richards**, his brother Max Richards, Dennis Ritchie and Alby Roberts. But there was almost no participation in the amateur ranks because these men needed money and the professional ring was their only avenue.

It wasn't until the 'decade of some hope', the 1960s, that amateur boxing became attractive to Aboriginal youth. It did so with a flourish. At the 1962 Commonwealth Games in Perth, the boxing team of ten had three Aboriginal boys, all from the Cherbourg community in Queensland: **Adrian Blair**, Eddie Barney (son of cricketer **Eddie Gilbert**) and **Jeff Dynevor**. Looking at the table, it is clear that boxing dominates: 19 of the Olympians and 15 of the Commonwealth Games representatives have been fighters.

The first Aboriginal Olympian was **Kevin Coombs** in wheelchair basketball at the Paralympics in 1960. His national representation may well be an Australian record — five Paralympics in all (1960, 1968, 1972, 1980 and 1984)! He and **Michael Ahmatt** are the only Aboriginal people in the Basketball Australia Hall of Fame. There can be few sporting achievements to match his. Several Commonwealth Games representatives are not in the Hall of Fame, but that does not devalue their fine achievements.

DISABLED SPORTS

Disabled or disability sports have come a long way since their recognition in the 1920s. The 1960s saw the beginnings of organised competition and the 1980s ushered in the beginnings of universal recognition and acceptance for those who have a physical, mental, permanent or temporary impairment. Several sports have been specifically created for people with a disability and have no equivalent in non-disabled sports. For that reason only we have discussed disabled sport members of this Hall in a separate chapter, mentioning but not defining in detail each achiever's internationally recognised category.

FAMOUS TEAMS

We have done something unusual by including nine notable and respected teams: five from Australian football, two from cricket, and two from rugby league. Some teams were remarkable for the consistency of their membership and for their successes; others are important because they illustrate the sole recreations allowed by missionaries and officials. Some were born out of racial discrimination; some were established by Whites in order that Aboriginal people could interact with the wider community; others were created by Aboriginal people to invigorate their identity. Dozens of Aboriginal teams have had spectacular achievements, often in the face of great hardship.

Enduring Obstacles

In many ways this is a celebratory book, one of achievement in the face of crushing adversity. But the new dawns are very slow in coming: in a speeded-up age of high technology and communication, Aboriginal people, and those who care about their experience, are justified in expecting much better than the permafrost of racism that refuses to melt, of the rusting inertia of bureaucrats and conservative politicians, of their refusal to see, let alone address, the issues that stand starkly before their eyes. We need to look at some of the dark spots in an era of enlightenment.

In Addendum III we locate Hall members in the eras that illustrate the Aboriginal experience. One of them is the 'era of (relative) liberation'. Relative is the correct word: there is certainly liberation from special draconian laws and control of movement but there is no real freedom in the social, political and economic senses. The outstanding achievements presented in this book mask the sharp reality that all is *not* well in many Aboriginal and Islander communities. The glory days, the accolades, the medals and the money suggest that the past is past — that racism, exclusion, oppression, disregard, of having to be twice as good in order to rate a semblance of equality, have come to an end with sudden enlightenment, good sense and a universal embrace of fairness. The past, regrettably, is also the present.

THE UNLEVEL PLAYING FIELDS

Much of Aboriginal life is unfair, unequal, unenviable — and stubbornly unaddressed. Remoteness and distance remain a problem for at least a third of the 750,000 people who form just on 3 per cent of the population. Technology and engineering skills make most things possible, yet the absence of adequate garbage and excreta disposal systems, of potable water, reliable electricity, of all-weather roads, readily available fuel, make for difficult lives. The geographic distribution of hospitals, treatment clinics, nurses and doctors ensures that what Aboriginal people receive in the way of health care is but a faint imitation of the facilities available to urban, peri-urban and rural Australians. [The gross disproportion of kidney transplant availability was brought into the public arena at the end of 2017.]

The facilities and services we take for granted in well-to-do or even poor suburbs are simply not there: adequate housing, running water, electricity or gas, access to cinemas, the internet, skateboard rinks, bicycle tracks, public pools, drop-in centres, counsellors and therapists of many kinds. Nor, of course, is there ready access, if any access at all, to sports arenas, lights, grass fields, change rooms, coaches, trainers, physios, equipment, funding and, importantly, inter-community competition. Colin once described these 'facilities' as looking like Afghanistan in war-time and Somalia in drought-time.

Some communities are blessed, as at Nguiu (Bathurst Island, NT) and Woorabinda (Qld), with football fields, lights, stands and first-rate competitions. Yet they have to rely heavily on pushing beer sales through local canteens to fund their sports enterprises. Most others have nothing but dusty dirt tracks, even salt pans in the Kimberley region, as football 'ovals'.

THE ABSENCE OF WELLNESS

Far too many of the remote communities are blighted by trachoma, leading to blindness unless attended to. The easiest prevention of trachoma — traditionally a disease of poverty — is a chlorinated swimming pool. Such facilities exist but only in a handful of places. The prevalence of hearing loss through chronic eardrum infection is quite catastrophic when compared to the norms in most nations, and there is evidence that deafness is correlated with suicide, a matter discussed briefly below. Many are also beset by the early onset of renal disease, type I and type II diabetes, an increased propensity to cardiac disease and to cancer. Malnutrition, that is, wrong nutrition rather than starvation, blunts the lives of the young. Obesity, which was rarely a factor in Aboriginal life before the 1960s, is now endemic.

Housing of an adequate and culturally acceptable nature has been a disaster for well over 50 years and those programs that have been funded usually do so minus electricity and reticulated water. In sum, Aboriginal health in remote and parts of rural Australia presents at the level of a third-world country, sometimes a fourth.

ABIDING ISSUES

Since 2007 governments have been hell-bent on 'closing-the-gap' on a range of social indicators, like infant mortality rates, life expectancy tables, levels of communicable diseases, general education, poverty levels and so on. A few markers have changed for the better over the past decade but some have escalated to the point of near-calamity. Youth suicide is but one such indicator. (In 2017 and in early 2018 the federal government decided to revise its objectives and targets on closing-the-gaps because things were not working the way that was hoped or predicted.)

There are no records of more than a rare Aboriginal suicide before the 1960s. A search of police, prison, missionary, settlement and assimilation home records, as well as the anthropology and psychiatry literature before that date, reveals Aboriginal suicide numbers that could be counted on perhaps two sets of hands. (Some suicide scholars insist that there must have been suicides before then but they can't find them — essentially because they aren't there to be found.)

History and geography (rather than the medical insistence and dogma that it is solely a matter of 'mental illness') offer explanations for the onset of dramatic and tragic clusters of suicide that place Aboriginal Australians, and youth in particular, in the 'top five' of world rates per 100,000 of a population — a statistic to cry about. Earlier we touched on some of the factors involved and certainly at the legacies of the genocidal eras of killing, incarceration in the name of protection and of forcible child removals.

Poverty and chronic unemployment continue despite several public and private sector initiatives. The Community Development Employment Project (CDEP) — which began when Northern Territory Aboriginal people sought to work for their social service benefits — gave both some labour satisfaction and certainly dignity to many across the country. But that project has bounced up and down like a yo-yo, constantly refashioned, cancelled, reinstated and, latterly, has been under attack as a form of serfdom or even slavery. It certainly has inherent and serious flaws but Aboriginal people wanted something better than 'sit-down money' — which remains the sole source of income for a great many people.

The incarceration rates of Aboriginal and Islander youth come close to defying belief. In the Northern Territory over 80 per cent of juveniles in detention are Aboriginal and their treatment there has been the subject of a royal commission following revelations of treatment that also defy belief about corrective and rehabilitation systems in a country that insists it has a clean record on human rights. In 2017 the Commission found that the Territory's youth detention centres were simply not accommodating, let alone rehabilitating, youth, that there was 'distressing mistreatment', humiliation and physical abuse. Isolation 'continues to be used inappropriately, punitively and inconsistently'. Children in the high security unit 'continue to be confined in a wholly inappropriate, oppressive, prison-like environment … in confined spaces with minimal out of cell time and little to do for long periods of time.'

Yet in the face of such findings, the federal government has declared that its expertise leads it to reject some of the findings, or those that relate to the effect of the detention system on mental health!

Aboriginal people, at 3 per cent of the population, form over 27 per cent of all prisoners, Aboriginal women form 34 per cent of the female incarcerated population and juveniles are a more than notable 48 per cent. In the 1960s Aboriginal people were shown to be far more law-abiding than the non-Aboriginal population in the Northern Territory. So something has gone terribly wrong in the past half-century, partly explained by Colin in his 2017 book, *Australia's Unthinkable Genocide*.

In the context of criminality one has to note that the conservative Coalition government went to extraordinary lengths to abolish section 18(c) of the federal *Racial Discrimination Act 1975* which had made the expression of racial hatred and vilification punishable. In an infamous episode in 2010, a right-wing Melbourne journalist, Andrew Bolt, claimed that a specified group of Aboriginal people were not 'real Aborigines' and were merely posing as such to gain benefits. A federal court found against Bolt, whereupon George Brandis, the federal Attorney-General, pledged to abolish the anti-vilification clause of 18(c) because 'we have a right to be bigots' in the land of 'free speech'. Australia still treats racism and expressions of racial hatred as forms of illness requiring therapy and counselling rather than punishment.

The whole identity question was thought to be resolved in 1969 by the late (Liberal) Minister for Aboriginal Affairs, W C (Bill) Wentworth. He introduced the formal definition of Aboriginal as those who identified as such and were recognised as such by other Aboriginal people. Self-identification is the only sane and moral approach to such matters but the Bolts of this world are still stuck with antiquated and unscientific notions of 'full blood', half blood, quarter, eighth and so on. For him and for so many Australians a 'real Aborigine' is a male hunter-gatherer, thin, semi-naked, bearded, head-banded, standing on one leg, spear in hand, gazing into the Dreamtime. They are also meant to be extinct, a Stone Age people doomed because of their inability to withstand the onslaught of Western capitalism and 'progress'.

A POLITICAL VOICE

Australia has previously flirted with designated parliamentary seats for Aboriginal people elected on an Aboriginal roll, akin to the (now) seven reserved seats for Māori in New Zealand. In 1944 **Pastor Doug Nicholls** sought one such federal seat for an Aboriginal person but 'if that be too much, then a white man of our choosing'.

In December 1973, 41 Aboriginal people were elected on a separate roll to sit on the National Aboriginal Consultative Committee (NACC), a body that Aboriginal Affairs Minister Gordon Bryant said was to 'advise' him 'on matters pertinent to Aboriginal citizens'. On polling day, Prime Minister Gough Whitlam told the committee that: 'Our most important objective now is to restore to Aborigines the power to make decisions about their own way of life.'

That looked and sounded promising. But when Senator Jim Cavanagh replaced Bryant as minister, he quickly declaimed: 'If your proposals are wise and logical, the government would reject them only at its own peril.' Cavanagh went on to define the committee as a *forum* for Aboriginal expression.

Deluded, by February 1974 the committee voted to become the National Aboriginal Congress, possibly with some of the connotations that the word 'congress' had in African colonisation politics. Its aim was to have the then Department of Aboriginal Affairs act as its secretariat. But their power, Cavanagh ruled, 'is only to advise' and he decided not to pay the members' salaries if they thought otherwise. The compromise was a new constitution for a National Aboriginal Conference, but still an advisory body.

In March 1990 the Labor government legislated for a 20-member Aboriginal and Torres Strait Islander Commission (ATSIC). It was to have an appointed chair, two appointed members and 17 elected commissioners. Seventeen zones (of tribal/land affiliation) were divided into 60 regional councils with 30 regional offices.

The Coalition saw ATSIC 'as a way forward'. In many ways it was. It catered to the reality that Aboriginal and Islander people are not 'one people' with a common history or a common past or present.

By 1993 ATSIC had a budget of A$800 million. It had wide-ranging programs, including oversight of the Royal Commission into Aboriginal Deaths in Custody's recommendations and finding ways for local people to participate in health promotion. [Twenty-five years later, the bulk of the Deaths in Custody recommendations remain unimplemented and Aboriginal people are still dying in custody, due — according to some coronial findings — to a mix of racism and negligence.]

Despite some nightmare scenarios of nepotism, poor accounting procedures and staffing difficulties, ATSIC gave Aboriginal people political participation, a voice independent of government, culturally appropriate programs, an avenue to state and territory co-operation and a distinct voice for Torres Strait Islanders. But by 2005 the Coalition government said 'enough'. The government abolished the Commission and replaced it in 2007 with a Mal Brough-designed 'Intervention'. This signalled that only he knew what was in their best interests — Aboriginal voices were of no matter or moment.

Remote Aboriginal communities were to be quarantined yet again as they were in 1896 and beyond, but this time to protect them *not* from predators who wanted to kill them or take their women and children but to save them from themselves. Nearly a century of resistance, resilience, self-help, economic enterprise, educational, artistic and sporting advancement was to be wiped in a moment.

In May 2017 Aboriginal and Islander leaders from across the country met at Uluru in Central Australia to formulate a proposal for the Referendum Council — that a legal body for an Aboriginal voice should be established and cemented into the constitution. The Uluru Statement — some eighteen months in preparation — was hailed as coming from the heart of both Aboriginal and Islander people and the nation in general, greeted in the main with a sense of achievement and a movement towards real progress.

By October 2017 the Coalition government declared that such a proposal was not 'desirable', not 'winnable' in a referendum and the 'Voice to Parliament' proposal undermined the principle of equality! Not winnable may have been a realistic assumption, given the few referenda that have passed in the federation's history. But not desirable? Unfair? Aboriginal Senator Pat Dodson described this decision as 'a real kick in the guts'. In a long history of disdain, this was possibly one of the worst examples.

MEMORIAL JUSTICE

We have seen the deficits suffered by Aboriginal and Islander people on the scale of human rights: personal freedoms, legal rights, social justice, a political voice, health and educational access, employment and income opportunities, access to sport and recreation. But denial of those deficits is another order of discrimination: Aboriginal and Islander people suffer killing, removal of their children, incarceration on reserves, destruction of their language and culture, and are then told by politicians, bureaucrats, journalists and teachers that these things never happened. Or if they happened, they happened in a 'lesser way' or in a way that was in their best interests and never intended as harmful. They are told that some of this treatment was 'good' for them and that their successes in life owed all or much to those earlier 'interventions'.

Most schools now embrace Aboriginal history and studies in the thirteen-year school program. We have had experience of adulterated or 'massaged' history taught by teachers at primary, secondary and even tertiary levels. We have yet to find teachers who teach from primary documents — findings of judicial inquiries and royal commissions, parliamentary debates, parliamentary committee findings, or trial records such as those of the Myall Creek murderers of 1838. [There were more than a hundred inquiries in the twentieth century.] Primary sources are much more dramatic and informative than secondary accounts. Using Trove and similar research engines you can find newspaper accounts from yesteryear that are a remarkably vibrant and compelling source of interest.

There is as yet almost nothing in the way of memorialisation of this Aboriginal history. Historian Henry Reynolds asserts that there is not a single public memorial to any Aboriginal group or community that suffered massacre or violent attack by government or state-sponsored agencies like the infamous Native Police Forces, judged by Reynolds to be the most violent organisations in Australian history. Nor does the Australian War Memorial in Canberra find the moral compass or the space to depict any of the frontier clashes between Aboriginal people and settlers as war. Henry Reynolds, Noel Loos, Lyndall Ryan, Russell McGregor, Geoffrey Bolton and other scholars have documented enough history to warrant physical representations of it, by way of statue, plaque, or park.

Ironically, what we do have is at least three public memorials to boxer **Dave Sands**; a restaurant in the name of Australian footballer **David Kantilla** at Nguiu's sports ground; a statue of rugby league star **Artie Beetson** at Lang Park Stadium in Brisbane; one of league legend **Laurie Daley** in Canberra; a football stand in the Canberra stadium in honour of rugby league giant **Mal Meninga**; a tennis stadium dedicated to **Evonne Goolagong-Cawley** in Melbourne; a statue of cricketer **Eddie Gilbert** in Queensland cricket headquarters in Brisbane; an oval in honour of cricketer **Johnny Mullagh** at Edenhope in Victoria; two streets in Queensland named after **Jerry Jerome**; a Perth freeway named after **Graham (Polly) Farmer**; and Samantha Riley Drive in Beaumont Hills (NSW) in honour of **Samantha Riley**. In the Victorian town of Bairnsdale there is a public memorial in honour of Gippsland sports achievers.

It is certain that other sports achievers will be honoured for their glory — but we also need statues to inglory.

CHAPTER 2
SINGULAR SPORTS

Aboriginal and Islander people don't participate in at least half of the 60 activities in the recognised sports catalogue. Many are expensive or operate at an elite level — ballooning, parachuting and hang gliding come to mind as do archery, canoeing, croquet, fencing, gymnastics, modern pentathlon, motor racing, polo, powerboating, rowing, triathlon, winter sports and yachting.

In recent times, and only on occasion, an Aboriginal sportsperson has emerged in an offbeat or unexpected sport. The world motocross champion **Chad Reed** is one of them; ice-skater **Harley Windsor** is another. Each decade Aboriginal people venture into these hitherto inaccessible or minority sports. In 2016 for example, the *Southern Excellence Two*, with an all-Aboriginal crew, participated in the iconic (and very expensive) Sydney to Hobart yacht race.

Increasingly, women are involved in national and international ball games like Australian football, basketball, cricket, rugby league, rugby union, softball, soccer, touch football, Oztag (a non-tackling form of touch football) and volleyball. All of this indicates a major change in the portrait of Aboriginal and Islander people in sport. Until at least 30 years ago — and in some instances only 20 years — these were events where Aboriginal people had no mutual support, no camaraderie and no heroes to emulate. There is now a new generation of men and women who will become the champions of tomorrow. There are, to date, no remarkable achievements in gymnastics, skiing and tenpin bowling, but Aboriginal people have begun to compete in hitherto 'unavailable' sports.

Seventeen singular sports are discussed alphabetically below and are followed by each Hall member's portrait and profile, 12 in number. Thus we mention five sports where there is some Aboriginal connection but in which there are no Hall members.

We are confident that in a relatively short time there will be more Aboriginal and Islander achievers in these singular sports, and that entries on them will become the richer.

AMERICAN FOOTBALL

In 2015 the Australian media went into overdrive with headline messages, pictures and news updates of every move by league footballer Jarryd Hayne and his participation in American football. There was never a mention of **Jesse Williams**, a 334 pound (151.5kg) Thursday Islander who had played for the University of Hawaii and for the Seattle Seahawks in 2013.

BODYBUILDING

Controversy abounds as to whether this activity is a sport in the usual sense. Unsuccessful attempts have been made to introduce it into the Olympics, even as a demonstration sport. We accept it as a sport — it requires dedicated training, special diets, and of course it always has audiences. Athletics has always been about the body as some kind of art form and this is certainly one them.

World recognition began with the exploits of the German, Eugen Sandow, at the turn of the last century. The activity gained prominence with the advent of Arnold Schwartzenegger, bodybuilder *extraordinaire* who turned actor and later became Governor of California.

CYCLING

Like horseracing and rowing at the turn of the twentieth century, cycling made some space for Aboriginal people. At the Australian Championships in 1907 there was a large attendance at the Brisbane Cricket Ground. Berty Brown won a 'Blackfellows' Race' over two laps. In Bairnsdale (Vic.) there is a monument in tribute to Aboriginal sports achievers from Gippsland and East Gippsland where four men are listed as cyclists of note: Phillip Pepper, William Thomas, Lardie Thomas and Mick Murray. Phillip Pepper's memoir, *You Are What You*

Paul Rowe was born and bred in Gunnaikurnai country located in East Gippsland, Victoria. He was Intermediate Mr Australia in 2006.
Photo: Paul Rowe

Make Yourself to Be, has fascinating things to say about a somewhat bizarre scene. Picture a Victorian town called Koo-wee-rup where George Colvan had a bike shop next to his 'eat-up joint' — called the Swastika Cafe. The bikes he assembled were called Swastikas, after a symbol that was a lucky sign before Hitler brought it into disfavour! Several cyclists did well in road races on these machines.

Nothing, it seems, happened between then and the emergence of two noteworthy riders in fairly recent times: **Brian Mansell** of Tasmania and Timothy Whittle from South Australia. Whittle represented his state in the national championships and Australia in the Oceania Games in Noumea, winning the gold medal in his age group. In the West, Henry Ugle, Ray Davis and Stuey Hansen were strong competitors in the York races. Of late we have **Amanda Reid**, a disabled swimmer who turned successful cyclist.

(left to right) Phillip Pepper, Georgie Rose, Sinclair Mills, 'Swastika Cafe', 1920s. Photo: Phillip Pepper

Scott Gardiner. Photo: Fairfax Photo Library/courtesy of John Fairfax Holdings

Cycling in Perth has initiated a development project to induce Aboriginal boys and girls to take up the sport. A similar venture started in rural New South Wales to foster cycling (and better health) among Aboriginal youth. Road events from Wilcannia to Wollongong have been popular, with cyclist Ben Russell in the forefront of the projects.

Cycling is an expensive sport. It requires costly equipment, clothing and training facilities as well as access to either indoor tracks or suitable road surfaces.

GOLF

Golf has hardly been within the Aboriginal grasp. Group 1 courses — those deemed worthy of holding championships — have annual dues of between $2,500 and $5,000 and joining fees can be three to four times that sum; and in 2017 terms, a reasonably good set of clubs and accessories was in the vicinity of $2,500 and closer to $3,500 for the best quality. An all-Aboriginal championship was first held in Sydney in 1987 but this annual event is more social than competitive golf.

May Chalker's feats were remarkable as indicated in the short biography under her portrait below. Her son Mark became the first Aboriginal club professional in Australia.

Scott Gardiner emerged in the amateur ranks in 1993; that year he was a member of the NSW and Australian junior teams and was NSW schoolboy champion. This young man from Tweed Heads was eleventh in the 1999 Australian Open. He played on the European tour, then on the American Nationwide Tour where he won the Chattanooga Classic in 2010. At last count there were only two professionals of Aboriginal descent: Wayne Smith from Perth who finished tenth in the Australian Order of Merit in 1999/2000 and Nicole Lowien of Queensland.

ICE-SKATING

A winter sport that is popular in Europe and North America but with little attention given to it in Australia, there are many forms of skating: ice hockey (a separate sport), figure skating, ice dancing, short and long track speed skating — all now feature in internal competition and in the Olympics.

It is not a sport that one usually associates with Aboriginal sportspeople. In the late 1980s Catherine Wright of Dubbo (NSW) won medals in Hong Kong and China and in 2013 Lowanna Gibson competed in the national figure-skating championships. She was followed by the remarkable rise of **Harley Windsor**.

JUDO

Lance Duncan is a man of singular talent. His judo students have achieved a great deal: Dean Duncan a second in the national titles in 1981 (in under 40 kg); Glen Duncan won the national under 50 kg title in 1983 and 1984, represented the New South Wales Police Citizens Youth Club in Japan and was third in the under 55 kg in 1985; Tasmania's Brian Thomas won the Young Men's National 78 kg title in 1987, the Young Men's Oceania Championship in 1988 and in 1989 took third in the Men's Scottish Open, also at 78 kg. In the West, Steven Oxenham, Nick Capewell, Dale Perry and Darren Gidgup were in the State teams with Gilmore and Perry winning individual titles.

Troy Smith won several state and national karate titles before he travelled to Kyoto in Japan for the 1991 World Championships. In the 15–16 year group he was runner-up to the champion. On his initiative he decided to compete in the Men's Middleweight Open where he placed third in a field of 120, handicapped by a fractured finger.

KICKBOXING/MIXED MARTIAL ARTS (MMA)

Kickboxing is in a group of stand-up combat sports based on kicking and punching, historically developed from karate and Muay Thai. Kickboxing is used for self-defence, general fitness or as a contact sport. **Shane Parker** is now a mixed martial arts (MMA) competitor.

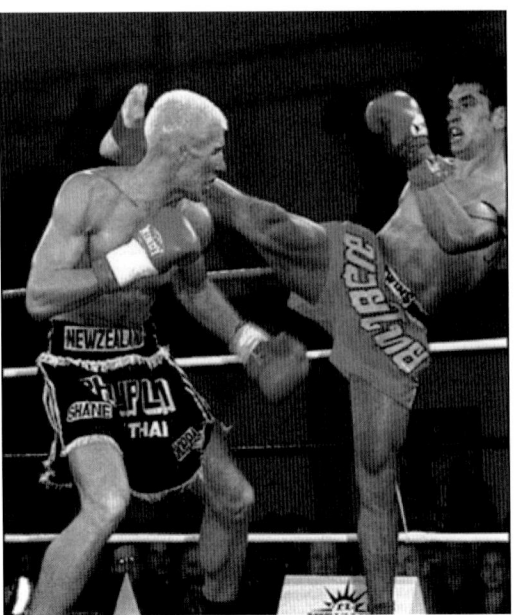

Fremantle's Chris Collard *(right)* began boxing in 1993. He won Australian and world kickboxing titles before switching to Muay Thai and competing in Thailand's prestigious King's Cup.
Photo: Chris Collard

Nick Landy-Ariel. At the end of 2017 Nick was MASA East Coast champion, WKA South Pacific champion, KBF world champion and the NSW light-heavyweight (normal) boxing champion. Photo: Nick Landy-Ariel

LAWN BOWLS

In addition to **Bob Appo**, Ike Bates is an important figure in lawn bowls. In Sydney in 1944 he joined the Redfern All Blacks for whom he played rugby league for the next eleven years. In 1983 he took to bowls at the Rosehill Bowling Club. He won the minor singles in 1988 and the fours in 1989 but his greatest achievement was to become president of Rosehill Bowling Club in 1988, a post he held for a long time. He may well have been the first Aboriginal president of an Australian club. Like Appo, Mary Ball, a member of the Kombumerri community on the Gold Coast, was a Queensland Champion of Champions in 1941.

MOTORSPORT

Motocross is a form of off-road motorcycle racing held on enclosed off-road circuits. Supercross racing, while related to motocross, involves off-road motorcycles on an artificial, man-made dirt track: it consists of steep jumps and obstacles. The tracks are usually built inside a sports stadium. Both forms of motorcycling — individual and team events — are hugely popular in the United States. The sport has a big following in Australia. See the **Char Reed** biography below.

ROWING

Of interest are early references to sports in which Aboriginal people were once involved: canoeing or rowing. From the mid-nineteenth century we have this description from North Queensland: 'The racing at this regatta started at 11 o'clock … A race was included for aboriginals, in six-oared gigs with cox's, the prize being — first, 100 lb. (45.3 kg) bag flour and 2 lb. tobacco; second, bag sugar; third, 6 lb. tobacco. At the early regattas these races

Isaac (Ike) Bates, possibly the only Aboriginal president of a lawn bowls club — the Rosehill Bowling Club in Sydney — was also once a member of the Redfern All Blacks rugby league side.
Photo: Ike Bates

Mary Ball, a member of the Kombumerri community of the Gold Coast, renowned for her World War II services and a Queensland champion of champions in lawn bowls in 1941.
Photo: Margaret Cooper

were the cause of much merriment, both to onlookers and competitors. The 'boys' used to row hard, and many a fine race has been seen between them.'

On 26 January 1848 in Moreton Bay (Qld), a race — 'in commemoration of the founding of the colony' — took place for two 'four-oared boats manned by aboriginal natives'. The boats, *Swiftsure* and *Pirates*, were given to the Blacks 'for their exertions in rescuing the survivors of the unfortunate Sovereign steamer'. The prizes for the crews, reported as 'the best of the day', were £2 10s each — 'to be expended on clothing' on their behalf. The 'sable crew exhibited skill and emulation in the race'; 'The spectators expressed their pleasure at the result of the race by loudly cheering both boats, to the evident delight of the natives.' A degree of paternalism was then indulged in as the reporter continues: 'Great praise is due to the Committee for arranging this match, as a means of convincing the blacks that, if we punish criminality, we can also reward merit ...'. There were to be no further examples of such races: expensive canoes, Great Public Schools and private clubs are not within the domains of Aboriginal communities.

RUGBY SEVENS

Sometimes called 'sevens', rugby sevens has a surprisingly long history: it began in Scotland in the 1880s, invented by two local butchers from the small town of Melrose. It derives from rugby union but is played seven-a-side in two seven-minute halves as opposed to 15-a-side rugby in two 40-minute halves. It is played on a full-sized field. There is a strong international competition with Australia faring well in world series events. **Shannon Walker**, **Bo de la Cruz** and **Jim Williams** have represented Australia in this game.

SHOOTING

Aboriginal people and guns don't mix. Historically, they were the targets of 'dispersal' — shooting to kill on sight — by Native Police Forces. Resistance was hardly possible given that most colonies banned Aboriginal people from having access to firearms. Yet, in the 1990s, a young man from Darwin emerged as a singular talent. Brett Hall was a member of the Northern Territory's Open and Junior Trap teams, the national junior high gun winner and twice Australian junior champion at the age of 17. (See the biographies of **Reuben Cooper** (chapter 4) and **Jerry Jerome** (chapter 7): both were skilled shooters.)

Brett Hall
Photo: Brett Hall

SURFING

Given the social values and ideals of the surf lifesaving movement in the 1960s, one would expect some Aboriginal participation in surfboard riding. Until the end of the last century the only surfers of prominence were Peter Cooley and Gavin Dickinson. Peter was a foundation member of the Eastern Zone All-Aboriginal board-riding association and won a prestigious Maroubra Open against world-class competition.

In 1993 Shane Martin organised the first national Aboriginal competition at Wreck Bay (ACT). Here is to be found a cohesive Aboriginal community, about 250 in number, with high employment and a strong control over its affairs. Competitors came from as far away as Carnarvon (WA). The first Open Final was won by Gavin Dickinson, with Scott Winch, the Illawarra regional champion, runner-up. Third was Andrew Ferguson from Coffs Harbour who described the problem of Aboriginal surfers: 'Most don't go to contests because they've got no one to travel with, or they just can't afford to'.

A moment of surfing history began when the Aboriginal team participated in the 1994 Coca Cola State of Origin Mark Richards Cup at Burleigh Heads (Qld). This was the first time that an all-Aboriginal team competed against Australia's best in interstate competition. Entering as a 'state' or a 'nation', the team called itself 'The Originals'. The team came fourth, ahead of Victoria and South Australia.

The surfing movement is likely to do more for Aboriginal people than perhaps any other sport. The Aboriginal Surfing Association was established and is affiliated with Surfing Australia. Scholarships are provided and national and international contests organised for Aboriginal and Islander surfers. The competitions are as much

Dale Richards, the first Aboriginal surfer to get into a world championship tour (2007). Photo: Justin McManis/Fairfax Syndication

about surfing as they are about cultural and inter-racial exchanges with, for example, Māori and Fijian participants.

From Fingal Beach in northern New South Wales, the Slabb brothers competed successfully in Hawai'i and Fiji. Kenny Dann from Western Australia was the first Aboriginal person to represent Australia in both junior and national competition. Aboriginal dancer Lucas Proudfoot comes from a long line of sporting Minjungbal people on the far north coast of New South Wales. In 1999 he was the NSW eight-foot longboard surf champion.

Where surfing differs from other sports is that the scholarships and financial assistance are provided for the sheer participation rather than the winning of medals.

The Aussie Indigenous Titles first began in 1992, but after an unhappy period it was discontinued in 1999. Revival was inevitable and the sixth titles were held at Bell's Beach in 2016.

Of probable Aboriginal (Darginung) heritage, Mark 'Sanga' Sainsbury was a pioneer of Australian surfing, winning a raft of titles, including the World Amateur Open Title in 1986, and responsible for developing the 'floater' manoeuvre — riding the back or rim of the wave. Sadly, Mark died of a possible brain aneurism at 25.

Dale Richards was the first Aboriginal surfer to compete in a WCT event in 2007. Jordie Campbell has won the Victorian Indigenous Title on 8 occasions. Russell Molony was the first winner of the Aboriginal Bell's Beach Title, gaining entry to the Australian Title — which he won. This gave him entry to the World Titles. Otis Carey and Robbie Page have been great surfers and promoters of Aboriginal events.

SWIMMING

There are four swimmers in this Hall of Fame: **Ben Austin**, **Tracey Lee Barrell**, **Amanda Reid** and **Samantha Riley**. The first three are in the disabled category (see chapter 10). The scarcity may well be due to Aboriginal lack of access to Olympic pools, coaching and regular training facilities, and to the costs involved in getting to swimming carnivals.

TRAMPOLINING

It is difficult to classify the sport of trampolining as this is another new venture for Aboriginal people. The first Australian trampolining championships were held in 1964. In 1987 Brian Devonshire of Newcastle won the national men's tumbling championship and came second in the Australian Open event. He was placed ninth in the world championships in 1988. Tanya Karpany was the first Aboriginal woman to make the South Australian squad.

In recent times, trampolining has become popular in several remote Aboriginal communities in the Northern Territory and northern South Australia. Public exhibitions of trampolining are now popular in city public spaces. Jacob Hunt who lives in Brisbane has been a notable success story.

VIGORO

The game, now distinctively Australian, was invented by an Englishman in 1901. Akin to cricket and originally played with tennis rackets, this is a 12-a-side game played with a ball lighter than a cricket ball and a bat that looks like a paddle. Bowling must be with an overarm action and if the bat hits the ball the batter has to run. Dismissals are identical to the cricket rules.

WEIGHTLIFTING AND POWERLIFTING

These two separate but related sports, have attracted a few men and at least one woman. **Bernie Devine** reached a world ranking of seventh while **Jodi Edwards** held three New South Wales and two Australian titles in both versions of this sport (see chapter 14).

BOB APPO

Bob Appo is a man of rare distinction: an Aboriginal lawn bowling champion. Bob encapsulates much of the Aboriginal experience. Born in 1932 at Childers (Qld), probably a Waka Waka man, he was one of eleven children. Educated to fifth grade, he left school to play football for a little money. He played with **Mal Meninga**'s father Norm, was a useful cricketer and as an adult played Australian football in Mt Isa. He was, in turn, pearler, cane- and timber-cutter, fisherman, and diamond-driller at the Mt Isa Mines. It was in that town that he began bowls at the Leichhardt Bowling Club. He represented Queensland against all states and was twice a member of the Queensland state premiership side. He won the Benson & Hedges Queensland Champion of Club Champions crown in 1980. His aptly titled book is *The Most Colourful Bowler in Australia*. Photo: Paul Tatz.

GEORGINA ARCHER

Georgina Archer had a remarkable sporting career as both hockey and vigoro player. Born in Cairns in 1952, Gina is of Torres Strait Islander descent. She started playing hockey at 10 and umpiring at 12. Gina has been player, umpire, coach, selector and administrator. In 1970 and 1971 she was in both the Queensland Schoolgirls and the Queensland state vigoro teams. Georgina was in the Queensland open hockey team in 1974, was appointed captain in 1976 and concluded her state representation in 1979. She continued playing for St Andrews and was a gold medallist at the World Masters Games in Brisbane in 1994. Her umpiring of state matches began in 1972, followed by achieving a State A badge in 1976, her Australian Badge in 1979 and her International Umpires Badge in 1980. Gina has umpired international matches and has capped a life in sport by holding a number of administrative positions. Photo: Georgina Archer.

SINGULAR SPORTS

SOLI BAILY

From the Yaegl people, Soli was born in 1995 and raised in Byron Bay (NSW). He was surfing from the age of 2, and was sponsored from 9 years of age. He represented Australia twice in the ISA World Championships placing fifth in the under-16s, then second in the under-18s a year later, as the Australian team captain. Soli turned professional, immediately placing fourth in his first year on Pro Junior Circuit, going on to win the 2014 Pro Junior Championship in 2014. The following year he won the Australian Indigenous Title. In 2016, Bailey competed in the World Qualifying Series, ranking a very credible eighteenth. Upon winning the 2017 Volcom Pipe Pro, he became the first Aboriginal surfer to win a world professional title. Photo: Michael Cain/Soli Bailey.

MAY CHALKER

One of ten children, May was born in the wheat-belt town of Wagin (WA) in 1940. With nothing to do in the Wialki district she began playing golf with four battered men's clubs: a 3- and 7-iron, a driver and a putter. She moved to Perth in 1970 and from such elementary beginnings proceeded to win the country championship in 1976. May 'got ambitious'. In 1982 she won the state singles title, captaining the state side that year. She played for Western Australia for six years and captained the state team twice. In 1979 she won the state mixed fourball title with her son Mark, later the first Aboriginal professional golfer in the country. In 1980 her daughter Marion played in the state junior side — alongside her mother who was playing in the senior team. May was a state selector for two years. Photo: Department of Aboriginal Affairs.

LESLIE (LANCE) DUNCAN

A First Dan in judo, an accredited national coach of the sport and an esteemed teacher, Lance was born in Moree (NSW) in 1941. A shearer for 25 years, a hand accident curtailed that career. A master judo technician, he teaches in the Japanese mode: minimum effort for maximum efficiency. He has been the backbone of the sport in rural New South Wales, keeping the sport alive through his commitment to the Police and Citizens Youth Club (PCYC) movement. In a town with difficult race relations, Lance was made Moree Citizen of the Year in 1983 and again in 1994; he was elected a Life Governor of the PCYC in 1988. He won an Anzac Award for his services to the community in 1994. Photo: Barbara Livet.

BRIAN MANSELL

There are six Tasmanians in this Hall, a remarkable achievement for so small a population of 23,572 Aboriginal people, as counted in the 2016 Census: Roger Brown (cricket), Justann Crawford (boxing), Daniel Geale (boxing), Des James (Australian Football), Greg Lovell (woodchopping) and Brian Mansell (cycling). Born in Launceston in 1949 Brian, of the Mansell clan, is the only male Aboriginal person to have achieved top honours in cycling. This sport was popular among Aboriginal people in the Gippsland area of Victoria in the 1930s and 1940s but no state champions emerged. Between 1967 and 1969 Brian won two silver and two bronze medals in sprint and road events at the Australian Amateur Championships. He won Queensland track and road championships for three consecutive years (1973–1975), won the Tasmanian Champion of Champions title in 1968 and was twice Tasmanian Cyclist of the Year in 1968 and 1969. Photo: Brian Mansell.

ANTHONY MARTIN

Anthony Martin was born in 1979. Originally from Brisbane, his later life was in Perth. As a schoolboy he played sports that built up his strength, like shot putting. Starting out in the heavyweight division in his teens, he won the Australian under-20 championship in the 108 kg+ category in 1995 and 1996 and was ninth in the world junior weightlifting championships in 1997. Anthony was an Australian world junior championships representative in 1997, 1998 and 1999, the year in which he became the Oceania junior champion in the super-heavyweight class. He lifted for Australia at the 2000 Sydney Olympics in the 105 kg+ class with a creditable 18th place. He was the first Aboriginal weightlifter to represent Australia in this sport. Anthony died suddenly in 2014, aged 33. Photo: Craig Golding/Fairfax Syndication.

CHAD REED, AM

Chad was born in Kurri Kurri (NSW) in 1982. Encouraged and supported by his family from an early age and starting on a Yamaha Pee Wee 50 cc bike, Chad's career finally took off in 1997 with his winning of the national Junior Motocross Championship. He moved to the USA in 2002 where he was rarely outside the top three in his class. He is a multiple Supercross and Motocross champion, winning four Australian Supercross, two World Supercross as well as the Junior and Senior Australian Motocross Championships. Between 1999 and 2009 he won a staggering 11 major national and international titles — proving himself to be Australia's most successful ever motocross rider. In 2011 he was named a Member of the Order of Australia for both his services to Motocross riding and to the community. Photo: Phil Hearne/Fairfax Syndication.

SAMANTHA RILEY, OAM

Born in 1972, Samantha hails from Brisbane. Her great career began at the 1991 world championships in Perth, followed by a bronze medal in the 100 m breaststroke at the 1992 Barcelona Olympics. In Victoria, Canada, Sam won both breaststroke events at the Commonwealth Games — and repeated that feat in the 1994 world championships in Rome. There she set a world record for the 100 m event, a feat that earned her the world Swimmer of the Year award. At the 1996 Atlanta Olympics she took bronze in the 100 m. In 1997 she was the Pacific Rim Swimmer of the Year. An infection caused her omission from Sydney 2000 Olympic selection, after which she retired. Such were her achievements that Samantha Riley Drive in the Sydney suburb of Beaumont Hills is named in her honour. Photo: Craig Golding/Fairfax Syndication.

SHANNON WALKER

Shannon Walker was born in Kyogle (NSW) in 1988. After playing junior rugby league in both Kyogle and Bundaberg he moved to the Gold Coast to further his career. Playing at full-back, Walker's astonishing speed and footwork impressed the Gold Coast Titans with whom he made his first-class debut in 2008. At that time many considered Shannon the fastest man in rugby league. His first grade career only amounted to four appearances. Shannon switched to rugby sevens, making an immediate impact: between 2012 and 2016 he represented Australia 55 times as both full-back and winger. An attempt to return to rugby league in 2016 was unsuccessful and at the cost of having to withdraw from the Rio Olympics Sevens team. Photo: Geoff McLachlan/Newspix.

SAMANTHA RILEY, OAM

Born in 1972, Samantha hails from Brisbane. Her great career began at the 1991 world championships in Perth, followed by a bronze medal in the 100 m breaststroke at the 1992 Barcelona Olympics. In Victoria, Canada, Sam won both breaststroke events at the Commonwealth Games — and repeated that feat in the 1994 world championships in Rome. There she set a world record for the 100 m event, a feat that earned her the world Swimmer of the Year award. At the 1996 Atlanta Olympics she took bronze in the 100 m. In 1997 she was the Pacific Rim Swimmer of the Year. An infection caused her omission from Sydney 2000 Olympic selection, after which she retired. Such were her achievements that Samantha Riley Drive in the Sydney suburb of Beaumont Hills is named in her honour. Photo: Craig Golding/Fairfax Syndication.

SHANNON WALKER

Shannon Walker was born in Kyogle (NSW) in 1988. After playing junior rugby league in both Kyogle and Bundaberg he moved to the Gold Coast to further his career. Playing at full-back, Walker's astonishing speed and footwork impressed the Gold Coast Titans with whom he made his first-class debut in 2008. At that time many considered Shannon the fastest man in rugby league. His first grade career only amounted to four appearances. Shannon switched to rugby sevens, making an immediate impact: between 2012 and 2016 he represented Australia 55 times as both full-back and winger. An attempt to return to rugby league in 2016 was unsuccessful and at the cost of having to withdraw from the Rio Olympics Sevens team. Photo: Geoff McLachlan/Newspix.

JESSE WILLIAMS

Born on Thursday Island in 1990, Jesse bears the nickname 'Tha Monstar'. The first Aboriginal player to be awarded a college football scholarship in America, he went on to play as a defensive tackle in the National Football League. He played in the very tough American college leagues for the University of Alabama, where he was on the defensive line for the 2011 and 2012 national championship teams. The Seattle Seahawks chose him in the fifth round of the 2013 NFL Draft. He was on the injury list for much of his career but nevertheless became the first Australian to win a Super Bowl ring as a member of the Seattle team in 2013. A kidney ailment ended his playing days but he went on to coaching. Photo: Danielle Cronin/Fairfax Syndication.

HARLEY WINDSOR

Born in Penrith (NSW) in 1996, Harley has an Aboriginal mother, Josie, from the Weilwyn and Gamilaraay people and father Peter is of Gamilaraay and Ngarrable descent. Harley and his Russian-born partner Ekaterina (Katia) Alexandrovskaya won the Junior Grand Prix event in Tallinn, Estonia in 2017 where they won the pairs title, overcoming the top three Russian teams. The pair had been skating together for less than a year. They took fifth place in France at the JGP Final. Competing at the 2017 World Junior Championships in Taipei they became the first Australian skaters to win gold at one of the ISU Figure Skating Championships. Harley became Australia's first Aboriginal Winter Olympian when he pairs with Ekaterina in Pyeongchang, South Korea, in 2018. Photo: James Brickwood/Fairfax Syndication.

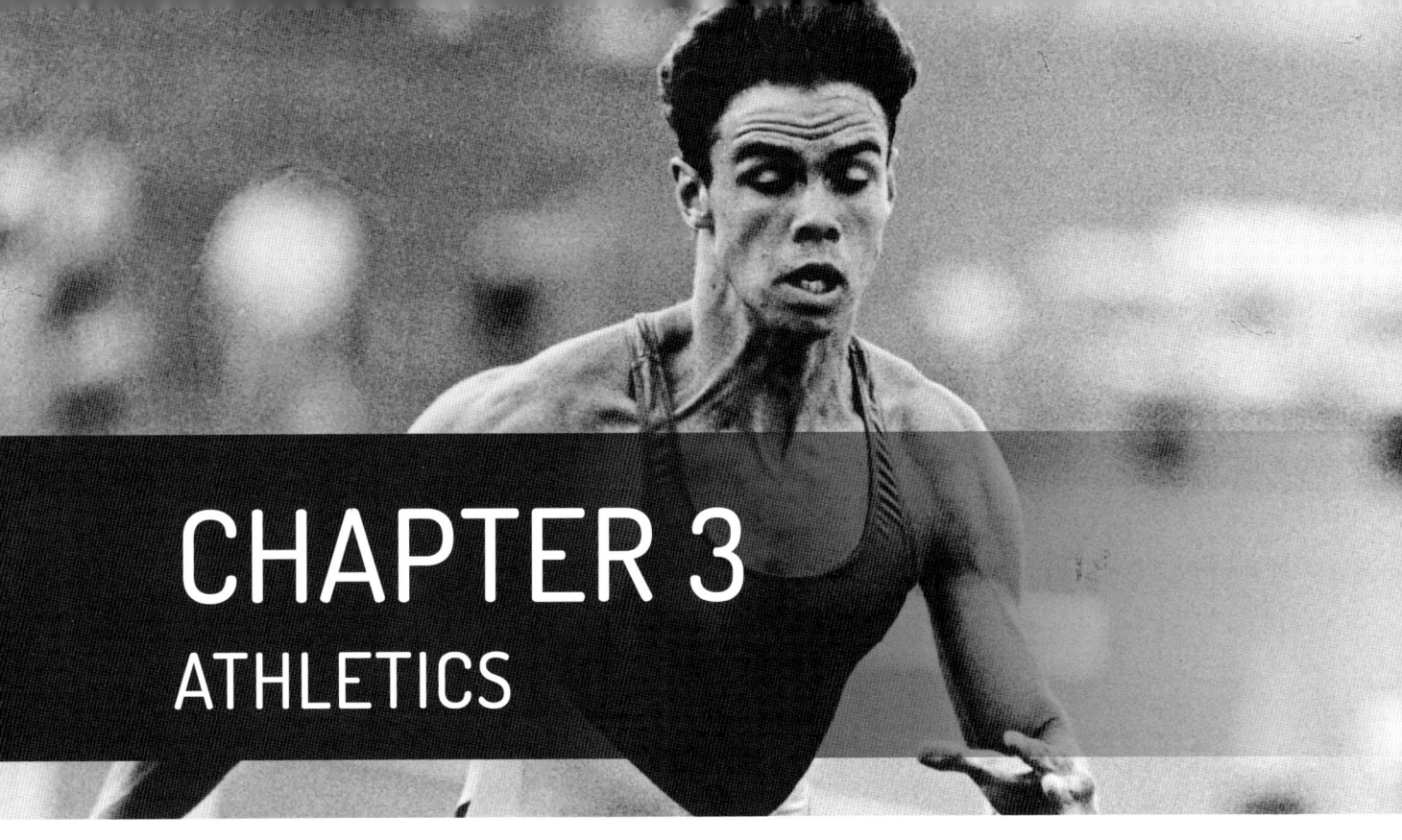

CHAPTER 3
ATHLETICS

From time immemorial athletes have been paid for their performances. In the Ancient Greek Olympics it wasn't simply the laurel wreaths that were sought by the winners: it was the jars of the purest olive oil, often delivered annually, that lured them into the sport.

In the late eighteenth century English landowners would allow races between the servants who used to run ahead of the masters' horse carriages; betting on the fast men became an organised sport, particularly at Powderhall Park in Scotland. And so pedestrianism — the name given to professional running — was born. Audiences of 10,000 and up to 17,000 were common.

'Ped' racing was a popular Australian sport in the 1870s but fell from grace because of heavy gambling and race-fixing. Corruption was rife, with athletes often running 'stiff' or 'dead' to gain extra handicaps or to fix race results. All races were based on a handicap system, with the fastest man running off 'scratch', that is, the full distance laid down for the event, and others were staggered with starts of up to 10 yards (9.1 m) over a 100 yard (91 m) dash, for example. Races ranged from a 75 yard (68.5 m) sprint to a mile (1.60 km).

In Australia, 'gift' races — like the Stawell, Warracknabeal and the Melbourne Thousand in Victoria, the Bay Sheffield at Glenelg in South Australia, the Carrington Cup at Botany in Sydney, the Charters Towers in Queensland, the York races in Western Australia — were prestigious events which attracted huge crowds and big betting. Prize money was huge: £1000 at Melbourne, £840 at Sydney — really big money even in those days. The Stawell Gift is the world's oldest and richest foot race: at present the first prize is A$40,000 for running 120 m in approximately 12 seconds.

Aboriginal people were both prominent and controversial athletes. Draconian state legislation, especially in Queensland and Victoria, prevented Aboriginal participation in virtually every economic enterprise while at the same time confining them to isolated mission stations and reserves for 'their own protection'. The Queensland Amateur Athletics Association even tried to disbar all Aboriginal people from athletics on the spurious grounds that they either 'lacked moral character', 'had insufficient intelligence' or 'couldn't resist white vice'. These appalling excuses were rejected by the national athletics body, leading to the Queensland Association deeming them all professionals in 1903!

Governments created obstacles as did athletics officialdom and athletes — some of whom wrote to the governor of Queensland asking him to ban all Aboriginal people at Fraser Island because they always won. When Aboriginal runners became so conspicuous, separate initials began appearing after a runner's name indicating whether they were 'a' (Aboriginal), 'h.c.' ('half-caste'), or 'c.p.' ('coloured person') in the official race programs. It was suggested that 'without these distinguishing marks ... the public are misled'. This bizarre practice lasted from the 1880s until about 1912.

The first account of an Aboriginal runner is Manuello in Victoria who, in 1851, beat Tom McLeod, then regarded as the fastest man in Australia over 100 yards (91 m). Other prominent early 'peds' included Combardello Billy (Billy Thompson) who ran 150 yards in 15 seconds in 1882 and was the man 'who beat them all'; **Patrick Bowman**, winner of the 1887 Carrington Cup; R R (Bobby) Williams, winner of the 1899 Carrington Cup; Fred Kingsmill, winner of the 1890 Carrington Cup and 'the best short distance runner in Australia'; and Larry and **Jack Marsh** who excelled in sprinting and cricket. **Alec Henry** also ran professionally while playing representative cricket for Queensland. **Bobby Kinnear**, a member of the Yurra Yurra tribe, won the prestigious Stawell Gift in 1883, the first

Charlie Muir, born at Cummeragunja (NSW), winner of the Maryborough Gift in 1936. Photo: Alick Jackolos Collection.

of four Aboriginal men [**Kinnear, Tom Dancey, Lynch Cooper** and **Joshua Ross**] to do so. **Bob Anderson** won the £100 Charters Towers in 1904, defeating the legendary sprinter, Arthur Postle, considered the world's fastest man in that era.

Perhaps the greatest of all Australian male runners was **Charlie Samuels**. Charlie was begrudgingly accorded the title of 'the champion foot runner in Australia' by the *Referee*, the most important sports newspaper in the country, after running 136 yards in 13.20 seconds and 300 yards in 30 seconds in 1886. In 1888 Samuels ran 100 yards in 9.10 seconds at Botany in Sydney, an astonishing time possibly because there was a tendency for promoters to shorten the distances! He enjoyed memorable wins

The exemption certificate that made Jim Murray a 'White man' in New South Wales.
Photo: Paul Tatz/Jim Murray

over the English and Irish champions Harry Hutchens and Tom Malone.

Bobby McDonald won several Gift races in the 1890s and early 1900s including the Maryborough Gift in 1901. He invented the 'crouch start' in 1887: Bobby developed this 'sitting style' to counter the cold and the strong winds while awaiting the starter's gun. **Tom Dancey** didn't achieve prominence until 1910 when he won the Stawell Gift and £1000 for his trainers!

Charlie Green, born in 1884, was raised at Lake Tyers mission in Gippsland. For twenty years he walked the 400 kilometres to Stawell to compete. His reward finally came in 1927 when he won the Old Timers race of 75 yards in 8.50 seconds.

In 1929 **Doug Nicholls** won the Nyah Gift and then the Warracknabeal, second only to Stawell in importance. The Warracknabeal purse was £110 — for 12 seconds of 'work'. Little wonder that professional running was so attractive. Gift races also offered mobility and the opportunity to leave the abysmal government settlements and stations. Exemption certificates were often granted to 'half-castes', initially in Queensland, then in Western Australia and later in New South Wales. These 'dog tags' allowed freedom — albeit mostly temporary — from the oppressive and proscriptive state laws.

Desperate for money in 1928, **Lynch Cooper** sold his fishing boat and with the remaining £20 backed himself at 60 to 1 to win the Stawell Easter Gift — which he did, covering the 130 yards in 11.93 seconds. Cooper was World Professional Sprint Champion in 1929. His running provided security for his family during the Depression.

Selwyn Briggs won the Echuca Gift in 1926 and Charlie Muir won the Maryborough Gift in 1936. But after Cooper, Aboriginal interest in professional running waned. In part this was due to the growing money and status of the 'stadium sports' — boxing, Australian football and rugby league — and also to the decline in major sprint events. Horse-racing had replaced pedestrianism as the premier gambling sport in the early part of the century, while growing involvement in the Olympic Games served to heighten the 'purity' of amateur athletics.

There were, of course, notable exceptions. **Norm McDonald** was a remarkable athlete: 128 games of Australian football played for Essendon and state representation in 1952. A promising professional boxer and a champion sprinter, he won the Wangaratta, Maryborough and Lancefield Gifts and was runner-up in the Stawell Gift in 1948. George Nelson of Echuca won a Stawell Handicap 880 yards race in 1957 and Jack Donaldson a 220 yards handicap event in 1961. He was the first and only Aboriginal trainer of Noel Hussey, a Stawell Gift Winner in 1964. **Ken Hampton** won the famous Bay Sheffield in 1961, also the Broken Hill and Murray Bridge Gifts. At the 1962 Commonwealth Games in Perth, **Percy Hobson** became the first Aboriginal person to win a gold medal for Australia.

Several Aboriginal sportsmen who went on to great success in other sports were outstanding athletes. Jim Murray from Cowra (NSW) won several Gifts, also boxing in Jimmy Sharman's circus tents, playing Australian football for St Kilda and first-division rugby league. Jim's grandfather Sam was runner-up at Stawell in 1899. **Wally McArthur**, a promising junior, turned professional and later enjoyed a sensational career as a rugby league winger in the United Kingdom. Wally Bux of Victoria came second at Stawell in 1971 and won the VFA Centenary in 1977.

The mid-1980s and the 1990s were a very positive period for Aboriginal athletes. **Karl Feifar**, **Peter Kirby** and Beverley Champion won a swag of gold medals at the World Championships for the Disabled and the Paralympics. **Kyle Vander Kuyp** consistently ran world-class 110 m hurdle times and was a finalist in the Atlanta Olympics in 1996; **Patrick Johnson** became Australia's fastest 100 m sprinter (with a time of 9.93 seconds); **Nova Peris** made the extraordinary transition from international hockey representative and Olympic gold-medallist to Commonwealth Games 200 m sprint champion; Tim Ewan emulated Kyle and won the national hurdles title in 2000; **Cathy Freeman** won everything there was to win and is venerated as the apotheosis of Aboriginality.

Joshua Ross won the Stawell Gift twice, in 2003 and 2005, the latter off the prestigious scratch position. He also competed at the 2004 Olympics. **Robert Crowther** won the world junior and the Australian long jump title with a personal best leap of 8.12 m. Shannon McCann followed in the spikes of **Kyle Vander Kuyp**, winning the world junior 100 m hurdles championship and racing for Australia in the 2014 Commonwealth Games. Discus thrower **Benn Harradine** competed in three Commonwealth Games, three Olympics and four World Championships.

There has been such a rich history of involvement — and success — in athletics due to the simple fact that, despite the many laws, restrictions, forced removals or removal to assimilation institutions, people cannot be prevented from running!

BOB ANDERSON

Bob Anderson, one of fourteen children, may have been related to the famous NSW district cricketer **Sam Anderson**. Born in Redbank in Queensland in 1885, he was raised at Deebing Creek Mission. Bob made big money when he won a Charters Towers £100 race in October 1904. On that occasion he beat Arthur Postle, the 'Crimson Flash', who held world records from 50 to 200 yards and who was acclaimed world sprint champion in 1910. Postle (*at left*) said he feared only two men: Maurice Buxton [*at right*] over 75 yards and Anderson over 120. Postle described Anderson 'as a magnificent specimen of the North Queensland Aborigine ... It took me all my time to give him 2 [yards] in 120 when he was at his best.' In 1901, at the Commonwealth Celebrations, Anderson won a race of 118.5 yards in 11.60 seconds. Legend has it that at the Ipswich Showgrounds he jumped six feet over a cross-cut saw with the teeth exposed. Photo: Mitchell Library.

PATRICK BOWMAN

Biographical details and photographs of many of the great Aboriginal sprinters of the nineteenth century are simply not available. Details of men like Combardello Billy, Fred Kingsmill, R R (Bobby) Williams and George Combo (brother of **Charlie Samuels**) can only be found in the results columns of the *Referee*. We do have this drawing of Patrick Bowman. Some of the early writers were fascinated by body shapes. Of Bowman, the *Referee* wrote: 'He is rather a peculiar made runner, having little or no calf and a tremendous thigh at the top of the leg. It is the most peculiar shaped leg I have ever seen on a runner and he has an easy way of gliding over the ground.' We don't know where he was born but the year was probably 1865 or 1867. He won many races in Sydney, the most important of which was the second Carrington Cup in 1887. A reporter was told 'that the party reaped a harvest of something like £500 for the win'. Sketch: *Referee*.

LYNCH COOPER

In April 1929 one of the most important achievements in Aboriginal sporting history occurred: Lynch Cooper won the World Professional Sprint Championship. The title was contested over four races: 75, 100, 130, and 220 yards with Cooper defeating Austin Robertson, Bundy Parker and Tom Miles. Born at Moira Lake near Cummeragunja (NSW) in 1906, this likeable man won the Warracknabeal Gift in 1926. He failed at the Stawell Easter Gift in 1926 and again in 1927. In 1928, desperate for money, he sold his fishing boat and with his remaining £20 backed himself at 60 to 1 to win the Stawell, which he won by covering the 130 yards in 11.93 seconds. In 23 professional gifts he won 19, had one second and three third placings. His running provided security for his family, especially during the Depression years. A generous man, he spent most of his later life coaching athletes. Lynch was the son of the renowned Aboriginal activist William Cooper. Photo: Stawell Athletics Club.

ROBERT CROWTHER

Robert was born in Cloncurry (Qld) in 1987. He acknowledges both Aboriginal and Torres Strait Islander descent. A competent sprinter and triple jumper, he was a national long jump champion with a personal best leap of 8.12 m achieved at a Stockholm Diamond League event in 2011. (The Australian record is held by Mitchell Watt with a jump of 8.54 m.) Following wins in both the long jump and the high jump in the Oceania Youth Championships in Townsville in 2004, he became the world junior long jump champion in Beijing in 2006 and then won the Universidade title in 2007. Robert won the national open title in Brisbane in 2008, was third in 2010 and second in 2011. He jumped for Australia at the 2014 Glasgow Commonwealth Games. Photo: Robert Crowther.

TOM DANCEY

Three Members of this Hall of Fame were born in or near Hebel and Cunnamulla in southern Queensland: jockey **Darby McCarthy**, boxer **Tommy Chapman**, and his cousin professional sprinter Tom Dancey. Dancey came from a large and well-known family, all of them good at sport and most of them educated at Dirranbandi State School. A stockman and boundary rider, Tom wasn't considered a great runner before 1910. In that year he went to Stawell, looking 'tall, lithe, sinewy, every inch a runner'. Tom 'had no difficulty in silencing the opposition in the final, leading over the last 50 yards and winning comfortably by four yards'. He won the 130 yard race in 11.60 seconds. He was the 4 to 1, after favourite beating a Queensland Aboriginal runner, J. McKinley who was the second favourite. Tom won £1000 for his trainers and the state governor decorated Tom with his blue ribbon, but it is unsure what Tommy got for his efforts. Photo: Oxley Library, Brisbane.

CATHERINE (CATHY) FREEMAN, OAM

At 16 Cathy Freeman became the first Aboriginal athlete to win a track gold medal — in the 4 x 100 m relay at the 1990 Auckland Commonwealth Games. Born in Mackay (Qld) in 1974, Cathy's career was remarkable: national and Commonwealth 200 m champion, British and Commonwealth 400 m titleholder, twice World Championships winner of that event. She won two gold and a silver at the 1994 Commonwealth Games in Victoria, Canada. Cathy represented Australia at the 1992 Barcelona Olympics, the World Athletics Championships in Stuttgart in 1993 and in Sweden in 1995, and at the Atlanta Olympic Games in 1996 where she won the 400 m silver medal. The 400 m gold medal came at the Sydney Olympic Games in 2000. Cathy has won a world title in the 400 m twice — in 1997 and 1999 — an achievement unequalled by any other Australian athlete. She was Young Australian of the Year in 1991, Commonwealth Track Athlete of the Year in 1994, Australian of the Year in 1997, and four times winner of the National Aboriginal and Torres Strait Islander Sportswoman of the Year. Photo: Fairfax Photo Library/courtesy John Fairfax Holdings.

KENNETH (KEN) HAMPTON, OAM

'I used to run to earn extra money' is the understatement by Ken Hampton who won the Broken Hill and Murray Bridge Gifts and the famous Bay Sheffield race in Glenelg (SA) in 1961. He ran that prestigious 130 yard race in 12.38 seconds. Born in Darwin in 1935, he had parents and ten brothers yet was institutionalised at age 3. Raised in the unpleasant conditions of Mulgoa Mission near Penrith (NSW), he was moved — as were inmates **Wally McArthur**, **Charles Perkins** and **John Moriarty** — to the St Francis Home in Adelaide. He tried to join the Navy but was rejected because he was Aboriginal. Public outcry led to the Navy accepting him, an offer which a disillusioned Ken rejected. An ordained minister and justice of the peace, Ken was made a Member of the Order of Australia in 1985 for his services to the Aboriginal community. In 1986 he and **Andrea Mason** were recognised as South Australian Sports Persons of the Year. Photo: Department of Aboriginal Affairs.

BENN HARRADINE

Benn is descended from the Wotjobaluk tribe in the Wimmera district of Victoria. Born in Newcastle in 1982, he has been a world-class discus thrower, winning the Commonwealth Games title at New Delhi in 2010 and finishing 9th at the London Olympics in 2012. A large man — at 198.cm tall and weighing 117 kg (258 pounds) — Benn competed at the 2008 Beijing Olympics, the 2012 London Olympics, the 2016 Rio Olympics and at the athletics World Cup in Croatia in 2010. He made the final at the 2006 Commonwealth Games in Melbourne, coming eighth, and four years later took that title in India. He was fourth in the 2014 Glasgow Commonwealth Games. Benn has broken the Australian record three times; his current personal best is 68.20 metres, thrown in Townsville in May 2013. Photo: Pat Scala/Fairfax Syndication.

PERCY HOBSON

Percy Hobson, the boy from Bourke (NSW), was born in 1943. As a youth he had to learn his craft by using a clothes-line strung up in the small back yard as his high jump apparatus. In 1962 he became the first Aboriginal youth to hold a national amateur athletics record, with a leap of 6 feet 7 inches (just over 2 metres). Chosen to represent Australia in the Commonwealth Games in Perth in 1962, he was urged by athletics administrators 'not to broadcast his ancestry'. (He told us that he regretted that acquiescence all his adult life.) This didn't stop him from becoming the first Aboriginal athlete to win a gold medal for Australia with a leap of 6 feet 11 inches (2.1 metres). Photo: Wesley Hobson.

PATRICK JOHNSON

Patrick, the son of an Aboriginal mother and an Irish father, was born in Cairns (Qld) in 1972. Raised on a fishing trawler, he became an outstanding sprinter in 100 m and 200 m events. Patrick remains the fastest Australian over the shorter distance, with a time of 9.93 seconds set in Japan. His best 200 m time was 20.35 recorded in Sweden. Patrick has had a remarkable representative career: he took part in six World Cup or World Championship competitions; ran for Australia in a Universidade competition, in the Sydney 2000 and Athens 2004 Olympic Games; and was in the national team for three Commonwealth Games (2002, 2006 and 2010), winning a silver and a bronze medal. In the 2004 Athens Olympics, he and **Josh Ross** were in the same 4 x 100 m relay team. Photo: Gregg Porteous/Newspix.

PERCY HOBSON

Percy Hobson, the boy from Bourke (NSW), was born in 1943. As a youth he had to learn his craft by using a clothes-line strung up in the small back yard as his high jump apparatus. In 1962 he became the first Aboriginal youth to hold a national amateur athletics record, with a leap of 6 feet 7 inches (just over 2 metres). Chosen to represent Australia in the Commonwealth Games in Perth in 1962, he was urged by athletics administrators 'not to broadcast his ancestry'. (He told us that he regretted that acquiescence all his adult life.) This didn't stop him from becoming the first Aboriginal athlete to win a gold medal for Australia with a leap of 6 feet 11 inches (2.1 metres). Photo: Wesley Hobson.

PATRICK JOHNSON

Patrick, the son of an Aboriginal mother and an Irish father, was born in Cairns (Qld) in 1972. Raised on a fishing trawler, he became an outstanding sprinter in 100 m and 200 m events. Patrick remains the fastest Australian over the shorter distance, with a time of 9.93 seconds set in Japan. His best 200 m time was 20.35 recorded in Sweden. Patrick has had a remarkable representative career: he took part in six World Cup or World Championship competitions; ran for Australia in a Universidade competition, in the Sydney 2000 and Athens 2004 Olympic Games; and was in the national team for three Commonwealth Games (2002, 2006 and 2010), winning a silver and a bronze medal. In the 2004 Athens Olympics, he and **Josh Ross** were in the same 4 x 100 m relay team. Photo: Gregg Porteous/Newspix.

ROBERT (BOBBY) KINNEAR

It is a pity that we don't know more about Bobby Kinnear, the first of four Aboriginal runners to win the prestigious Stawell Easter Gift. He was born in Avoca, Victoria in 1851 or 1861, a member of the Yurra Yurra tribe, and raised at Antwerp Mission, Dimboola. Almost certainly he derived his name from the Kinnear Station nearby. Backed heavily after easy wins in the heats, Bobby won the Gift in 1883, covering the 130 yards in 12.50 seconds. The official history says Kinnear was 'greatly fancied' and 'jumped away with the lead, which he maintained throughout the distance, breasting the tape with his hands in the air, nearly three yards in advance ... amidst the deafening cheering of the spectators'. A stone memorial to Kinnear is in the Dimboola cemetery. There is no photograph of him in his prime — only this portrait with his wife and grandchild. Photo: State Library of Victoria.

BOBBY MCDONALD

The birth place of Bobby McDonald is not certain — either Bourke (NSW) or Nathalia in Victoria. The year was 1859. As a professional runner he won several Gift races in the 1880s and 1890s. Bobby, not D H (Harry) Bushell of Richmond (NSW), was the inventor of the crouch start in athletics. He explained his invention to the *Referee* in 1913: 'I first got the idea of the sitting style of start (as I always called it) to dodge the strong winds, which made me feel cold and miserable while waiting for the starter to send us away. One day while sitting down, almost, the starter sent us away, and I found that I could get off the mark much quicker than ever I could standing, and afterwards I always used the sitting or crouch start. I never saw anyone using what is known as the crouch start before I did.' Photo: Stawell Athletics Club.

JOSHUA (JOSH) ROSS

Josh hails from Sydney where he was born in 1981. He began his sporting career in the NSW Central Coast as a rugby league player and began sprinting from the age of 19. In 2003 he won the famous Stawell Gift off a handicap of seven metres. In 2005 he again won, this time off the prestigious 'scratch' mark, only the second person to achieve that feat and only the third runner to have taken out the event twice. Josh made the semi-finals at the 2004 Athens Olympics and at the 2005 World Championships. He won four consecutive national 100 m titles. His best 100 m time was 10.08 seconds and his best 200 m was 20.52. After Josh won his fifth national 100 m title in 2009 he retired, and in 2012 returned to win his sixth, and then his seventh in 2013. Photo: Darren Pateman/Fairfax Syndication.

CHARLIE SAMUELS

His birth name was Sambo Combo and he was born at Jimbour Station, Dalby (Qld) in 1863. But it was as Charlie Samuels that he went on to become one of the greatest sprinters in Australian track history. The famous *Referee* wrote that while it would have liked to say a white man was champion foot runner of Australia, 'a black aboriginal has to be accorded the laurel crown'. Charlie won many events in Sydney. In 1886 he ran 136 yards in 13.20 seconds, and 300 yards in 30 seconds. In 1888 he ran 100 yards in 9.10 seconds at Botany in Sydney. However, race organisers had a shady habit of shortening distances so as to excite patrons with fast times. He had an eye for White ladies and trained on 'a box of cigars, pipe and tobacco, and plenty of sherry'. In match races he overwhelmed Harold Hutchens, the world's fastest sprinter of the nineteenth century, and Tom Malone, the man who held world records over five sprint distances. Photo: Herbert Hall.

KYLE VANDER KUYP

Kyle Vander Kuyp was born in Melbourne in 1972 and adopted by a non-Aboriginal family. As a teenager he won the Pacific School Games and the Australian All Schools hurdles titles and then represented Australia at the Commonwealth Games in Auckland in 1990. Four years later he made the finals of the 110 m hurdles at the Commonwealth Games in Canada. Kyle missed selection for the 1992 Barcelona Olympics but was chosen for the World Championships in Germany in 1993 and in Sweden in 1995. It was in Goteborg in 1995 that Kyle broke his national record: he hurdled the 110 m in 13.29 seconds in the World Championships. Kyle was national titleholder in this event for several years. In 1996 Kyle achieved his life's ambition when he made the finals in the Atlanta Olympics, finishing seventh. Kyle was in the world's top ten hurdlers for close on a decade, a record matched by few athletes. Photo: *Herald & Weekly Times*.

ROBERT (BOBBY) WANDIN

Coranderrk, rescued from historical oblivion by the late Dr Diane Barwick, is now suburban Healesville, Victoria. Only a quarter-acre cemetery remains of the famous Aboriginal mission of the nineteenth century. It produced many talented farmers, especially of hops, as well as musicians, political figures and athletes, including Robert (Bobby) Wandin, born at the Mission in 1874. He played Australian football for, and was captain of the Badger Creek Football team in the early 1900s. But his major sport was in professional athletics as a hurdler. The Stawell Easter competition comprises many races apart from the famous 120 m (130 yards) Gift. Robert won the Stawell Hurdles over 220 yards in 1900 and the 120 yards hurdles in 1901. He had third placing in the 130 yards hurdles in 1902 and again in 1906. Photo: Stawell Athletics Club.

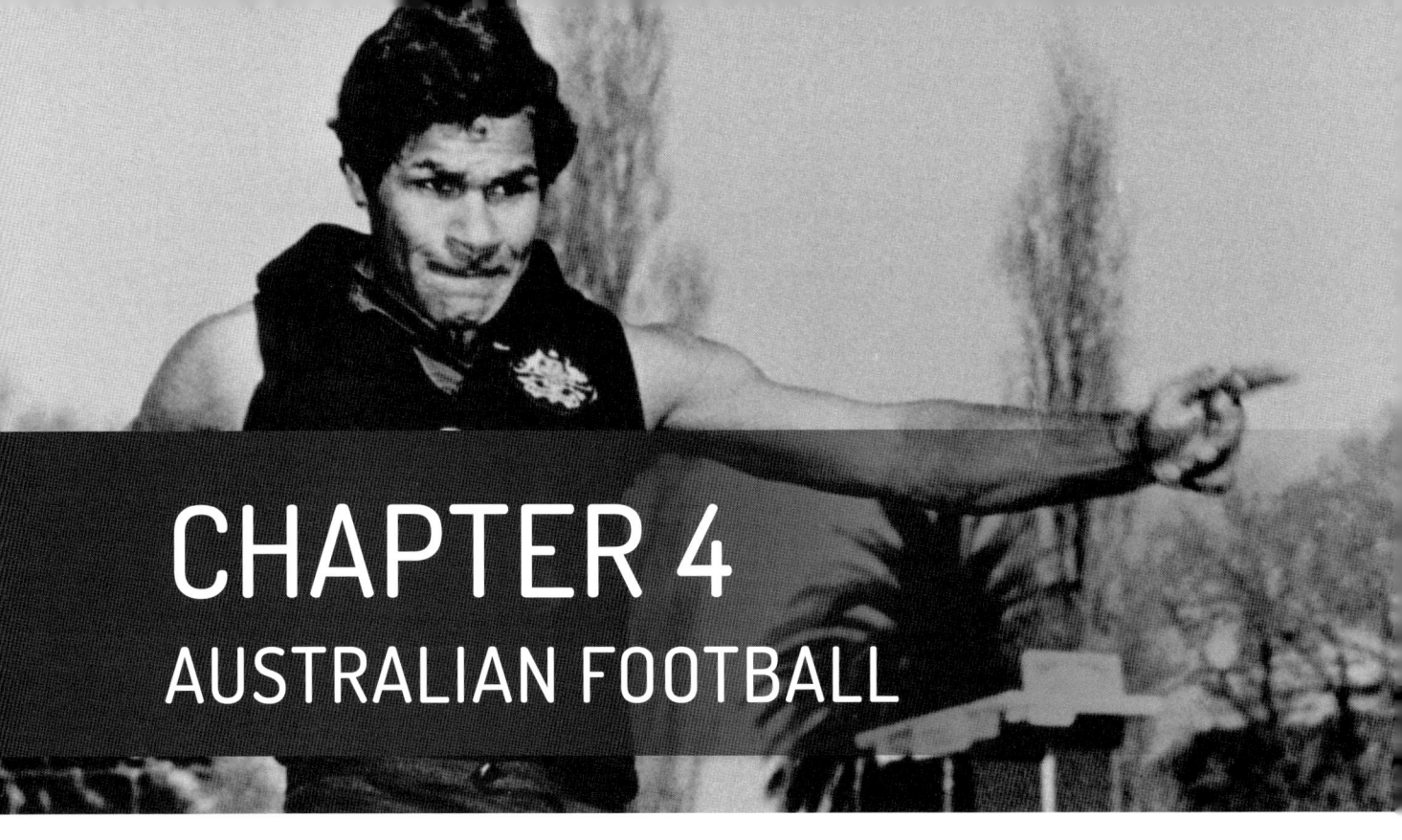

CHAPTER 4
AUSTRALIAN FOOTBALL

Racism and exclusion have a long history in a sport that Aboriginal people may have invented. The game may have started out as marngrook, said to be an Aboriginal game of high marking and the basis for a famous match between Melbourne Grammar School and Scotch College in 1858. Whatever the origins, competition in the Victorian Football League (VFL) began in 1897 and was renamed the Australian Football League (AFL) in 1990.

John Moriarty, a prominent Aboriginal soccer player in the 1960s, once told us that Australian football was 'a colonial bastion with colonial attitudes'. While the last decade of the twentieth century looked like, and was, a golden era for Aboriginal players in that sport, there can be no denial of the past. The ugly period helps us understand the present climate of recognition and celebration of extraordinary Aboriginal achievements. (Just under 20 per cent of this Hall of Fame membership stems from this singularly Australian code of football.)

We searched for refutation of Moriarty's assertion but couldn't find an Aboriginal name between the 1870s and the arrival of regular players in the last two decades of the twentieth century. The story of **Pompey Austin**, an athlete and Australian football player in the early 1870s, has come to light through the work of Melbourne historian Roy Hay. At best there were seven or eight players in the 80 years between the 1870s and the end of the 1940s. It is ludicrous to argue that Aboriginal people didn't have the strength, speed or reaction skills needed: their prowess in cricket, boxing and especially professional athletics has been well demonstrated in the intervening 80-year period. This fast-running, handling, kicking game on a large field seemed 'natural', especially if marngrook was the prevailing pastime of local tribesmen.

In the years 1904 to 1906, **Joe Johnson** starred for Fitzroy in a career which included two winning grand final games. As the Aboriginality of Vic Thorp, the outstanding defender for Richmond between 1910 and 1925, is still not certain, we cannot include him in this Hall of Fame. George Simmonds played a few games for Melbourne in 1924. Unfortunately we still cannot verify the Aboriginality of Cec Gomez who played for North Melbourne and Essendon between 1925 and 1928.

Perhaps greatness lies with those who not only showed superb skills but who overcame the most serious obstacles on the way. In the Gnowangerup district of Western Australia, the Hayward brothers — Eric, Bill and Maley — began by kicking the ball with bare feet through forks in trees and walking to games 40 km distant. **Maley Hayward** was the first to break the colour bar by playing eighteen games for Claremont in the 1928 season. South Fremantle managed to secure travel permits from the Chief Protector of Natives that enabled the Hayward brothers to begin a strong tradition of Aboriginal people playing as clan and family members. Western Australia, South Australia and the Northern Territory produced 'tribes' of brothers and cousins named Betts, Bonson, Burgoyne, Collard, Johncock, Kickett, Krakouer, Lew Fatt, Lewis, Long, Matera, McAdam, Mitchell, Motlop, Narkle and Rioli. An important book on families is Lois Tilbrook's *Nyungar Tradition: Glimpses of Aborigines of South-Western Australia 1829-1914* (Aboriginal Studies Press e-book). An outstanding facet of Aboriginal players in Australian Football in the West is to be found in a video made by Paul Roberts in 1999, *Black Magic* (Ronin Films).

Doug Nicholls was the only player in the 1920s and 1930s. Small in stature but immensely fast, he represented Victoria in 1934. With 'Shady' James, **Norm McDonald** and the brilliant Eddie Jackson as the three prominent players of the 1940s, by 1950 — 53 years after the VFL's inception — there

Sony Morey played 215 games for Central Districts (SA) and four matches for South Australia in a career spanning 1964 to 1977.
Photo: *Advertiser*

were six (possibly eight) black men in VFL. Among the several hundred fine Aboriginal players across the continent in the twentieth century, only **Polly Farmer** and **Barry Cable** have been elevated to the AFL Hall of Fame (in Melbourne) and the Australian Sports Hall of Fame.

There was a trickle in the 1950s: Jimmy ('Juby') Wandin in 1952–1953; Percy Johnson in 1951–1955 and Cyril Collard in 1957–1958. Then followed a void until the great stars of the 1960s: **Polly Farmer** and **Syd Jackson** (both from WA); Bert Johnson (SA); Derek Peardon (Tas.); Percy Cummings, Robert Muir, Ted Lovett and Elkin Reilly (Vic.). The 1970s had only **Barry Cable** and Colin Graham playing for North Melbourne and

AUSTRALIAN FOOTBALL

Jimmy ('Juby') Wandin was a Healesville player, descended from the famous Wandin family from the now defunct Coranderrk Mission in Victoria. Juby played for St Kilda in the early 1950s.
Photo: *Mountain Views*

Melbourne respectively, **Syd Jackson** for Carlton and Robert Muir for St Kilda. In short, there were as few as 20 top players in the VFL in the first 80 years of the competition! The (relative) flood of Aboriginal players began in the 1980s with perhaps six times that earlier number emerging in the next 30 years.

Until the advent of **Michael Graham**, **Gavin Wanganeen**, **Andrew McLeod**, **Peter Burgoyne**, **Shaun Burgoyne** and **Eddie Betts**, South Australian quality players were overlooked. There were great performances by Bert Johnson, Roger Rigney, Sony Morey and Wilbur Wilson (see pictures and statistics below).

Tasmania is the state so many wrongly believe no longer has any Aboriginal people. Yet the 2016 census records 23,572 Aboriginal Tasmanians! Derek Peardon, a Cape Barren Islander, played 20 games for Richmond in the late 1960s, **Des James** (from Shepparton in Victoria) played an astonishing 32 games for Tasmania, Darryl West and Neil Maynard both played well for North Launceston and Ritchie Maynard for La Trobe. Of recent vintage was the ever-talented Andy Lovell — with 121 games for Melbourne and 43 for West Coast Eagles. (Andy's father **Greg Lovell**, a world woodchopping champion, is in this Hall of Fame.)

Some three-fifths of the players in this Hall of Fame hail from Western Australia and the Northern Territory. The Territory has been the real nursery for AFL champions, particularly since the birth of **St Mary's** club in 1954. Some of the great players moved inter-state after learning their craft in the north.

The golden decades were also the periods of ugly attitudes and behaviour. Earlier racism was about exclusion, rejection and non-selection. The later racism has seen inclusion but with insults, degradation and vilification. **Glenn James**, qualified teacher, Vietnam war veteran (brother of **Des James**) became the first black 'Man in White', umpiring the 1982 and 1984 VFL grand finals. He reached a sporting pinnacle yet was subjected to gross racial vilification from fans and players — not simply as an umpire but because he was Aboriginal.

In 1982 the *Age* reported that every time North Melbourne's **Jim Krakouer** went near the boundary line he could hear the chorus of voices singing out: 'you black bastard'. The taunts were from fans — and players. Five years later, the poet and writer Martin Flanagan described how the MCG crowd 'bayed for the blood' of Krakouer, how nice young men in the Members' Stand went pink from the exertion of yelling 'hit him' whenever the black man came near. He suggested that Jim and brother Phil attracted so much abuse because of their sheer wizardry: no one before them 'had played in such an obviously, and threateningly, Aboriginal way'.

Martin Flanagan has argued that 'the more complex the game of Australian football becomes, the more precious and valuable … are Aboriginal footballers'. This was evident as Victorians saw the play of Western Australian players in Melbourne teams; it was even more evident when the West Coast Eagles landed in the AFL competition, winning the grand finals in 1992 and 1994. **Chris Lewis**, **Peter Matera**, Phillip Matera, Wally Matera, **Phil Narkle** and Troy Ugle were major figures in the western invasion. To add to Victorian delight, and at times discomfort, Fremantle Dockers brought to light the remarkable trio of Winston Abraham, Scott Chisholm and Gary Dhurrkay.

In 1993 Essendon's **Michael Long** was suspended for striking an opponent. His defence was provocation arising from racist comments. Following a 1993 match won by St Kilda against Collingwood, the *Sydney Morning Herald* commented:

> The Collingwood cheer-squad had decided to remind **Nicky Winmar**, an Aborigine … that he was one of them rather than one of us, and they did so in the manner for which they are justly notorious … After the final siren he gave the 'Pie cheer squad as good as he had received, lifting his jumper and pointing to his skin. As spectacularly talented as he is with or near a football, Winmar has never been more eloquent or effective for his cause or his colour than he was in that moment.

Wilbur Wilson played 171 games for Central Districts (SA) between 1975 and 1986.
Photo: *Advertiser*.

That photograph (page 7) is destined to become one of the most famous, certainly the most significant, photo in Australian football history. Matthew Klugman and Gary Osmond have written a book on this iconic image, *Black and Proud*. Collingwood president Allan McAlister told the television world that as long as 'they' behaved themselves like White folks off the field, they would be admired and respected; nay, it would be better, he said, if 'they' behaved themselves 'like human beings'. By this time the matter of racial vilification on the sports field had become an issue of public concern and serious media debate, resulting in the establishment of a meaningful Code of Conduct that attempts to deal with this racial problem.

As a result of the national outcry over Collingwood's attitudes, apologies were offered and by way of atonement Collingwood arranged a match against the Aboriginal All Stars in February 1994 — in

Between 1959 and 1971 Roger Rigney played 210 games for Sturt (SA) and one match for South Australia. Photo: *Advertiser*

part to say sorry and in part to 'prove' to the world their egalitarian spirit and their contribution to reconciliation. The Aboriginal team won that seriously contested match by 88 to 68.

While the past has hardly been pleasant, it must be said that Aboriginal players now have an enormous impact on the game across the country, becoming almost essential to any team's success. It is certain that 276 have played senior football in the VFL/AFL between 1897 and 2017. Aboriginal players now form at least 10 per cent of all AFL players. The teams with most Aboriginal players have been: first, Fremantle; co-equal second Melbourne, North Melbourne, West Coast Eagles, Melbourne, Essendon, Fitzroy/Brisbane Lions; followed by co-equal West Coast Eagles, St Kilda, and Port Adelaide. At the other end of the scale, leaving aside the newly established teams like Greater Western Sydney and Gold Coast, Geelong (surprisingly, given the hero status of **Polly Farmer**), Collingwood (much less surprisingly) and South Melbourne/Sydney Swans — despite the brilliant trio of **Michael O'Loughlin**, **Adam Goodes** and **Lance Franklin** — have had the fewest.

For those interested in statistics, four players have notched up over 300 games: **Shaun Burgoyne**, **Adam Goodes**, **Andrew McLeod**, **Michael O'Loughlin**; thirteen players had over 200 games: **Peter Burgoyne**, Leon Davis, Shane Edwards, Graham Johncock, Mitchell Johnson, **Peter Matera**, Ashley McGrath, Lindsay Thomas, **Andrew Walker (1)**, **Daniel Wells**, **Darryl White**, **Nicky Winmar**, **David Wirrpanda**. Another 34 players chalked up over 100 games. Note that selection for the All-Australian team at the end of each season is composed of the star players of that year. It is a 'paper team', an honours board and not a physical team.

The Aboriginal Team of the [Twentieth] Century, voted on by an expert panel, is: **Peter Burgoyne**, **Barry Cable**, **Billy Dempsey**, **Graham Farmer**, **Adam Goodes**, **Michael Graham**, **Syd Jackson**, **Glenn James** (umpire), **Chris Johnson**, **David Kantilla**, **Ted Kilmurray**, **Jim Krakouer**, **Chris Lewis**, **Michael Long**, **Peter Matera**, **Norman McDonald**, **Michael McLean**, **Andrew McLeod**, **Stephen Michael**, **Michael O'Loughlin**, **Byron Pickett**, **Maurice Rioli**, **Byron Pickett**, **Darryl White**, and **Nicky Winmar**. Sean Gorman published *Legends: The AFL Indigenous team of the Century*, a book about this team (Aboriginal Studies Press, 2011).

Each season spawns a crop of new talents. For most young Aboriginal men this is clearly the sport of choice. When the previous Hall of Fame was updated in 2008, the number of Aboriginal players in senior VFL was 105; nine years later the figure had nearly trebled to 276.

TEAMS

At the start of the twentieth century, when they were victims of prejudice, Aboriginal people managed to assemble teams to compete in rural competitions. The Badger Creek Football Club was part of the once proud and successful Aboriginal community at Coranderrk. The Lake Tyers Australian footballers battled to play in competitions in the 1930s and were still fighting exclusion as late as the 1990s. The Mallee Park Football Club enjoyed a long period of supremacy in South Australia, winning the Port Lincoln Football League premiership fifteen times between 1985 and 2016. **Byron Pickett**, **Peter Burgoyne** and **Shaun Burgoyne**, among others, began their careers with Mallee Park.

'Superlative brilliance' was the phrase used about 'Gentleman Ted', Eddie Jackson. He played 84 games for Melbourne and was a contemporary of Norm McDonald.
Photo: *Herald & Weekly Times*

Between 1994 and 2003, Che Cockatoo-Collins, often at the receiving end of racial abuse, played 85 games for Essendon and 75 for Port Adelaide.
Photo: Che Cockatoo-Collins

The Hayward brothers, Eric (*left*) and Bill, who played for South Fremantle in the 1930s.
Photo: Eric Hayward

Bert Johnson, the lightning fast winger was the first 'Croweater' in the VFL/AFL competition.
Bert played 84 games for West Adelaide and 31 games for North Melbourne in the mid-1960s.
Photo: *Herald & Weekly Times*

WILLIE ALLEN

The son of a Larrakia mother and a White father, Willie was born in 1886. Employed by Charles Herbert, later the Northern Territory Government Resident, Allen played in Darwin's first interschool cricket game in 1899. After schooling in Adelaide (1901–1905) Allen broke through Darwin's racial caste barriers, paving the way for others. Between 1906 and 1917 he competed in athletics, cricket, rifle shooting and Australian football. In 1911 he represented Darwin in its first soccer match, won trophies in rifle shooting and cricket and so became the Territory's first Aboriginal sports champion. Australian football began in Darwin in February 1916. Allen and **Reuben Cooper** were the only Aboriginal players to play in the league's first season. Allen enlisted in the AIF, serving in Egypt and Palestine. He returned briefly to Darwin before moving to Cairns where he continued playing cricket into his forties. Photo: Matthew Stephen.

ALBERT (POMPEY) AUSTIN

Born in the mid-1840s near Camperdown (Vic.), Pompey was a Djargurd Wurrung man. He was the first Aboriginal man to play Australian football at the highest level. In 1861, living at Framlingham Mission (often called 'Fram'), he first appeared at the [adjacent] Warrnambool Cricket Club's annual sports where he had an immediate impact, winning three events, among them the high jump with a leap of 5 ft. 6 in. He was successful as a hurdler and sprinter in Western District competitions during the 1870s. At the Geelong Easter Sports in 1872 he defeated all comers, winning the £10 Grand Easter Gift. Pompey was invited to the next big Geelong event in May that year and was selected to play for the Geelong Football Club against the reigning premier Carlton the day after. In 1873 he was in Framlingham's first cricket team alongside **Johnny Cuzens**, and he was the star of 'Fram's' football team in 1877. He died aged about 40. Photo: Roy Hay.

BADGER CREEK TEAM

The Badger Creek Football Club consisted of players from Coranderrk in Victoria. They were Wurundjeri people. Coranderrk was a remarkably successful community of good farmers, fine cricketers and determined politically-minded leaders. The community was destroyed ultimately by White greed, prejudice, as well as jealousy at the Aboriginal economic success. Part of the community's land became a popular zoo at Healesville and today there is a tiny remnant plot with a plaque commemorating family names. For an excellent history see Diane Barwick's *Rebellion at Coranderrk* (1998).

The 1906 team: *Back row, left to right*: Frank Wandin, Charlie Tissear, Fred Smith, Wally Roach, Wilfred Hull, Charlie Wilkinson, Phillip Laing, John Terrick, Woodford Robinson, uknown, Willie Russell. *Centre row*: Willy King, Henry McCrae, Alick McCrae, Joseph Wandin (the first ever Aboriginal headmaster of a state school, Badger Creek Primary), **Robert Wandin** (captain), Jack Gibbs, Jacob Harrison, Alfred Davis, Edward Foster. *Front row*: Willie Condon, Fred Hunter, George Peck.

Photo: Les Harastal and Frank Endacott.

EDDIE BETTS

Born in 1986 in Port Lincoln (SA), raised in Kalgoorlie (WA), after some early troubles Eddie was mentored by **Phil Krakouer**. He began senior football with Carlton in 2005. Between that year and 2013 he played 184 games for the Blues, kicking 290 goals. In 2014 he moved to the Adelaide team, notching up 244 goals in 93 games for the Crows. He has thrice been selected in All-Australian sides. Eddie's goal kicking improved as the seasons went by and his 500-plus goals up to 2017 is remarkable by any standards. On two occasions he won the Goal of the Year award. There is a nice Aboriginal connection here: in 2017, the aptly named Sir Douglas Nicholls Indigenous Round, Eddie kicked three goals in the Crows' 100-point win against Fremantle. Photo: Adam Trafford/AFL Media.

PETER BURGOYNE

A player with beautiful balance, great skill and remarkable speed, Peter was born in Darwin in 1978, identifying with the Kothaka clans of northern South Australia. He spent his early years there and began his football life playing rugby union for an under-20 Territory side and Australian football for **St Mary's**. Recruited to the Port Adelaide Magpies, he began his senior career with Port Adelaide in 1997 when that team joined the SANFL. By the end of 2009 he had amassed 240 games. A defender, he was in the premiership side in 2004. He played two state matches, two International Rules games and is a member of the Aboriginal Team of the Century. Son of Peter Burgoyne Sr, a renowned Port player, Peter and brother **Shaun Burgoyne** have helped Port Adelaide to major achievements, including the 2004 AFL premiership. Photo: Jamie McDonald/AFL Media.

SHAUN BURGOYNE

Shaun, a brother of **Peter Burgoyne** and son of Peter Burgoyne Sr (of **Mallee Football Club** fame) was born in Darwin in 1982. He is a descendant of the Kokatha people of northern South Australia. Shaun played 157 games for Port Adelaide (2002–2009) and then 184 games for Hawthorn (2010–2017), a remarkable tally of 341 senior games and 276 goals. Only sixteen players in football history have played more games, and in that context he has played one more than **Andrew McLeod**. With 32 finals appearances, Shaun is second to Michael Tuck who has most finals appearances of any AFL footballer. He was in two premiership teams and was selected for the All-Australian side in 2006. A midfield player, Shaun's hallmarks were his great ability to dispose of the ball and his hard running. Photo: Adam Trafford/AFL Media.

BARRY CABLE, MBE

Critics regard Barry Cable as one of the most brilliant rovers of all time. He was born in Narrogin (WA) in 1943 to a Nyungar mother. Possibly the most decorated player in Australian football history, Barry won three Sandover Medals (1964, 1968, 1973), four Simpson Medals (1966–1969), a Tassie Medal (1966) and was selected for the All-Australians in 1966 and 1969. Between 1960 and 1973 he played 225 games for Perth, 42 for East Perth, 115 for North Melbourne and 23 for Western Australia. He was in two premiership sides (1975, 1979) and had a successful coaching career with North Melbourne (1981–1984) and the Western Australia team (1990–1991). Cable and **Polly Farmer** are the two Aboriginal players in the Australian Football Hall of Fame. Barry was appointed coach of the Western Australian state team in 1990 and 1991 followed by a new career encouraging and promoting Aboriginal sporting talent in the West. Photo: Department of Aboriginal Affairs.

REUBEN COOPER

The Northern Territory has been a major nursery of Black talent: sixteen football members of this Hall hail from the Territory. It took an outstanding sportsman, Reuben Cooper, to bring Aboriginal players into Territory sport. Born in Pine Creek in 1898, the child of an English father and an Aboriginal mother, he was educated at Prince Alfred College in Adelaide. He helped found the Waratahs Club in 1917 and later played for Vesteys. He won the NTFL best and fairest in 1921–1922 as an outstanding defender as well as utility man. He was the first Aboriginal person to play Australian football in the Territory, among the first to play anywhere in Australia, and the leading campaigner to fight the colour bar in hotels. His son Ron played for Buffaloes [Darwin] in the 1940s and '50s and grandson Reuben Junior played a few games for South Melbourne. Photo: Michael Barfoot.

WILLIAM (BILLY) DEMPSEY, MBE

Billy was born in Birdum (NT) in 1942. He was raised in an assimilation home — in his case the Retta Dixon Home which grew out of the pre-war Kahlin 'half-caste' home. He began his Australian football career in 1958 with the famous Buffaloes [Darwin] Club in Darwin. Billy is still regarded as that club's most celebrated footballer. He moved to Perth where he played a staggering 343 games for West Perth, four times as captain and once winner of a season's best and fairest. His career lasted until 1976 during which time he played 14 games for Western Australia, once as captain. In 1969 he won the Simpson Medal for the best player in a grand final or interstate match. Like **Stephen Michael** and **Ted Kilmurray** he elected not to go east to play in the Victorian (now Australian) Football League. Photo: Department of Aboriginal Affairs.

GRAHAM (POLLY) FARMER, MBE

The 'Steel Cat' was one of football's greatest champions. Born in Perth in 1935, he was raised in Sister Kate's Orphanage, the first of the assimilation homes in the West, alongside lifelong friend **Ted Kilmurray**. He began his career with 176 games for East Perth and 80 for West Perth. He then moved to Geelong where his 101 games for the Cats remain in the memory of fans and scribes. He revolutionised ruck play, revived the art of the handball and played 'near perfect football'. Between 1955 and 1962 Farmer played 31 games for WA and five for Victoria, won two Sandover Medals (1956, 1960), a Tassie Medal (1956), three Simpson Medals (1956, 1958, 1959) and was selected in the All-Australians team in 1956, 1958 and 1961. He also coached Geelong from 1973 to 1975. Farmer has a rightful place in the Australian Football Hall of Fame. Photo: *Herald & Weekly Times*.

JEFF FARMER

South-west Western Australia was the birthplace of many Aboriginal football greats. Jeff was one, born in Tambellup (WA) in 1977. He was the first Aboriginal player to kick 400 goals in Australian football. He scored 483 goals in a total of 249 senior games. Jeff started with Melbourne in 1999 and moved to Fremantle in 2002, ending his career there in 2008. He had a remarkable talent for creating goal opportunities, seemingly out of nowhere and was suitably nicknamed 'The Wizard' (or 'Wiz'), Jeff had a wonderful game against Collingwood at the MCG in 2000 and in that year was duly selected in the All-Australian side. Jeff's record of 483 goals places him 49th in the history of goal scorers in Australian football. He was very popular with team mates and fans. Photo: GSP Images/AFL Media.

LANCE ('BUDDY') FRANKLIN

Born in Perth in 1987 of Nyungar-Wujak or Balladong descent, Lance's mother is from the Kickett family and he is a cousin of **Dale Kickett and Byron Pickett**, a nephew of **Derek Kickett** and a brother to **Bianca Franklin (Giteau)**. This remarkable footballer has kicked 860 goals to date, making him the tenth highest scorer in football history. Lance began football life with Hawthorn for whom he played 182 games and scored 580 goals between 2005 and 2013. He then joined the Sydney Swans, playing 89 games for 280 goals. Lance has been selected for the All-Australian team on no less than eight occasions, he won two Coleman Medals (for the most home-and-away goals in a season) and represented Australia in the 2013 International Rules Series. He has been in two premiership sides and twice won the Goal of the Year award. Audiences love his every move. Photo: Michael Willson/AFL Media.

ADAM GOODES

Born in Wallaroo (SA) in 1980, son of a Adnyamathanha and Narungga mother, Adam is an Aboriginal role model and champion on and off the sports field: brilliant and attractive to watch. One of sport's most decorated players, Adam was made Australian of the Year in 2014; he was twice the recipient of the ultimate football prize, the Brownlow Medal (2003, 2006); winner of three Bob Skilton Medals (for the best and fairest at Sydney Swans); four times selected for the All-Australian team; and is a member of the Aboriginal Team of the Century. Adam played 372 senior games for the Sydney Swans, kicking 464 goals. Adam was often vilified by racist spectators and after incessant booing and racial taunting he chose to retire in 2015. Goodes was awarded an honorary doctorate by the University of Sydney for his contribution to Australian society. He contributes his services to Aboriginal youth programs. Photo: Michael Willson/AFL Media.

MICHAEL GRAHAM

Footballers from South Australia are sometimes overlooked. Star players were Bert Johnson, Roger Rigney, Sony Morey, Wilbur Wilson, Eddie Hocking, **Gilbert McAdam**, Greg McAdam, the Johncock, Motlop and Bond boys. The arrival of two new teams in the AFL competition in the 1990s, Adelaide and Port Adelaide, showed the public just how good they are. Several 'Croweaters' are in this Hall of Fame: **David Kantilla**, **Andrew McLeod**, **Michael O'Loughlin**, **Gavin Wanganeen** and Michael Graham. Born in Wallaroo (SA) in 1952, Michael played 282 games for Sturt, scoring 455 goals. His career overlapped, in part, with two outstanding team mates, Eddie Fry and Roger Rigney. He was picked for the South Australian side on 11 occasions between 1973 and 1982 — crowning a long career in top football, which began in 1971 and ended in 1986. In 1973 he was runner-up for the Magarey Medal, the most prestigious award in that state. Photo: *Advertiser*.

MALEY HAYWARD

Maley Hayward (*right*) was the first Aboriginal player to break the colour bar in first-division Australian football in Western Australia. The year was 1928 and Maley, one of three athletic brothers, played eighteen games for Claremont. Maley was born in 1902 in Tambellup in the Katanning district (WA). He joined his brothers Eric and Bill in the South Fremantle team in 1937. The club president Clive Doig was able to secure permits from the Chief Protector of Natives so that the boys could travel. Maley played eighteen games for the Bulldogs. A champion sprinter, he won the Kellerberrin Championship Test in 1928 and the Kellerberrin 440 yards Handicap in 1930. When **Lynch Cooper** visited the West he ran a special match race against Bill (on a one-yard handicap) and Maley (on scratch). Maley and Lynch dead-heated. Photo: (Maley) Lois Tilbrook.

STEPHEN HILL

Born in 1990, Stephen began football life with West Perth and as a junior was named in the Australian under-18 team. His senior career has been with Fremantle for whom he has played 190 games since 2009, scoring 108 goals. In 2013 he and brother Bradley Hill, playing for Hawthorn, became the second pair of brothers (since 1912) to oppose each other in a grand final. By then end of 2017 Bradley had played 95 games for Hawthorn and 22 for Fremantle. Stephen is noted as a thinking player and is extremely fast with the ball. In the 2017 State of Origin match (in which Western Australia beat Victoria 134 to 71), Stephen Hill, Bradley Hill and **Lance Franklin** were in the winning side. Photo: Daniel Carlson/AFL Media.

SYDNEY (SYD) JACKSON

One of the most volatile and stylish players of the 1960s and 1970s, Syd began life in an assimilation institution after being removed at the age of two from his parents. Born in Leonora (WA) in 1945, he grew up at Roelands Native Mission. Syd is one of very few 'rescued' men who has a kind word to say about those institutions. He played 105 Australian rules games for East Perth and 136 for Carlton between 1969 and 1976. He was in three grand finals, in the losing side in 1969 and the winning teams in 1970 and 1972. Fiercely Aboriginal, he was quick to retaliate against racist slurs on the field. In the 1970 grand final he said he was conscious of the feeling that all 121,696 spectators were aware that he was an Aboriginal person. Syd was a member of the first national Aboriginal Sports Foundation. A keen and good golfer, he made a career in sports administration. Photo: AIATSIS.

DES JAMES

Overlooked by writers, critics and statisticians, Des played more interstate games of Australian football than any other player — 32 for Tasmania, one more than the legendary John Nicholls played for Victoria. His 'low profile' is clearly due to the fact that he didn't play in the VFL/AFL and he chose Tasmania as his arena. Unlike brother **Glenn James**, the AFL umpire, Des was lucky not to have experienced racial vilification. Born in Shepparton, Victoria in 1952, he began his football life in the Lemnos team in the Goulburn Valley Football League. Des moved to Sydney to play for Newtown. There he was spotted and signed up for the Sandy Bay team in Hobart — for whom he played 235 games. His crowning achievement was to be named, as a back pocket player, in the All-Australians team of 1979 following the national football carnival in Perth. Des is now a horticulturalist in Hobart. Photo: Des James.

GLENN JAMES, OAM

Glenn was born in Shepparton (Vic.) in 1948. He and brother Des played together with the Lemnos team in the Goulburn Valley Football League in rural Victoria. In 1970 his jaw was broken during the GVFL final series and he never played again but became a football umpire. He was the first (and only) black 'Man in White' (umpire) in first-division Australian football. He endured some of the worst racist abuse ever to come out of the MCG — more because of his Aboriginality than his (recognised and praised) umpiring ability. He had to be doubly good in order to be awarded the 1982 Carlton *versus* Richmond and in 1984 the Essendon *versus* Hawthorn grand finals. He also officiated at three night grand finals and two interstate games. Glenn was a school teacher, a Vietnam war veteran, an adviser to the AFL's cadet umpire squad and a Swinburne University lecturer. Photo: *Herald & Weekly Times*.

CHRIS JOHNSON

Chris has several claims to a place in the history of Australian football, not least that he was the last of the original Fitzroy team (now Brisbane Lions) to be an active player. A Victorian, Chris was born in 1976. In a long career, he played 264 senior games: 59 for Fitzroy from 1994 to 1996 and 205 for the Brisbane Lions between 1997 and 2007. He was a key member of the Lions' three glory years of successive AFL premierships (2001, 2002, 2003). He captained Brisbane in 2007, won the club's best and fairest in 2003 and was selected for the All-Australians in 2002, 2003 and 2004. Chris played six International Rules matches against Ireland. He is one of three Aboriginal players to captain an AFL side, with **Gavin Wanganeen** (Port Adelaide) and **Michael Long** (Essendon). He is a member of the Aboriginal Team of the Century. Photo: GSP Images/AFL Media.

JOE JOHNSON

Between 1897 and the glimmerings of a golden era in the 1960s, only seven identified Aboriginal players appeared in the VFL: at the start of the twentieth century, Joe Johnson was one of them. Johnson was the godfather of a sport now synonymous with Aboriginal sporting achievement. Joe was born in the early 1880s, but we don't know where. He played for Northcote in the Victorian Football Association competition in 1902–1903, then joined Fitzroy in 1904. He played 55 games in varying positions for the Lions until the end of the 1906 season and was in the 1904 and 1905 premiership sides. From 1907 to 1911 he was player-coach of Brunswick in the VFA and he re-joined Northcote in the VFA for the 1912–1914 season. Photo: Fitzroy Football Club Archives.

AUSTRALIAN FOOTBALL

DAVID KANTILLA

His birth name was Amparralamtua and he was born in Nguiu (Bathurst Island, NT) in 1940. David began his career as a ruckman with the famous **St Mary's** team in the late 1950s. He was recruited to South Adelaide in 1961 and thus became the first traditional Aboriginal man to play in a southern league. David played 113 games for that side until 1966, winning the Knuckey Cup — for that team's best and fairest — in 1961 and 1962. He represented South Australia in 1964 and 1965. In the 1968–1969 season he was captain and coach of **St Mary's**. David died in a motor smash at Nguiu aged 37. In honour of this man, the new football ground at Marrara in Darwin named its restaurant 'Kantillas'. Photo: *Advertiser*.

DALE KICKETT

Dale was born in 1968 and raised as a Balladong Nyungar man in Tammin (WA) — yet another great player from that south-western region of Western Australia. He is related to both **Derek Kickett** and **Lance Franklin**. He began playing for Claremont in the West, then recruited to Fitzroy for 15 games before being traded to the West Coast Eagles for two games. He moved to St Kilda for 21 matches, to Essendon for eight games and then finally to the Fremantle Dockers for whom he played 135 matches as the mainstay of their defence. These switches made him one of only three men who have played for five clubs in the AFL. Dale played in three Claremont premiership sides, winning a Simpson Medal as the best player in a grand final. In his final match in 2002 the crowd and the opposing Port Adelaide stayed on the ground to pay tribute to him. Photo: GSP Images/AFL Media.

DEREK KICKETT

Of Balladong Nyungar descent, Derek was born in 1962. He was a great attraction in three states. He played 32 games for Claremont starting in 1986, 25 games for Central Districts in the SANFL in 1988, twelve games for North Melbourne in 1989, 77 for Essendon between 1990 and 1993, and then 63 excellent games for Sydney Swans from 1994 to the end of 1996. With Paul Kelly, Tony Lockett and Aboriginal star **Michael O'Loughlin** he helped raise the Swans to the level where more Sydneysiders were watching this 'foreign' game than rugby league. He was in the Aboriginal All Stars team that beat Collingwood in Darwin in 1994 and played in six interstate matches. Derek has three nephews in this Hall: **Dale Kickett**, **Lance Franklin** and **Byron Pickett**. Photo: Fairfax Photo Library/courtesy John Fairfax Holdings.

TED ('SQUARE') KILMURRAY

Ted was born in Wiluna (WA) in 1934. He was raised in an assimilation home, Sister Kate's Orphanage in Perth. There he and **Polly Farmer** forged a lifelong friendship and both remember it with some affection — the place where they learned independence. Both admit that their apparently clairvoyant understanding was the result of practising endlessly together to ameliorate the boredom of the institution. As a pairing they were an unbeatable football combination for East Perth. 'Square' played 256 matches for East Perth from 1952 to 1967. He played five matches for Western Australia, won the prestigious Sandover Medal in 1958 (best and fairest in the season's league matches), was runner-up to Farmer for the same Medal in 1960. Unlike so many who were tempted to play in the glamorous game in Victoria, he stayed in the West. Photo: West Australian Newspapers Limited.

JIM KRAKOUER

In 1982 a new dimension was added to Australian football in Victoria's capital. The Krakouer brothers arrived from Claremont in Perth to play for North Melbourne. **Jim Krakouer**, brother to Phil, was born in Mt Barker (WA) in 1958. With 88 games for Claremont as experience, this fiery little man played brilliant football for North Melbourne in 134 games. He then had a short stint with St Kilda, playing thirteen games with the Saints. Jim's style was scintillating, artistic and at times turbulent: perhaps more than any other Aboriginal footballer he was the target of racial abuse by the crowds at the MCG. His career spanned 1977 to 1991 during which time he won the Simpson Medal in 1991, North Melbourne's best and fairest in 1986 and was selected for the All-Australians team in 1986 and 1987. A long gaol term for drug offences was a sad end to a brilliant career. Photo: *Herald & Weekly Times*.

PHIL KRAKOUER

Martin Flanagan of the *Age* describes the Krakouers' play as 'a most audaciously clairvoyant act ... the long looping handballs apparent to no one but always mysteriously, at the last moment, to the other'. Phil was born in Mt Barker (WA) in 1960. He was a more laid-back player than brother Jim, less prone to engage in confrontation. Of his style, Flanagan says he had 'the appearance of a semi-interested schoolboy'. Phil played 90 matches for Claremont, 141 for North Melbourne and then seven for Footscray. His career began in 1978 and ended in 1991. 'I suppose we were both very lucky we were given some sort of gift by God', said Phil. Perhaps, but they both worked very hard to perfect their talents. In their father Eric's words: 'They were determined players who hated to get beat'. Photo: *Herald & Weekly Times*.

LAKE TYERS TEAM

The Lake Tyers community in East Gippsland (Vic.) has a long and painful history. It was established as an Anglican church mission station in 1863. Despite some schemes to sell off the beautiful site to commercial interests in the 1960s, the local people fought some tough battles to keep it Aboriginal (documented in Richard Broome's 2015 book, *Fighting Hard*). In the 1930s and '40s White farmers in the area successfully pressed the state government to stop Aboriginal people from growing peas and other vegetables because they were considered to be engaging in 'unfair competition', that is, asking cheaper prices for their produce.

Lake Tyers Football Club in the late 1930s. *Back row, standing, left to right*: Les Green, Stewart Hood, Norman O'Rourke, Jimmy O'Rourke, Herbie Bull, Foster Moffatt, Harry Hayes, Alec McRae, Keith Bryant. *Sitting*: Gordon Marks, Charlie Green, Jack Hood, Jim Wandin, Con Edwards, Alec Harrison, Bert Stevens. *Front row*: Neville White, Billy Tregonning (mascot), Allan McDougall. (Stewart Hood was the grandfather of **Lionel Rose**; Harry Hayes the grandfather of Australian flyweight champion also named Harry Hayes.)

Photo: Alick Jackomos Collection.

CLIFFORD (GYMPIE) LEW FATT

Walter Lew Fatt — born in the Maningrida (Bawinanga) community — was the head of a famous Darwin family and a great footballer with the Buffaloes team. Walter is in the NT Football Hall of Fame as are his sons Clifford pictured here, Terry and Bennie. Clifford was always known as Gympie even in the official death notices in 2010. Born in 1945, he first played for **St Mary's** in 1960. His first football award in the 1960–1961 season was the Steve Abala Colts Medal. Gympie won the Saints best and fairest award for the first time in 1963–1964, winning again in 1964–1965. He was the club's leading goal scorer and winner of the NT Football League's highest honour, the Nichols Medal. In 1967–1968 he was again the leading goal-kicker and was selected to play in the 1967 NTFL All Star Team against the VFL All Stars team. Gympie played for Saints until his mid-40s and coached several Saints teams. Photo: Bennie Lew Fatt.

TERRY LEW FATT

Born in 1937, Terry was the eldest of the three sporting brothers. He was one of the Northern Territory's outstanding sportsmen in the 1950s and 1960s, playing Australian football, basketball and soccer (to keep fit, he said). He is fondly remembered as the fairest sportsman to grace a field. His entire career was with **St Mary's**, beginning with his debut in the premiership win in the 1954–1955 season. By the end of his playing career in 1968–1969 he had been in seven premiership sides, played over 200 games for the Saints, won their best and fairest award three times and for seven seasons he was either captain or captain-coach. In basketball Terry was one of the great players of the 1950s and 1960s: he was still playing A-grade at the age of 44. Photo: Bennie Lew Fatt.

CHRIS LEWIS

The Lewis family is unusual in sport. Irwin Lewis was the first Aboriginal man in the West to attend university. He didn't graduate, preferring to play 75 games for Claremont. Son Clayton played 25 games for Claremont; son Cameron played 92, moved to East Perth and played one game for Western Australia after which he had a successful coaching career. Son Chris, born in Perth in 1960, was the family's greatest achiever: nine matches for Claremont and then an outstanding 212 games for the West Coast Eagles between 1987 and 1998. Chris played five matches for Western Australia, won the Eagles' best and fairest in 1990 and was in no less than two AFL premiership sides, in 1992 and again in 1994. A somewhat tempestuous and erratic player, he was often pure genius against Melbourne sides, a fact rarely appreciated by that city's fans. Photo: GSP Images/AFL Media.

MICHAEL LONG

One of the truly great Australian footballers of the 1990s, Michael was born in Darwin in 1969. Starting at 16, this 'skinny youngster' played 52 games for **St Mary's**, then moved to West Torrens in the SANFL, for whom he played 22 matches in 1988. Recruited by Essendon, he starred in most of his 160 games for the Dons. In 1989 he was AFL Rookie of the Year. Michael has represented the Territory on five occasions. His glory day was in the 1993 grand final against Carlton: he was clearly the best player on the field and the Norm Smith Medal was duly presented to him — by **Polly Farmer**! In 1995 he came fourth in the Brownlow Medal competition and was selected for the All-Australians team in 1988. Michael has worked hard to end racial abuse in this code of football. Photo: Fairfax Photo Library/courtesy John Fairfax Holdings.

MALLEE PARK FOOTBALL CLUB

Mallee Park Football Club, Port Lincoln (SA) were premiers in 1985, 1987 to 1990, 1993 to 1996, 1999, 2001, 2005, 2009, 2010, 2011, 2015 and 2016. [We have no date for this 1980s or 1990s photograph.]

Back row, left to right: Rodney Johncock, John Coaby, Richard Miller, Max Thomas, Terry Miller, Jack Johncock, David Dudley, Trevor Johncock, Russell Miller (vice-president), Peter Burgoyne (president/team manager), Kirt Dudley (head trainer). *Middle row*: Fabian Davey (vice-captain), Byron Burgoyne, James Miller, Joe Burgoyne (captain-coach), Dean Miller, Lincoln Dudley, Roger Johncock, Tony Burgoyne. *Front row*: Darren Miller, Dion Betts, Warren Miller, Michael Burgoyne, Bobby-Shane Dudley.

Photo: Mallee Park Football Club.

PETER MATERA

Peter Matera was one of three outstanding Aboriginal players in the West Coast Eagles side that won the AFL premiership in 1992 and 1994. Born in Wagin (WA) in 1969, he is a brother of Phillip and Wally Matera, also members of the Eagles team. Peter is every inch as distinguished as the other greats from the West. He began his career with South Fremantle in 1987, completing 59 games for them before switching to the Eagles. By the end of the 1999 season he had played 200 games for the Eagles, scoring 182 goals. Peter represented his state on five occasions, was chosen in the All-Australians on five occasions (1991, 1993, 1994, 1996, 1997), won two premiership side medals, the club's best and fairest in 1997, and the Norm Smith Medal for the best player on the field in the AFL grand final in 1992. Photo: GSP Images/AFL Media.

GILBERT McADAM

The first and only Aboriginal player to win the prestigious Magarey Medal in South Australian football was Gilbert McAdam. Born in Alice Springs (NT) in 1967, Gilbert and brother Greg had good careers in the NT, SA and AFL competitions. Greg played 110 games for North Adelaide and then ten for St Kilda. Gilbert began with Waratahs and South Alice in the NT, played 73 matches for Central Districts in South Australia, 53 games for St Kilda and by the end of 1996 had played 58 games for Brisbane. He also played in two interstate matches for the Territory. Brother Greg played three matches for South Australia. When the racial vilification issue was at its height in 1990s Gilbert was appointed by the AFL as the liaison man, the one who could best discourage racism on the field and among the players. He has had an outstanding career in sports media. Photo: *Herald & Weekly Times*.

NORMAN McDONALD

Norman McDonald and **Doug Nicholls** rank as two of the greatest all-rounders in Australian sport: as boxers, professional sprinters and Australian footballers. Born in Richmond (Vic.) in 1925, Norm joined Essendon after leaving the Royal Australian Air Force. He played 128 games for the Dons between 1947 and 1953. This attacking half-back played in six grand finals, two of them in the winning side (1949 and 1950). Norm was Essendon's top vote-scorer in the Brownlow Medal for three years. He represented Victoria twice in 1952. He won the Wangaratta, Maryborough and Lancefield sprint Gifts and was runner-up to Essendon colleague Lance Mann in the 1948 Stawell Easter Gift. He had a short career as a professional boxer. McDonald says he had total acceptance: 'there was no backlash or anything like that against me'. **Michael Long** wore Norman's number 4 guernsey in the 1993 grand final. Photo: *Herald & Weekly Times*.

MICHAEL McLEAN

Michael, born in Darwin in 1965, began his sporting life with Nightcliff who regard him as their most celebrated player. He won two important under-age medals before being selected for the 1981 All-Australian Schoolboys. Michael had an outstanding 95 games career with Footscray. He had an even more successful relationship with Brisbane for whom he played 86 games to the end of 1997. He won the Brisbane Bears Club Trophy for best and fairest in 1991 and 1993, played seven games for the NT and was captain of the Aboriginal All Stars team that beat Collingwood in Darwin in 1994. He was selected for the All-Australians in 1998. Michael was the prime mover in recruiting Territory Aboriginal players to the Brisbane Bears, a team he has coached with much success especially in the 1999 season. Photo: Fairfax Photo Library/ courtesy John Fairfax Holdings.

ANDREW McLEOD

Andrew was a stellar footballer for Adelaide from 1995 to 2010. Born in Darwin in 1976, his early football was with a Darwin team and then Port Adelaide. He began life with the Crows in 1995 and remained there until retirement in 2010, playing no less than 340 games and scoring 275 goals for the team. Andrew has a long list of achievements. He was in two premiership sides (1997 and 1998), was Adelaide's best and fairest on three occasions, won the Norm Smith Medal twice for best player in a grand final, a Michael Tuck Medal, and was selected for the All Australian side on five occasions. He also played in three International Rules football matches and in the 150th anniversary Tribute Match between the Dream Team side that played Victoria in 2008. Andrew was a natural choice for the Aboriginal Team of the Century. Photo: GSP Images/AFL Media.

STEPHEN MICHAEL

In the 1980s several critics contended that Stephen was the best player in the country. Football authority Alan East rated him a better footballer than **Polly Farmer** and **Barry Cable**. Farmer was the incomparable ruckman and Cable the best rover, he said, but Michael played both roles superbly. Born in Wagin (WA) in 1956, Stephen played 243 games for South Fremantle including 216 in a row — a feat that speaks volumes for his fitness and dedication. A man of phenomenal speed, people flocked to see the combination of Michael rucking and **Maurice Rioli** playing centre. Radio commentators were serious about Michael 'having eyes at the back of his head'. His senior career started in 1975 and ended in 1985. He won the Sandover Medal twice, in 1980 and 1981. His triumphant year was 1983 when he won the Simpson Medal, the Tassie Medal and was selected as captain of the All-Australians. Photo: Paul Roberts.

PHIL NARKLE

Six little towns in the south-west of Western Australia — Bunbury, Gnowangerup, Narrogin, Wagin, Tambellup, and Kellerberrin — with an Aboriginal population of about 5000, have produced a staggering number of champion footballers: the **Haywards**, the **Kickett** clan, the **Krakouers**, **Syd Jackson**, **Polly Farmer**, **Ted Kilmurray**, **Barry Cable**, **Nicky Winmar** and the Narkle boys — Dempsey, Keith and Phil. Phil was born in Bunbury in 1961. He played 134 games for Swan Districts and was in their premiership side in 1982, 1983 and 1990. Phil moved east where he played 48 games for St Kilda, then west again to play eighteen games for the West Coast Eagles. He won the coveted Sandover Medal — for the best and fairest in the season's league games — in 1982 and was runner-up in that trophy in 1991. In 1987 he was selected for the All-Australians team. Phil twice represented WA in interstate matches. Photo: *Herald & Weekly Times*.

PASTOR SIR DOUGLAS NICHOLLS, KCVO, OBE, KSTJ

The great role model for Aboriginal players, plain 'Doug' became Pastor Doug, then progressed to Sir Doug as Governor of South Australia in 1976. This tiny, courageous Yorta Yorta man — born in Cummeragunja (NSW) in 1906 — tried out for Carlton, who rejected him because of his colour. Fitzroy signed him on for a magnificent career of 54 games in which he played wing alongside football's greatest legend, Haydn Bunton. In life with the Lions (1932–1937) he won the club's best and fairest in 1934 and 1935 and represented Victoria in 1934. He boxed in Jimmy Sharman's tents and as a professional sprinter won the Warracknabeal and Nyah Gifts in 1929. Retiring in 1937, Doug went into church and welfare work, becoming a leading figure in the Aborigines Advancement League. A great-nephew of political leader William Cooper, Doug participated in the 1938 'Day of Mourning' protest. In a Melbourne public address he once said his people were 'the skeleton in the cupboard of Australia's national life … outcasts in our own land'. Photo: *Herald & Weekly Times*.

MICHAEL O'LOUGHLIN

Of mixed ancestry, including a paternal Czech Jewish grandfather, Michael was born in South Australia in 1977 and grew up in Adelaide. He began playing with Central Districts, then moved to Sydney where he was recruited by the Swans. Michael was in that side from 1995 to 2009, playing a remarkable 303 games for 521 goals. A strong, fast and agile half-forward flanker and later as a full forward, he joined **Adam Goodes** in enthralling the crowds. Michael was twice selected for the All-Australian side. He won club's best and fairest in 1998, was the leading goal kicker in 2000 and 2001, played in the 2005 premiership side, was selected for the All-Australian team in 1997 and 2000 and was a member of the Indigenous Team of the Century. He played two State representative games as well as four International Rules matches. Photo: GSP Images/AFL Media.

BYRON PICKETT

Born in Kellerberrin (WA) in 1977, Byron is acknowledged as one of the finest of the many Aboriginal footballers in history. A nephew of **Derek Kickett** and related to the Kickett clan and to **Lance Franklin**, Byron's junior playing days were in Port Lincoln (SA). In all, Byron played 120 games for North Melbourne between 1997 and 2002, 55 games for Port Adelaide from 2003 to 2005 and 29 games for Melbourne in 2006 and 2007. A tough and aggressive player given to controversies, he was in two premiership sides, won the Norm Smith Medal for the best player in the 2004 grand final, and was selected twice for the All-Australia side. Despite troubled times he has worked hard in Aboriginal youth programs. Photo: GSP Images/AFL Media.

CYRIL RIOLI

The nephew of both the great **Maurice Rioli** and **Michael Long**, Cyril was born in the Tiwi Islands north of Darwin in 1989. At 14 he attend Scotch College in Melbourne on a scholarship and when unhappy there he was mentored and encouraged to stay by **Michael Long** and **Derek Kickett**. Cyril made his debut for Hawthorn in 2008 playing every game that year including a sensational performance in the winning premiership side. Cyril has been in four premiership sides (2008, 2013, 2014 and 2015) and won the Norm Smith Medal for the 2015 final. He had three selections for the All-Australian sides and in 2009 won the Goal of the Year award. 'Polished brilliance' is a common observation of his play; 'a delicious player' is another acclamation. Photo: Michael Willson/AFL Media.

MAURICE RIOLI

Few footballers can match the record of the talented Maurice, born at Garden Point (Pularumpi), Melville Island, NT) in 1957. Starting with sixteen senior games for **St Mary's**, Maurice moved West to play 168 games for South Fremantle (1975–1981 and 1988–1990), captaining the team in 1988–1989. In between, he played 118 games for Richmond in the AFL competition, kicking 80 goals (1982–1987). His mastery, touch and physical strength won him Richmond's best and fairest in 1982 and 1983, three Simpson Medals (1980, 1981, 1984), runner-up in the 1983 Brownlow Medal, the Norm Smith best and fairest in 1982 and three All-Australians selections in 1983, 1986 and 1988. He played thirteen games for WA. He was a member of the Legislative Council in the NT. Maurice coached the victorious Aboriginal All Stars against Collingwood in 1994. In many ways he is rightly regarded as 'Mr Aboriginal Football'. Photo: Department of Aboriginal Affairs.

BILLY ROE, BEM

A legend in the Northern Territory, Billy excelled in Australian football and in basketball. Born in Broome (WA) in 1934, he began his long football career — from 1954 to 1967 — with the famous **St Mary's** team in Darwin. He played in seven grand finals in the Top End league. He was awarded a best and fairest by his club and won the prestigious Nichols Medal — the NTFLs best and fairest for the season — in 1954–1955. He moved to the West and played 13 games for East Perth, including the 1956 premiership game in which he was voted best player. Billy represented the Northern Territory in the Australian basketball championships, played professional basketball in Perth and coached the first Aboriginal football team to go abroad on the Papua New Guinea tour in 1972. Photo: *NT News*.

ROVERS FOOTBALL CLUB

One hundred years ago the outstanding Australian rules team from the Ceduna area of South Australia, the Koonibba Football Club, was born with the help of Lutheran missionaries. It is the oldest surviving Aboriginal team in Australia. In the 1950s, with too many Aboriginal men wanting to play, a sister team, Rovers, was admitted to the league — and within a year had won the 1958 premiership. We are constantly reminded that, statistically, there is a 17- to 19-year gap between Aboriginal male and non-Aboriginal male life expectancy (59 to 78). Rovers is an example of a far starker reality. Of the eighteen men in that team, only one, Keith Willoughby, was alive in 1987: the other seventeen men didn't make it to the age of 50. Keith died in 1995.

The Rovers Football Club, Ceduna (SA), winners of the 1958 premiership. *Back row, left to right*: Doug Benbolt, Cyril McCarthy, Brenz Saunders, Spencer Weetra, Gordon Ware, Don Kelly, Mervyn Edwards, Dennis Kelly, Francis Willoughby, Herbert Miller, Eric Richards. *Front row*: Edwin Kent, Alf Peel, Reg Betts, Cecil Betts (captain), Keith Willoughby, Eddie Betts (who died in custody), Glen Bilney.

Photo: John Gascoyne.

ST MARY'S FOOTBALL CLUB

In the 1940s and early 1950s many young men from Bathurst and Melville Islands went to Darwin for three-month spells to work for the Army or Air Force. Despite the uniforms, they were not allowed to be servicemen and worked as mere domestic servants. The Bishop of Darwin felt that football might be 'a good thing' for the men. Despite objections from the town's administrators who did not want 'too many blackfellas around', the team was born in 1952, formed with the help of Ted Egan (then a young patrol officer with the Department of Native Affairs). He initially coached and captained St Mary's. In 1954–1955 they won the first of many premierships. St Mary's was the training ground and nursery for such famous players as **Billy Roe**, Benny Vigona, **Bennie Lew Fatt**, **Terry Lew Fatt**, **Gympie Lew Fatt**, **David Kantilla**, **Michael Graham**, **Maurice Rioli** and **Michael Long**. (St Mary's had won 32 NTFL premierships by the end of the 2017 season.)

St Mary's first premiership team 1954–1955: *Back row, left to right*: H Sherlock (coach), Benny Cubillo, Arthur Smith, **Terry Lew Fatt**, Ken Bowman, **Billy Roe**, Terry Connolly, Brian Pobjoy, Gordon Roe, Anastasius Vigona. *Middle row*: Edmund Johnson, Urban Tipiloura, Phillip Babui, Ted Egan (captain), Saturninus Kantilla, Jerome Kerinaiua, Raphael Apuatimi. *Front row*: Jacob Pautjimi, Bertram Kantilla, Dermot Tipungwuti, Paul Kerinaiua.

Photo: Ted Egan.

ANDREW WALKER (1)

Born in Echuca (Vic.) in 1986, a Yorta Yorta man, Andrew was educated at good schools. He came to football notice playing in Bendigo. He made his debut for Carlton in 2004. By the end of 2017 he had played 202 games for the Cats, scoring 139 goals. In 2016 he became the first Aboriginal player to achieve 200 goals for Carlton. Several injuries caused loss of games and of form but he played well in 2006, establishing himself as a key player as a forward in the Carlton side. Following retirement in 2016 he became a coach for Carlton's development program for young players. He was given life membership of the club. [See the rugby league chapter for another **Andrew Walker (2)**.] Photo: Lachlan Cunningham/AFL Media.

GAVIN WANGANEEN

It was only a matter of time before an Aboriginal player would win the Brownlow Medal, awarded to the best and fairest player in all the season's games leading to the finals. Gavin won in 1993. Born in Mt Gambier (SA) in 1973, this brilliant young man played 24 games for Port Adelaide in the South Australian Football League and then moved into the AFL competition where he played 127 matches for Essendon, including in the premiership side in 1993. He went on to captain Port Adelaide when that team entered the AFL. By the end of 1999 he had played 51 games for Port Power. He won the Michael Tuck Medal in 1993 and was selected for the All-Australians on four occasions. The *Age* describes him as 'inventing skills of his own, controlling circumstances with a serenity that mocks the mayhem around him'. Photo: *Herald & Weekly Times*.

DANIEL WELLS

Born in 1985 in Port Lincoln (SA), Daniel began his scintillating career with North Melbourne in 2003, staying with that team until 2016. In that time he played 243 games, scoring 150 goals for the Kangaroos. In 2017 he changed to Collingwood, playing ten games for the 'Pies. He came to prominence in 2004, kicking the Goal of the Year in a match against Fremantle. In 2008 he was selected in the Australian side that lost to Ireland in that year's International Rules Series. Twice winner of the Syd Barker Medal for the Kangaroos' best and fairest player of the season, following the 2013 season he was chosen to represent Australia in the International Rules Series — a game in which Gaelic footballers from Ireland play Australian Rules footballers — and appointed captain of the exclusively Aboriginal team, a rare and memorable honour. Leroy and Lewis Jetta were in that team as was **Lance Franklin**. Photo: Sean Garnsworthy/AFL Media.

GAVIN WANGANEEN

It was only a matter of time before an Aboriginal player would win the Brownlow Medal, awarded to the best and fairest player in all the season's games leading to the finals. Gavin won in 1993. Born in Mt Gambier (SA) in 1973, this brilliant young man played 24 games for Port Adelaide in the South Australian Football League and then moved into the AFL competition where he played 127 matches for Essendon, including in the premiership side in 1993. He went on to captain Port Adelaide when that team entered the AFL. By the end of 1999 he had played 51 games for Port Power. He won the Michael Tuck Medal in 1993 and was selected for the All-Australians on four occasions. The *Age* describes him as 'inventing skills of his own, controlling circumstances with a serenity that mocks the mayhem around him'. Photo: *Herald & Weekly Times*.

DANIEL WELLS

Born in 1985 in Port Lincoln (SA), Daniel began his scintillating career with North Melbourne in 2003, staying with that team until 2016. In that time he played 243 games, scoring 150 goals for the Kangaroos. In 2017 he changed to Collingwood, playing ten games for the 'Pies. He came to prominence in 2004, kicking the Goal of the Year in a match against Fremantle. In 2008 he was selected in the Australian side that lost to Ireland in that year's International Rules Series. Twice winner of the Syd Barker Medal for the Kangaroos' best and fairest player of the season, following the 2013 season he was chosen to represent Australia in the International Rules Series — a game in which Gaelic footballers from Ireland play Australian Rules footballers — and appointed captain of the exclusively Aboriginal team, a rare and memorable honour. Leroy and Lewis Jetta were in that team as was **Lance Franklin**. Photo: Sean Garnsworthy/AFL Media.

DARRYL WHITE

Martin Flanagan describes Darryl as 'the scribbly gum of Australian football, totally novel and a great crowd favourite'. Born in 1973 in Alice Springs, this 'erratic youth' began playing with Pioneers in the Central Australian league. Between 1992 and 2005 he played 268 games for the Brisbane Lions scoring 165 goals. He had five representative games, for Queensland and the Northern Territory, played one International Rules match and was in three Lions premiership sides (2001, 2002, 2003). Darryl was a member of the Aboriginal All Stars team that played Collingwood in Darwin in February 1994, a match intended to heal some deep-seated racism shown by Collingwood fans towards **Nicky Winmar**. He is a member of the Aboriginal Team of the Century. In the NTFL 2005–2006 season he was in the Darwin Football Club's premiership side. He then played in a Queensland league premiership side. Since retirement he has worked in Aboriginal youth support. Photo: GSP Images/AFL Media.

NEIL (NICKY) WINMAR

Nicky was born in Pingelly (WA) in 1965. He played 58 games for South Fremantle and 230 for St Kilda, scoring 283 goals between 1987 and 1998. He played 21 games for Footscray in 1999. He was winner of St Kilda's best and fairest in 1989 and 1995, selected for the All-Australians in 1991 and 1995, and played eight matches for Western Australia. Winmar is shown here with **Derek Kickett** (*right*). Nicky will long be remembered for his amazing skills, his ability to turn a game around and his dignity in the face of some appalling abuse on and off the field. The issue of racial abuse came to a head in 1993 when the Collingwood crowd vilified Nicky. He lifted his jumper and pointed proudly to his skin, an action supported by most Australians and all sports reporters [see picture in chapter 1]. Further abuse of **Michael Long** in 1995 led to the Australian Football League introducing a code of conduct prohibiting racist behaviour. Photo: West Australian Newspapers Ltd.

DAVID WIRRPANDA

Born in Melbourne in 1979, David began his remarkable football career with Healesville (once the site of the famous Coranderrk Mission). He is descended from the **Doug Nicholls** clan. Most Western Australian Aboriginal footballers have migrated to the Victorian clubs but David moved West. Between 1996 and 2008 he played 227 games for the West Coast Eagles, scoring 131 goals. He was in the winning premiership side in 2006, played two International Rules matches against Ireland and was honoured by an All-Australians selection in 2005. He established the David Wirrpanda Foundation to support Aboriginal advancement and is considered a potential leader. He was an unsuccessful candidate in the 2013 Federal Senate elections. Photo: GSP Images/AFL Media.

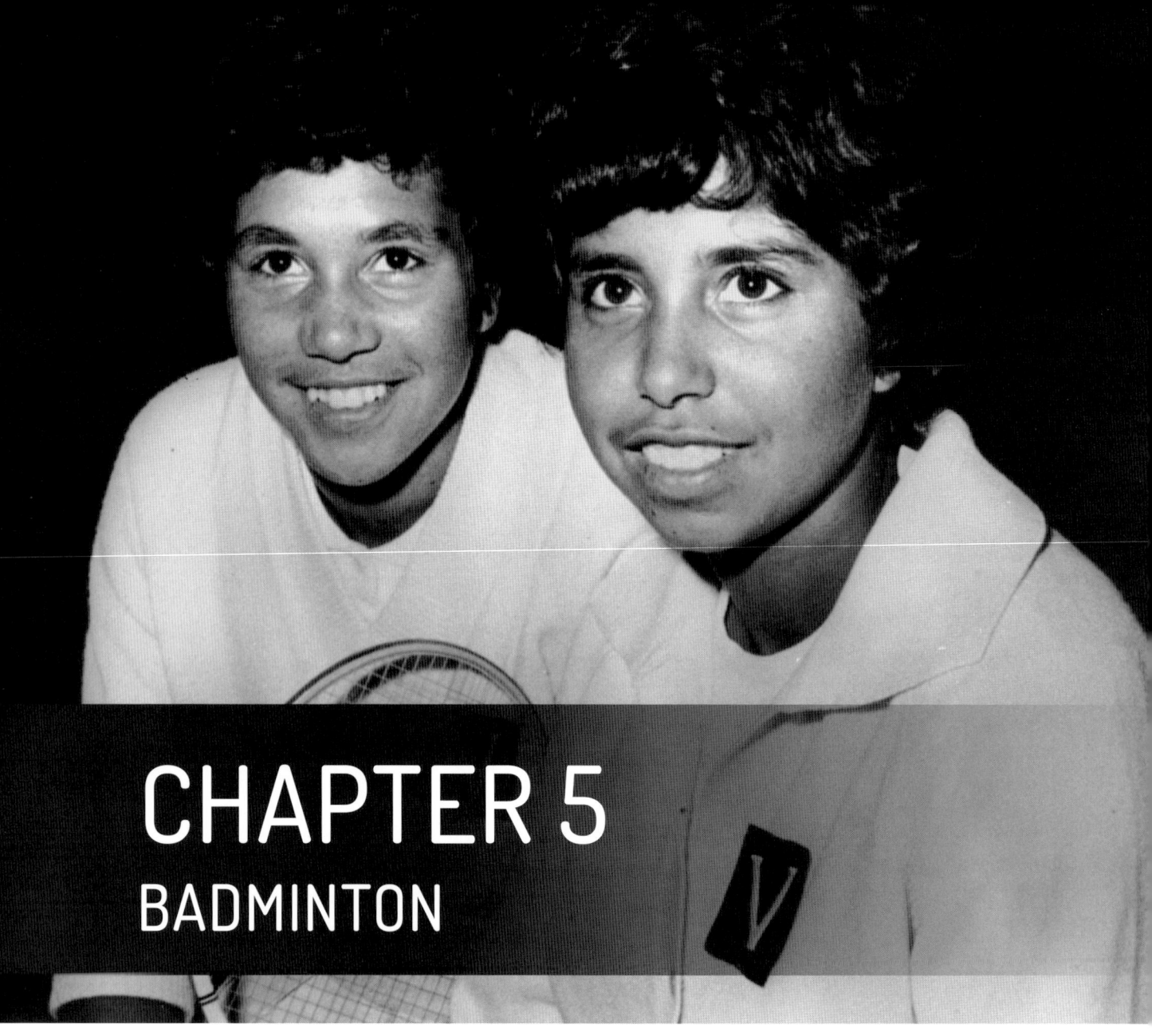

CHAPTER 5
BADMINTON

This is an indoor racquet game, played as singles, doubles and mixed doubles matches. The 'ball' that has to cross the high net is called a shuttlecock, or commonly, a shuttle, originally hand-made of feathers. Developed in India, it became a worldwide game once dominated by the Danes and now by Chinese and Indonesian players. An exciting, fast and athletic sport, it ought to be more popular in Australia than it is. It is possible that increasing Asian immigration to Australia will make the game a more popular one.

The Aboriginal involvement in this game arose by chance. Dick Hine was a dairy farmer at Labertouche in Victoria's Gippsland. He befriended a neighbouring Aboriginal community at Jacksons Track — and history was made. (It also made history as the birthplace and early childhood domain of boxer **Lionel Rose**.) Dick taught most of the twelve Mullett siblings to play badminton, and Cheryl, Sandra, Pauline, Linda, Phillip and Russell all went on to win state or national titles.

CHERYL MULLETT (DRAYTON)

Cheryl became a player of international status. Born at Jackson's Track near Drouin (Vic.), Cheryl won three Australian junior singles, the Australian women's doubles and mixed doubles titles, five titles at the Australian Championships in 1969 and five major doubles titles with her sister **Sandra Mullett**. The years 1968 and 1969 were the highlights for her: she was chosen to play for Australia in the Uber Cup, the women's world team championship and in the Whyte Trophy (Australia v New Zealand). All the Mullett family say they owe their start in life to their badminton days. They also symbolised the 'era of hope', the 1960s. Cheryl had a long career in the Victorian public service. Photo: Dorothy Proctor.

SANDRA MULLETT

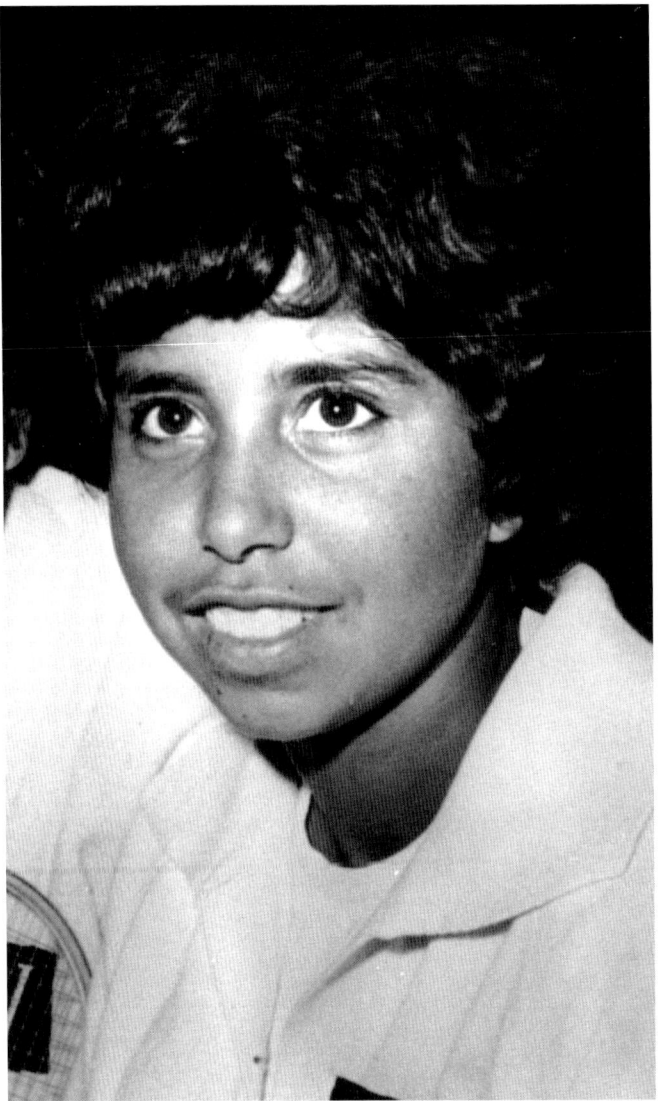

Sandra Mullett, sister to **Cheryl Mullett (Drayton)**, was also born at Jackson's Track near Drouin (Vic.), in 1953. As a junior she won no less than ten Victorian titles, ranging from state under-15 schoolgirls champion to state under-19 mixed doubles and women's doubles titles. She won five under-age Victorian singles and five doubles titles, one with brother Phillip and one with brother Russell. Sandra also won six Australian singles titles: three under-17 national singles (1968, 1969, 1970), three under-17 doubles (one with sister Cheryl), and three under-17 mixed doubles championships (all with brother Russell). She beat sister Cheryl for the under-17 Victorian title in 1967. Russell won four Victorian under age titles and one Australian championship; brother Phillip won six Victorian under-age and one Australian championship, the Junior Singles, in 1967. The Mullett and other families are celebrated in *Jackson's Track—Memoir of a Dreamtime Place*, by Sandra's father Daryl Tonkin and Carolyn Landon. Photo: Sandra Mullett.

CHAPTER 6
BASKETBALL

Basketball originated in the United States in 1891 and is now a truly worldwide sport. For long a city-based game, rural basketball began to make progress in the 1970s. But for Aboriginal people there was virtually no participation. This may seem odd given that in Queensland the Kalkadoon people played a game called *kerentan*, a form of ball-catching much in the mould of modern basketball.

Missions and government settlements didn't have the halls or gymnasiums to house courts. At best, some communities had an outdoor or dirt or asphalt area with poor-quality hoops. The town of Geraldton in Western Australian once had a regular Aboriginal basketball carnival. Today it has resurfaced as a 'midnight competition' aimed at distracting youth from anti-social behaviour. In the 1980s and 1990s basketball flourished in a few Aboriginal communities, especially in Western Australia, North Queensland and the Top End of the Territory. For us, Aboriginal male

Andrea Collins was a Queensland representative in basketball and managed the Aboriginal and Torres Strait Islander team that toured Canada and the United States in 1998.
Photo: *Courier Mail*

under-participation still remains something of a surprise, especially as Aboriginal women have done so well in this sport and in the related game of netball.

The pioneers, so to speak, were **Michael Ahmatt**, **Kevin Coombes** (in disabled basketball), **Bennie**, **Terry and Gympie Lew Fatt**, **Danny Morseu** and **Billy Roe**. Joe Clarke played for South Australia and in New South Wales. Brian Dixon represented the Northern Territory in both basketball and baseball. He became captain-coach of the Glenelg baseball side in Adelaide for several seasons. Robert Baldwin and Kane Muir were the first Aboriginal players in Victorian state metropolitan sides with Robert playing in the NBL. At the end of 1988 two teams went to Canada and the United States for a short tour. Called Aboriginal Australia, the object of the tour was to help players gain international experience by competing against teams in the college circuit. In the 1999–2000 season Tim Duggan of Darwin played for the Territory and New South Wales and was a member of the Cairns Taipans in the National Basketball League.

In the current era, William McDowell-White, son of Australian footballer **Darryl White**, has played professional basketball in Germany. Cousins **Patrick Mills** and **Nathan Jawai** became stellar players not only for Australia at the Olympic level but in the American NBL competition, possibly the fiercest tournament arena in sport.

Joe Clark was a powerful force in the South Australian side.
Photo: *Advertiser*

MICHAEL AHMATT

Although born in Townsville (Qld), in 1942, Michael spent his short life in the Northern Territory and South Australia. He first played basketball for the Territory aged 17. The outstanding player in the Australian side which came ninth in the 1964 Tokyo Olympics, he was also in the national side for the 1968 Mexico Olympics. Michael played an amazing 588 games for South Adelaide and represented South Australia for ten years. Chris White, the former national coaching director, revered Ahmatt: 'a fantastic basketballer, a real whiz kid, a great ball-handler. The man who excited the crowds and was idolised by the kids.' Michael was a member of the original Aboriginal Sports Foundation. Like so many Hall Members he died young, aged 41. His son Shane played under-16 basketball for South Australia, daughter Michelle captained the under-20 state side and was a member of the state's senior basketball team. Photo: *Advertiser*.

SCOTT BUTLER

Scott, born in Rockhampton (Qld) in 1971, officiated at a remarkable number of National Basketball League (NBL) games, 500 in all, and was named NBL Referee of the Year in 2005, 2006, 2007 and 2009. His high standard of refereeing led to his appointment for twelve NBL Grand Final series between 2002 to 2012. Scott had an international role as well, refereeing at two Olympic Games and two FIBA World Championships, in 2006 and 2010. Scott took charge of the women's bronze game at the 2008 Beijing Games and was the emergency referee for the gold medal final at the 2004 Athens Games. His first major game was in 1992 and his career ended, through an injury, twenty years later. He has the distinction of being named Head of Referees. Photo: Basketball Australia.

LOUISA COLLINS

Louisa represents the liberation of Aboriginal women in northern Australia — legally, socially, economically and sportingly. Born in Broome (WA) in 1938, Louisa lived her sporting life in the Northern Territory. With freedom for 'half-castes' in the late 1950s, women had their first real chance to move about, join clubs and enter competition. Louisa was exceptional: she represented the Territory in basketball on ten occasions, won nine best and fairest awards and was a member of the Aboriginal team that toured New Zealand in 1975. She played in three outdoor soccer premiership finals in Darwin, winning six top goal scorer awards. Louisa represented the Territory in hockey four times and played in eight hockey grand finals. She won the season's hockey best and fairest on fifteen occasions, a truly remarkable feat by any athlete in any sport. Photo: Louisa Collins.

ROHANEE COX

Rohanee was born in Broome (WA) in 1980. Following a scholarship to the Australian Institute of Sport, Rohanee played for the Perth Lynx, the Townsville Firebirds, and the West Coast Waves, among other teams. Honours have come: in 2007 she won the Maher Medal for International Player of the Year and in 2009 she won a Deadly Award for Female Sportsperson of the Year. Rohanee had 53 caps with Australia's junior national team. She was one of the first Aboriginal players to represent Australia in basketball at the Olympics and won a silver medal with the Opals at the Beijing Games in 2008, the first Aboriginal basketballer to win an Olympic medal. The Opals won seven straight games at Beijing, losing only to the United States in the final. Photo: David Tease/Fairfax Syndication.

ROSE DAMASO

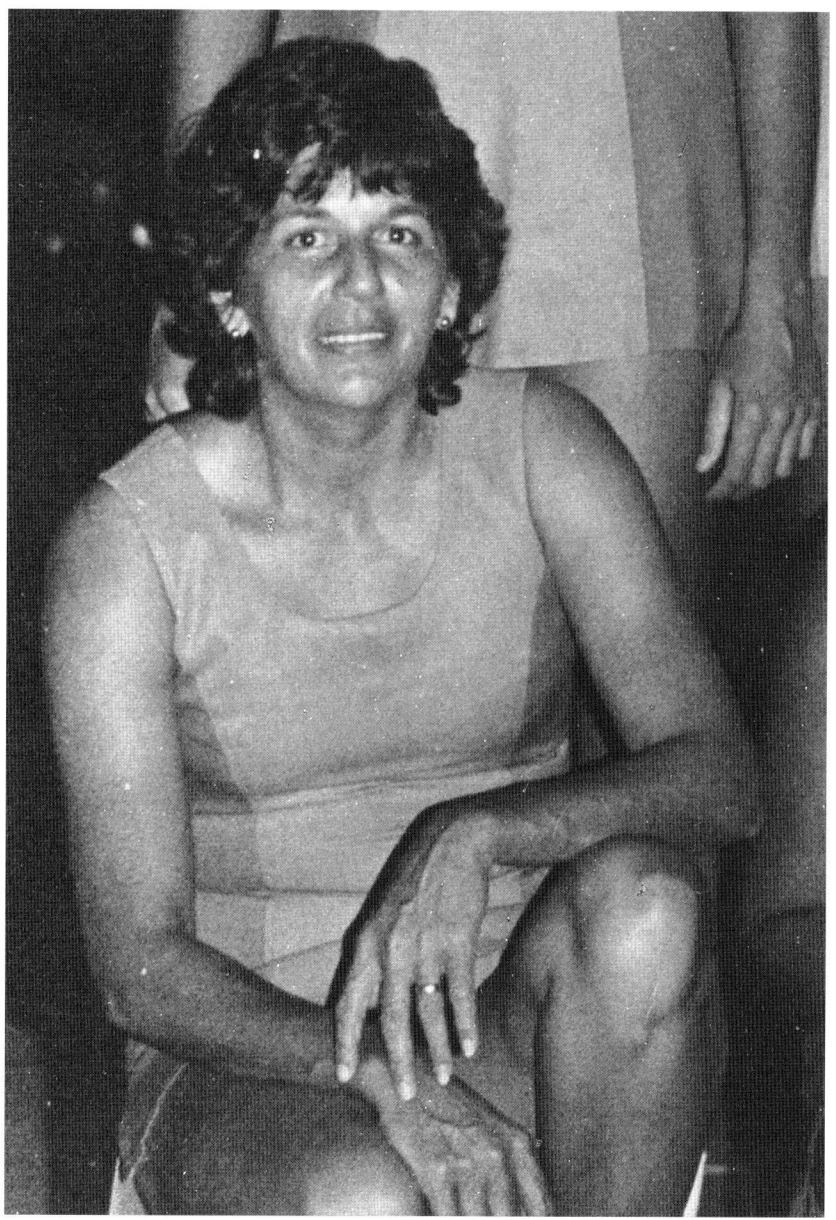

Aboriginal women have proven their quality as champions in several sports simultaneously. In the Northern Territory, **Louisa Collins**, **Karmi Dunn**, **Donna Hunter** and Rose Damaso are excellent examples. Although Rose was born in Sydney, in 1942, she lives in the Territory. There, in a career lasting from 1960 to 1984, she represented the Territory on 36 occasions — in four sports. Rose played basketball, netball, softball and hockey. If one sport has to be singled out it would be basketball, the sport in which she was named All-Australian coach. She was coach of the All-Aboriginal netball team in 1976, a member of the Darwin Football Club and leading hockey goal scorer. There can be few sportspeople in Australia who have matched this level of consistency in so many sports over such a long period. Photo: Rose Damaso.

CARMELITA (KARMI) DUNN

Louisa Collins and **Rose Damaso** represent the first liberation of women in northern Australia, emerging just as the restrictive special legislation applying to people considered less than 'full blood' was repealed. **Donna Hunter** and Karmi Dunn are a generation later but they are nevertheless examples of how great all-round athletes can emerge when given access to competitive sport. Born at Nguiu (Bathurst Island, NT) in 1954, Karmi comes from a large family of sports achievers. Like Rose Damaso, Karmi played four sports for the Territory: basketball from 1982 to 1993, netball from 1976 to 1979, softball from 1974 to 1987 and soccer in 1981. For good measure she played touch for Darwin. In basketball she captained Rebels, the Northern Territory premiership team and played 350 first grade games, scoring just on 3000 points in the Darwin Basketball Association league. Karmi had a long career in the NT public service. Karmi, her husband and their two daughters, were tragically killed in a plane crash in 2013. Photo: Karmi Dunn.

NATHAN JAWAI

This huge Torres Strait Islander man is a nephew of **Danny Morseu**, and was born in Sydney in 1986. Standing 209 cm tall and weighing in at 140 kg, Nathan grew up in the small and remote community of Bamaga (Qld) — almost at the tip of the Cape York Peninsula. A move to Cairns led Nathan to take up basketball. As a power forward and centre, he was drafted to the NBA in 2008. Jawai played a total of 45 games for Toronto and Minnesota, then signed to Partizan Belgrade (Serbia) in 2010. Further seasons were with UNICS Kazan (Russia), Barcelona Regal (Spain) and Galatasaray (Turkey) before Nathan returned to Australia to play for the Perth Wildcats (WA). Finally, in 2016, there was a home-coming to the Cairns Taipans. Nathan has an NBL, a Serbian League, and an Adriatic League Championship to his credit. Photo: Australian Sports Commission Image Library.

BENNIE LEW FATT

It is difficult to position Bennie as he is both an Australian footballer and a basketballer of note. Born in 1938 in Darwin, son of the legendary Walter Lew Fatt of Buffalo Football Club fame, Bennie played in nine Australian basketball championships from 1959 to 1967. In the 1963 tournament at Devonport (Tas.) one newspaper voted him best player of the series. After the 1961 Melbourne championships he joined fellow Darwinian, John Bonson, in the Australian team that played ten provincial matches in New Zealand. This honour makes him the first Aboriginal man to represent Australia in basketball. At 16 Bennie played the first of his 200-plus games of Australian football for Nightcliff, and won a prized Nichols Medal in the 1963–1964 season. He played from 1954 to 1968. Photo: Bennie Lew Fatt.

PATRICK MILLS

Patrick is only the third Aboriginal or Islander to play for Basketball for Australia, and the youngest ever male representative for this country. 'Patty' was born in Canberra (ACT) in 1988, and is of Torres Strait Islander and Ynunga heritage. His mother is one of the Stolen Generation. Mills was drafted by the (American) Portland Trail Blazers in 2009, and is currently with the San Antonio Spurs. To date he has played an incredible 441 NBA games, and is the only Aboriginal player to have attained an NBA championship (2014). He has represented the national Boomers side at three Olympic Games (2008, 2012, 2016). Patrick has been a very outspoken and effective voice in Aboriginal affairs and racism in sport. He was named NAIDOC Sportsperson of the Year in 2017. Photo: Brendan Esposito/Fairfax Syndication.

DANNY MORSEU

Danny Morseu was born on Thursday Island in the Torres Straits in 1958. A more robust and solid player in style than **Michael Ahmatt**, Danny played a total of 217 senior basketball games for St Kilda, the Brisbane Bullets, Toowoomba Mountaineers and Brisbane Southern Districts Spartans. He was in two St Kilda premiership sides and was in the Brisbane Bullets team which won the NBL title in 1987. As a junior he represented Queensland, Victoria and Australia in under20 teams. Danny played 27 internationals for Australia, touring in Europe, Canada and the United States. His internationals include twelve World Cup games, seven games in the 1980 Moscow Olympic Games and eight games in the 1984 Los Angeles Olympic Games. Since retirement he has had a successful coaching and public service career. In the latter, he is dedicated to improving Aboriginal and Islander access to sport. Photo: *Australian Basketballer*.

MICHELLE MUSSELWHITE (COSIER)

Victoria's Gippsland region has produced some great Aboriginal achievers: the two badminton sisters **Cheryl** and **Sandra Mullett** and **Lionel Rose** in boxing. Born in Bairnsdale (Vic) in 1982 Michelle played junior basketball for the Bairnsdale Bullets and then senior baskets for the Dandenong Rangers, the Sydney Uni Flames and the Canberra Capitals. Michelle played 34 junior games for Australia and was capped 17 times for the national senior team. She was a member of the national team in the 2003 Young World Championships in which the team came in fifth. Michelle Cosier works with Aboriginal children promoting healthier lifestyles. She and partner Simon have the rare distinction of both having been Women's' National Basketball League referees. Photo: Tim Clayton/Fairfax Syndication.

CLAUDE WILLIAMS

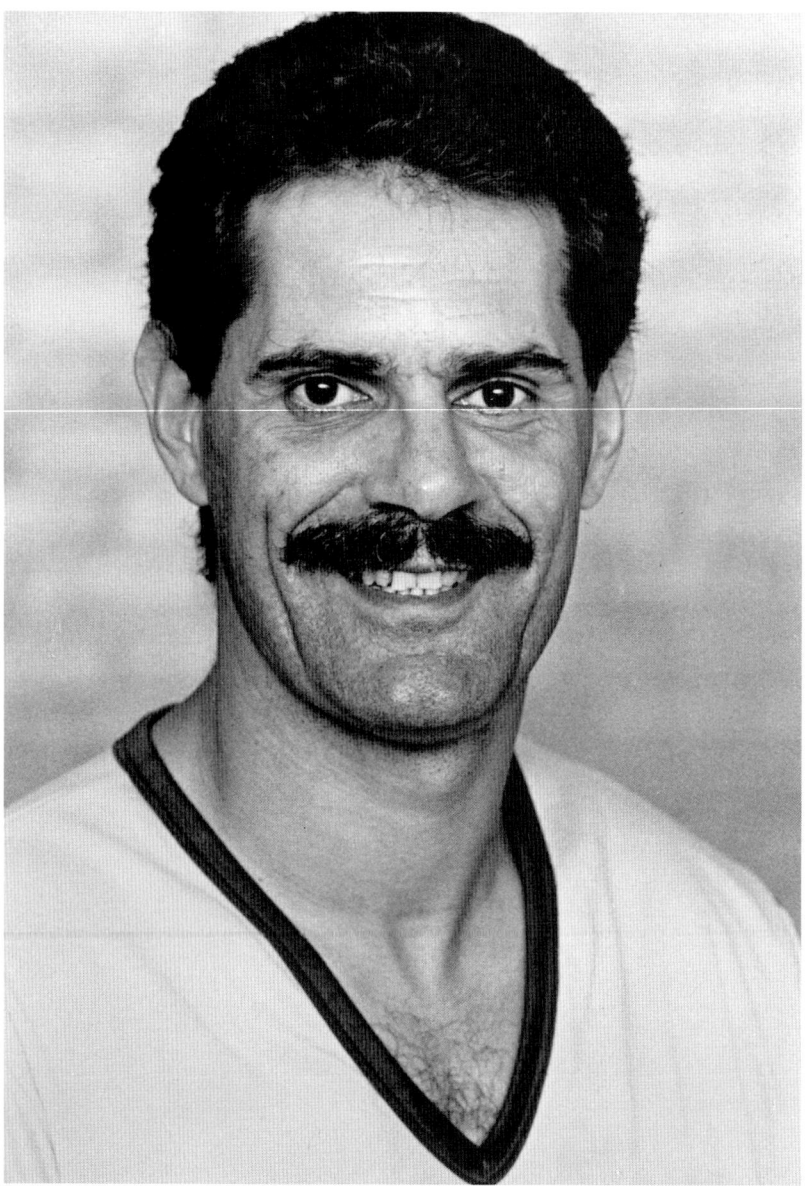

There are many all-rounders in this Hall of Fame, especially among the women. Another fine example is Claude Williams. He played first-division rugby league and basketball for New South Wales. Born in Camperdown, NSW in 1952 Claude had twelve games on the wing for South Sydney in the years 1972–1973. He was in the New South Wales basketball side in 1976, 1977, 1979 and 1981. Not many players go on to successful coaching careers but several Hall members did so, notably **Artie Beetson, Barry Cable, Lynch Cooper, Rose Damaso, Gary Ella, Glen Ella, Mark Ella, Jason Gillespie, Ian King, Karen Menzies, Danny Morseu, Billy Roe** and **Claude Williams**. In 1986–1987 Claude was assistant coach of the Supersonics, followed by a year as coach of the Sydney Kings in 1988. From there he became assistant coach of the Newcastle Falcons in 1989–1990. Photo: Sydney Kings.

CHAPTER 7
BOXING

One of America's most accomplished journalists, A J Liebling, called it 'the sweet science'. Boxing is just that for many. For others, probably the majority, it is the ultimate in barbarity. 'Fascinating' said British novelist and sports writer Brian Glanville about boxing — albeit a sport 'blemished by its essential brutality, its exploitation of the poor and simple'. The remarkable American writer Joyce Carol Oates commented that 'boxing's very image is repulsive to many people because it cannot be assimilated into what we wish to know about civilised man'. And then she wrote passionate and marvelous stuff about the sport.

Boxing is close to the bone. Under harsh lights, two men (and now women) engage in undisguised aggression with courage, skill, resilience and power. But boxing — in the opinion of historian Jeffrey Sammons — needs to be viewed 'beyond the ring', at its role in American and, indeed, in our history.

Whether or not one likes boxing (we do and we don't), it has political and social roles

John Jarratt was Australian professional bantamweight champion in 1958.
Photo: Michael Clarke

in society that can't simply be shrugged off with shudders of dismay or disgust. There is an especial political dimension to black boxing. It was one of the first sports to present young men with a way out of poverty; a chance to escape racism and discrimination, however briefly; a way to gain respect from one's opponents and even from fans notorious for their collective hates and loves. For racial minorities boxing was the glory sport. In the United States and South Africa boxing was once the only road possible for black men to escape poverty but even so there was an element of gross exploitation. Fans would pay to see gladiators in battle and the more blood the more coins would be thrown into the ring in appreciation. In the United States boxing was once a 'Jewish' sport — between the two world wars and during the Depression period there was no other avenue of income. When living conditions improved and anti-Semitism waned after World War II, so did Jewish boxing. It is now fading for African-Americans and has become the sport of Filipinos, Hispanic people and several Asian populations.

Australian historian Richard Broome argued that boxing has 'done more to reinforce the basic oppression of Aborigines than to overcome it'. In what way? The answer is that for Aboriginal peaople the odds have always been tough: entrapment in Australia's inherent and often vicious racism, unending stereotyping and the almost universal exploitation of the fighters. There were crippling percentages scooped off the top by managers and sometimes the full per cent by the Aboriginal Protectors, especially in Queensland. Aboriginal boxers were all too often regarded as a separate biological class of people — always described as quick, reflexive, strong, tough, enduring. They were seen as especially 'explosive' and 'exciting' — hence as a special breed

Harry Grogan won a version of the Australian welterweight championship in 1957, a title not universally recognised.
Photo: Ern McQuillan Jr

of gladiator and entertainer. The famous West Indian writer C L R James always deplored Caribbean cricketers being called 'spontaneous' as it suggested they were an instinctive people, incapable of thought. In similar vein, Aboriginal boxers were always 'naturally' exciting fighters, 'always a credit to their race'; they were rarely individuals, always — to use activist Paul Coe's words — bodies rather than brains.

In the broadest sense of the word 'political' it can be said that Aboriginal boxers had a political purpose. True, many boxed for 'the quick quid', but for others it was a route to some social mobility, a break through the caste barrier to a temporary (often sweet) victory over chronic powerlessness and over White privilege. Henry Collins of Framlingham in western Victoria offered this telling example. Gaoled and bashed in Coffs Harbour in the 1950s for refusing to move out of a 'Whites only' section of the cinema, Collins's view of boxing was this:

George Kapeen was Australian welterweight champion in 1953. He had 118 fights in all, but such was the exploitation that in 1946 he had fifteen fights in the space of 60 days.
Photo: Michael Clarke

I felt good when I knocked white blokes out. I felt good. I knew I was boss in the boxing ring. I showed my superiority … they showed it outside.

Boxing seemed to offer a chance of self-identity, some dignity, certainly a collective pride and a heightening of Aboriginal consciousness for both the city and the riverbank people as they barracked for their heroes. In several instances it did all of these things, but in a limited and transient way.

Aboriginal statistics are most impressive. In 1980 Richard Broome reported that while [then] forming only 1.5 per cent of the population, Aboriginal people had produced 30 of the 225 champions (or 15 per cent) in eight boxing divisions. With the advent of numerous 'junior' divisions, Aboriginal achievement has become even more spectacular. By the end of 1993, 45 men had won 65 professional titles. By the end of 1999, 51 men had held 71 national titles. Aboriginal boxers have held at least eight Commonwealth titles and the world bantamweight, light-welterweight, welterweight, light-middleweight and middleweight championships. The late boxing authority Ray Mitchell stated that there were more Aboriginal boxers per their head of population than among any other group in the world. (That was in the 1960s to 1980s, before Aboriginal men turned to other sports.)

At the start of the twentieth century Aboriginal men were playing cricket in a small way in scattered parts of the country (chapter 8) but most of their participation was in professional athletics (chapter 3). From about 1910 Aboriginal boxers began to appear in the ring: Black Paddy from Perth, Black Wand and Black Chris from Queensland. The major pioneer was **Jerry Jerome**, horse-breaker, rifleman and professional runner from Jimbour Station near Dalby (Qld) who turned to boxing at the advanced age of 33 or 34. He won the Australian middleweight title in 1912, the first of a great many national championships to be held by Aboriginal boxers.

There was something of a gap between Jerome and the arrival of Billy Samuels in 1922, Alby Roberts in 1927, **Ron Richards** in 1928 and Merv Blandon in 1931. During this intervening period much Aboriginal boxing took place in the boxing tents of Jimmy Sharman, Harry Johns and other troupes. This form of pugilism, said Richard Broome, was not motivated by a desire to get into 'the big time'; rather it was to chase 'the quick quid'. In 1928 a remarkable event occurred: Jack Deshong of Maryborough won the Queensland heavyweight title at the age of 48. But it was the 1930s that saw what author Peter Corris called 'Ron Richards and the rise of the Blacks' (in his book *Lords of the Ring*).

Richards was in so many ways the greatest fighter of his time and certainly at the very top of Australia's sporting hall of fame. Fast, a strong counter-puncher, resilient, a strong hitter, he was the complete boxer. In 1938 he thrashed Gus Lesnevitch who was considered one of the best light-heavyweights of the twentieth century. Ron achieved third world-ranking in the middleweights and fourth in the lightheavies. Legendary champion Vic Patrick declared him the best fighter he had ever seen. Had the chance come his way, wrote boxing author and referee Ray Mitchell, he would have been the world champion. Richards fought often, too often. Bad management, exploitation and the death of his (first) Aboriginal wife, led to a period of degradation: drinking, charges of vagrancy, removal to Woorabinda settlement, a beating by louts in the Sydney Haymarket area for the glory of saying 'I ko'd Ron Richards', and finally removal to remote Palm Island where he died, penniless, in 1967 at the age of 56. [Author Colin Tatz met him there in 1962: he wouldn't talk about boxing.]

Not all boxing stories end this way but more do in this sport than in any other. Alfie Sands had an incredible 151 fights. This number was due to exploiters who encouraged his drinking binges after fights so that he would need to return to 'work' sooner for more money. In 1946 George Kapeen had eight fights in October and seven in November: fifteen in 60 days is, indeed, an indictment of boxing administration. One suspects that this exploitation was greater in the case of black fighters.

Richards was the model for the legendary **Dave Sands** who held national titles in three divisions and was British Empire middleweight champion; the man destined to fight Sugar Ray Robinson or Randolph Turpin for the world title had he not been killed in a truck accident at the tender age of 26. Less exploited than Richards and dying in his prime, his career and charisma leave a better taste in the mouth and mind. Sands was then to be the role model for the astonishing talents that followed: **Elley Bennett**, **Jack Hassen** and **George Bracken**, with Bracken in turn the role model for **Lionel Rose** and Rose in turn the model for so many others.

Most writers have diminished Aboriginal achievement somewhat by presenting the 'standard' list of boxers — **Ron Richards**, **Dave**

Beaufort Dinah (*centre*), one of the great tent fighters in the West was invested as 'king of his tribe'.
Photo: Fiona Whittles

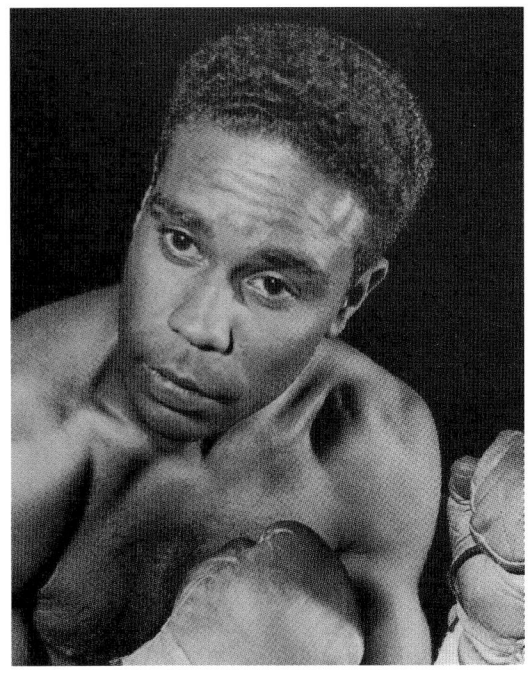

Rated the best gymnasium boxer and sparring partner in New South Wales, Keith Saunders 'froze' in stadium fights. His Book, *Learning the Ropes*, is a significant account of Aboriginal life in boxing. Photo: Ern McQuillan Jr

Sands, **Elley Bennett**, **Jack Hassen**, **George Bracken**, **Lionel Rose**, **Hector Thompson**, **Tony Mundine**, **Anthony Mundine**, **Daniel Geale** — as if that was complete. The 'forgotten men' should be remembered, especially some early pioneers like **Jerry Jerome**, Alby Roberts, Jack Deshong, **Rollo Hinton**, **Tommy Chapman** and later George Kapeen, Alfie Sands, **Bobby Sinn**, Jackie Ryan, **Gary Cowburn**, Alfie Clay, **Lawrence Austin**, **Steve Dennis**, **Wally Carr**, Pat Leglise, Bindi Jack and Big Jim West.

One notable change in the pattern has been the willingness of Aboriginal youth to turn to and remain in amateur boxing. Following the remarkable feats of **Joe Donovan**, **Jeff Dynevor**, **Adrian Blair** and **Frank Roberts** in the 1960s, the pattern was set for brothers **Bobby** and **Gary Williams**, and for Norman Stevens, **Robert Peden**, **James Swan**, **Justann Crawford** and **Daniel Geale**. But again there is a noticeable change: given that most youth receive unemployment benefits there is no longer the burning need to 'earn a quid' in either tent boxing, the amateur ranks or in the paid sport. Rugby league, even professional rugby union, Australian football and basketball are now seen as easier routes to some social mobility.

Despite these attractive alternatives, and the fact that boxing is a declining, unpopular sport, Aboriginal boxers are still very much involved. As the last century ended there were several Aboriginal professional champions: Lyall Appo won the strawweight championship in 1993; Johnny Binge from Moree (NSW) was bantamweight champion in 1999; Gilbert Hooper of St George was yet another in the long line of national featherweight champions, winning the title in 1995; Cliff Sarmardin was junior-lightweight titleholder in 1994; Quentin Donohue of Mareeba (Qld) held that title in 1998 and Colin Graham from Ipswich (Qld) won the same crown in 1999. Two brothers from La Perouse in Sydney, Kevin Kelly and Glen Kelly, achieved an outstanding double: Kevin Kelly was Australian junior-middleweight champion in 1995 and twice held the Commonwealth title at that weight; brother Glen was Australian light-heavyweight champion in 1997. Binge and Glen Kelly were the champions in 2000.

The Olympic tradition continued: young Henry Collins, **Daniel Geale** and **James Swan** were in the Olympic squad for the 2000 games. James Pittman and Anthony Little boxed in 2004, Little again in 2008, together with Luke Boyd and Paul Fleming. Cameron Hammond, Damien Hooper and Jesse Ross participated in the 2012 London Olympics. There were no Aboriginal boxers at the Olympics in Rio in 2016, an indication of Aboriginal attention diverting to other arenas.

BLACK PEARLS

Dennis Ritchie, father of AIATSIS Chief Executive Officer Craig Ritchie.
Photo: Craig Ritchie

Harry Hayes, cousin of **Lionel Rose**, was Australian flyweight champion in 1969, despite disliking the way he earned his living.
Photo: Department of Aboriginal Affairs

Russell Sands Jr, son of Australian middleweight champion Alfie Sands and nephew of **Dave Sands**, was Australian welterweight champion in 1984.
Photo: News Limited

Big Jim West was the man who could juggle the scales: He was both Australian flyweight champion in 1973 and junior lightweight titleholder in 1979, four divisions heavier.
Photo: Ern McQuillan Jr

Alfie Sands, brother of **Dave Sands**, beat the (non-Aboriginal) Harry Hayes for a version of the Australian middleweight crown in 1954, a title not universally recognised.
Photo: Michael Clarke

Neil Pattel was a magnificent ringman of the highest order. There have not been many boxers in Australia who have held three Australian Titles, but Pattel did: Lightweight, Junior-Welterweight and Welterweight. Little more needs to be said of his worth.

Neil Pattel hailed from Winton in Queensland. He was Australian lightweight champion in 1978 and lost the title a year later to **Steve Dennis**.
Photo: Michael Clarke.

Graeme Brooke was British Commonwealth lightweight champion in 1984.
Photo: Alick Jackomos Collection

LAWRENCE ('BABY CASIUS') AUSTIN

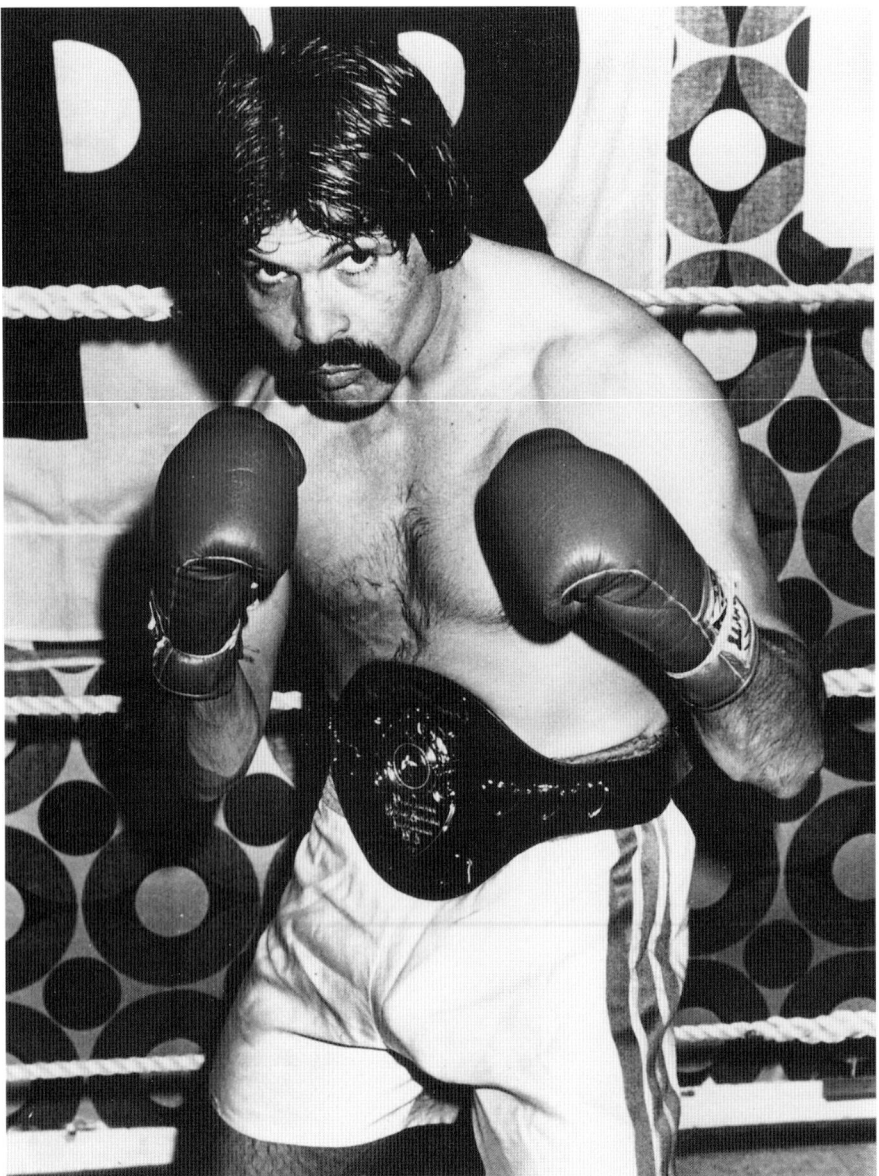

The Framlingham community near Warrnambool (Vic.) produced a number of great sports achievers including three of the famous cricket team which toured England in 1868: **Johnny Cuzens**, Jim Crow and Mosquito. There was also a legion of boxing tent fighters, including Henry Collins and Banjo Clarke. It was Banjo who taught the supreme achiever Lawrence, born at Framlingham in 1954. Like so many Aboriginal champions Austin was able to move between weight divisions and as with so many, he held Australian titles in three boxing divisions. Austin was welterweight, junior welterweight and lightweight champion, twice holder of the Commonwealth junior welterweight championship, 1977–1978. He lost twice to Aboriginal champion **Hector Thompson** and beat Thompson once. Austin had 48 fights with 34 wins, two draws, and 12 losses. Photo: West Australian Newspapers Ltd.

ELLIOTT (ELLEY) BENNETT

Elley was born at Barambah Settlement (Cherbourg, Qld) in 1924. He became a bullock-driver, fisherman, cane- and fruit-picker before he had his first tent fight in Maryborough. Badly managed and exploited, 'The Smile' won both the Australian bantamweight crown (1948–1951) and the featherweight title (1951–1954). Rated 'the hardest hitting man of his weight in the world', Elley had 59 fights, winning 44 (40 on KOs), drawing one, losing thirteen, and one declared no contest. 'Boxing's greatest sportsman' was *Ring Digest*'s opinion of him. Elley's earnings were controlled by the Aboriginal Sub-Department of Health and Home Affairs. He was a member of the Aboriginal Sports Foundation. After a long battle with alcohol he died in 1981. The grave marker 445 in Bundaberg cemetery was replaced with a black granite plaque depicting the Aboriginal flag, Elley's boxing stance and his championship fight records. Photo: News Limited.

ADRIAN BLAIR

Four men held nine national boxing titles in the space of five years. All four hailed from one small community — Cherbourg (Qld). Jim Edwards junior was featherweight and lightweight champion in 1960 and 1961, respectively; **Jeff Dynevor** was bantamweight champion of Australia in 1960, 1961 and 1962; Eddie Barney won the national flyweight title in 1962 and Adrian Blair, born at Cherbourg in 1943, was national featherweight champion in 1961 and then lightweight titleholder in 1962 and 1964. Adrian lost his second-round lightweight bout in the 1962 Commonwealth Games but was still strong enough in his division to be selected for the Australian Olympic team in 1964. **Francis Roberts** was the other Aboriginal member of the ten-man boxing team. The boxing magazines of the time were sometimes patronising but often positive about these men: 'they stir crowds with their flashy style, hard punching, natural skill and unpredictable character'. Photo: *Australian Ring*.

GEORGE BRACKEN

Born as George Brakenridge at Palm Island (Qld) in 1934, 'the most polished ring man Australia has produced' began life in Sharman's tents and went on to become Australian lightweight champion from 1956 to 1958, and again from 1959 to 1962. The role model for **Lionel Rose**, Bracken fought memorable battles against fellow Aboriginal champions Russell Sands and **Gary Cowburn**, negating the general belief that Aboriginal boxers were 'soft' on each other. George was debilitated by an undiagnosed chronic hepatitis. As singer, rock music composer and television showman, he spoke out strongly against the incarceration of Aboriginal people in settlements and missions and the exploitation of Aboriginal boxers. Later he trained youngsters in 'body boxing', a sport in which no blows are allowed to the head. He had 59 fights, winning 42, drawing two, and losing 15. George has spent many years as a liaison officer with the NSW Police Service. Photo: Department of Aboriginal Affairs.

WALLY CARR

Tony Mundine held titles in four divisions and four Aboriginal boxers have held crowns in three categories: **Ron Richards**, **Dave Sands**, **Lawrence Austin** and **Wally Carr**. Wally warrants more praise than the critics have given him. Ern McQuillan Jr said he could have been a world-beater but for want of self-discipline. He was born in Warren (NSW) in 1954. He had what George Bracken calls the 'Aboriginal style' of boxing, possessing the quick movements and the evasiveness, but unlike most he loved to stand up toe-to-toe and slug it out with his opponents. Perhaps this quality lost him more fights than should have been the case. In 1977 he won the Australian junior-middleweight title, he held the middleweight crown from 1978 to 1981 and won the light-heavyweight championship in 1984. He won 53 fights, drew nine and lost 38. Gaele Sobott's *My Longest Round* (2010) records Wally's highs and lows in life. Photo: Fairfax Photo Library/courtesy John Fairfax Holdings.

TOMMY CHAPMAN

Tommy was born in 1922 in the small Queensland town of Hebel. There were perhaps no more than a dozen professional Aboriginal boxers in the 1920s and 1930s, including **Rollo Hinton**, lightweight champion Alby Roberts and Jack Bowden. In the 1940s there weren't many Aboriginal boxers but the few were outstanding, especially the legendary **Ron Richards**. Chapman was the fifth Aboriginal boxer to win a national title: **Jerry Jerome**, Merv Blandon, **Ron Richards** and **Rollo Hinton** came before him. Tommy was a clever, hard-punching featherweight who went to Newcastle to be trained by the famous Tom Maguire. One of fifteen children, he had never seen a train or the ocean until he came to Newcastle. He knocked out Eddie Miller to win the national featherweight title in 1944. He had 74 fights of which he won 48, drew three and lost 23. His cousin was **Tom Dancey**. Photo: Ken Edwards.

TREVOR CHRISTIAN, AM

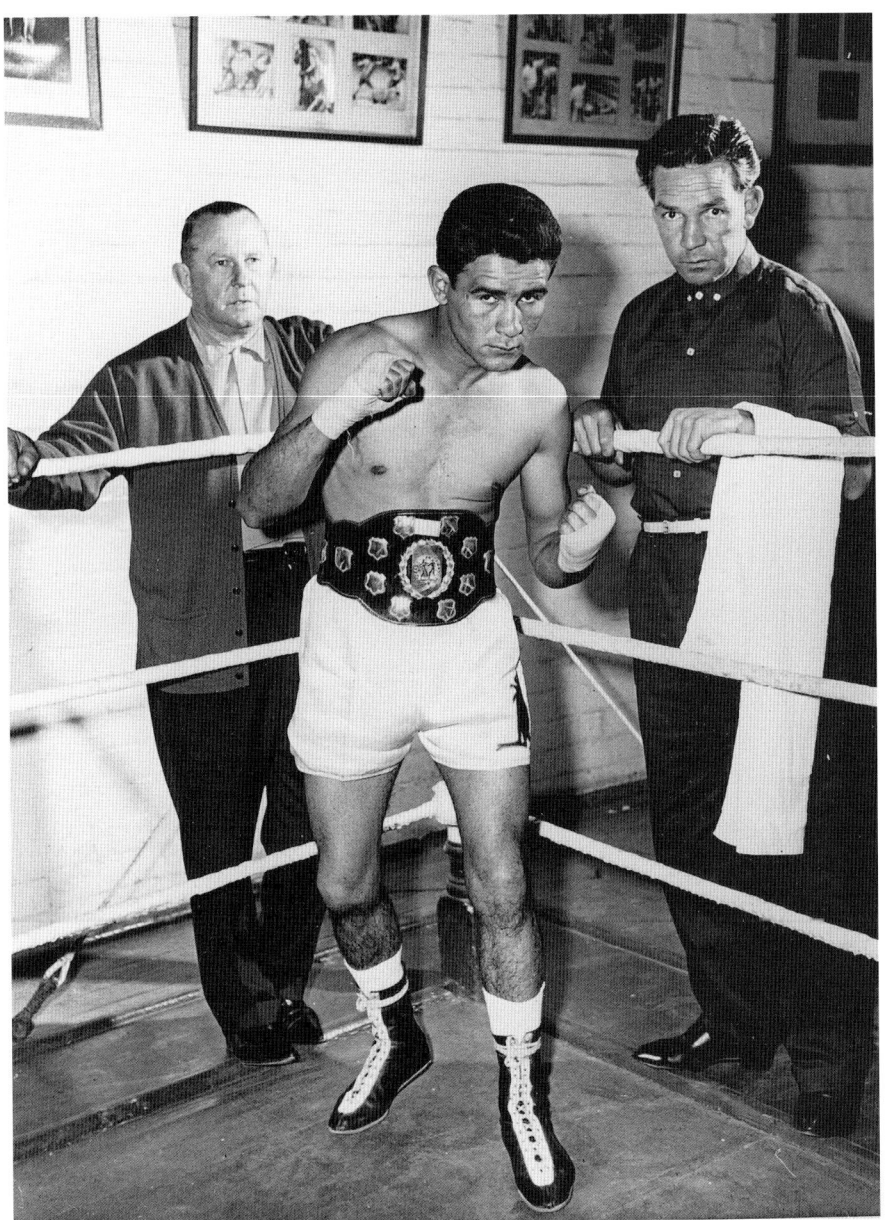

Born in Narrandera (NSW) in 1942, at age 7 Trevor went to live at the Erambie Mission in Cowra and at that age began boxing. He began professional boxing in 1960. By 1963 he was Australian junior-middleweight champion, beating Roy Carroll in what was described as the best fight of the year. Trevor had only 25 professional fights for 16 wins, two draws and 7 losses. Very stylish, he was a very fair and clean fighter. Smart in the ring, he used evasive tactics and wasn't hurt often. He saw boxing as too difficult a way to make a living and treated his ring days as a hobby. Trevor became the first Aboriginal person to referee a world title fight. His working life has been dedicated to Aboriginal service. At *left* is his manager Ern McQuillan Snr, at *right* Roy Carroll, the first Aboriginal man to gain a trainer's licence. Photo: Trevor Christian.

GARY COWBURN

Born in Gayndah (Qld) in 1937, Gary Cobbo took the boxing name of Gary Cowburn. In a good amateur career, he won the national featherweight title in 1955. As a professional he was both brilliant and erratic. Tall for his weight, he was both a fast and awkward opponent. He too used 'the Aboriginal style', relying on speed and evasion rather than outright aggression. Gary was Australian welterweight champion in 1962–1963, and then held the Australian junior welterweight title in 1965–1966. He fought two excellent bouts against **George Bracken**, winning one and losing one. He is the only man to have knocked out the seemingly indestructible former British Empire welterweight champion, George Barnes, who held that title from 1954 to 1956. Gary had 41 fights for 24 wins, two draws and 15 losses. Photo: Bernie Cox Collection, Mitchell Library.

JUSTANN CRAWFORD

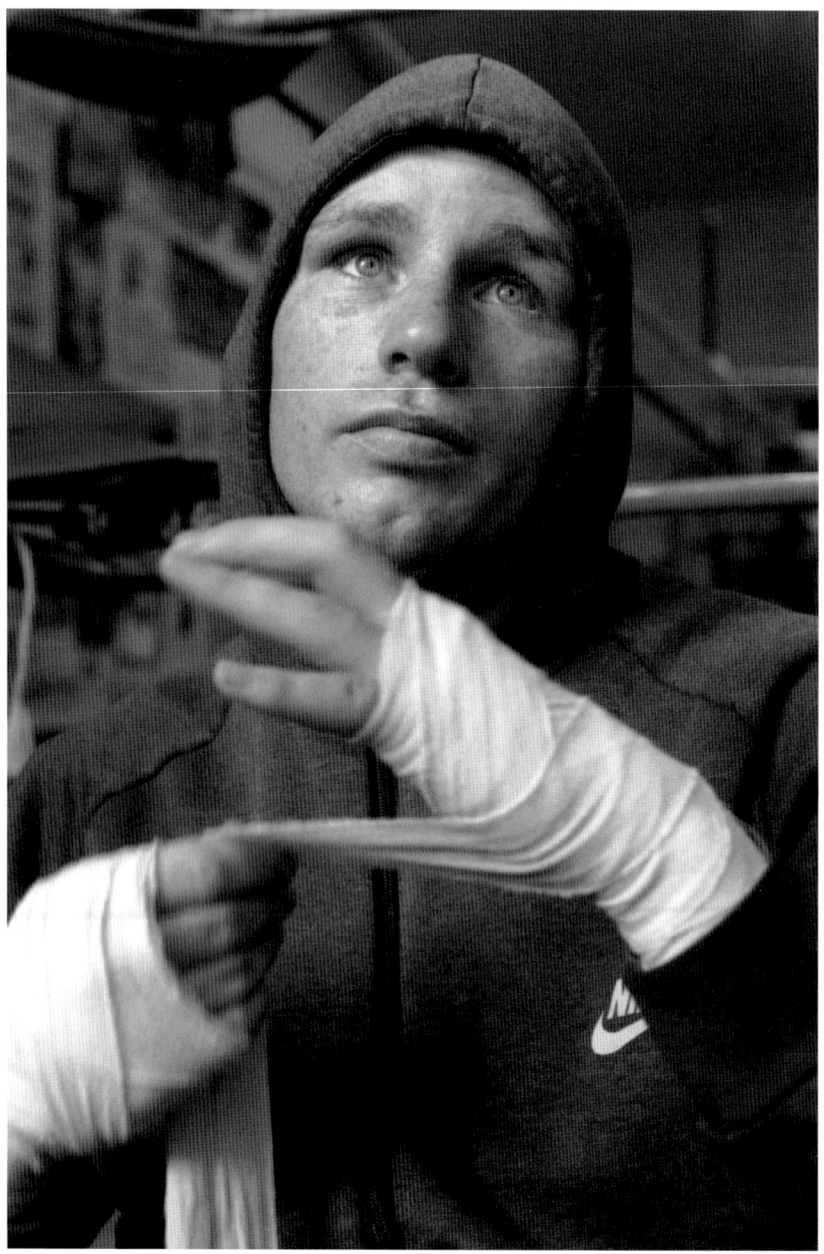

Justann Crawford was born in Burnie (Tas.) in 1973. After early training he moved to Sydney under the mentorship of Pat Hailwood and Andrew Tatrai. As an amateur Justann fought as a super middleweight and as a light-heavyweight, usually at 75 kg, winning nine Australian titles. Crawford represented his country at the 1992 Barcelona and 1996 Atlanta Olympic Games as well as the 1994 Commonwealth Games in Canada. In both Olympics he lost to the Russian Aleksandr Lebzyak who won that division in the Sydney 2000 Olympics. Justann retired in 1998 due to a mysterious illness, with a career record of 123 fights for 98 wins, 25 losses and a haul of nine international gold medals. Photo: Tim Clayton/Fairfax Syndication.

GARY COWBURN

Born in Gayndah (Qld) in 1937, Gary Cobbo took the boxing name of Gary Cowburn. In a good amateur career, he won the national featherweight title in 1955. As a professional he was both brilliant and erratic. Tall for his weight, he was both a fast and awkward opponent. He too used 'the Aboriginal style', relying on speed and evasion rather than outright aggression. Gary was Australian welterweight champion in 1962–1963, and then held the Australian junior welterweight title in 1965–1966. He fought two excellent bouts against **George Bracken**, winning one and losing one. He is the only man to have knocked out the seemingly indestructible former British Empire welterweight champion, George Barnes, who held that title from 1954 to 1956. Gary had 41 fights for 24 wins, two draws and 15 losses. Photo: Bernie Cox Collection, Mitchell Library.

JUSTANN CRAWFORD

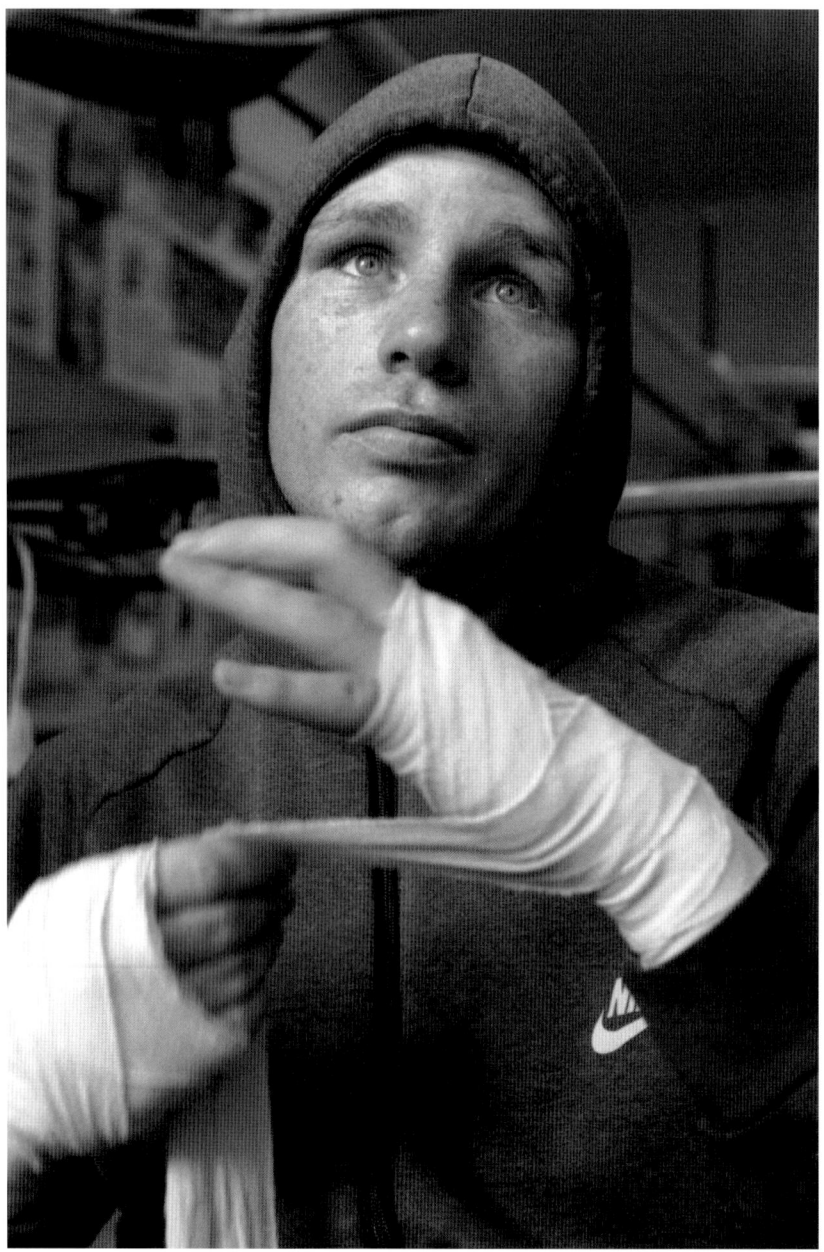

Justann Crawford was born in Burnie (Tas.) in 1973. After early training he moved to Sydney under the mentorship of Pat Hailwood and Andrew Tatrai. As an amateur Justann fought as a super middleweight and as a light-heavyweight, usually at 75 kg, winning nine Australian titles. Crawford represented his country at the 1992 Barcelona and 1996 Atlanta Olympic Games as well as the 1994 Commonwealth Games in Canada. In both Olympics he lost to the Russian Aleksandr Lebzyak who won that division in the Sydney 2000 Olympics. Justann retired in 1998 due to a mysterious illness, with a career record of 123 fights for 98 wins, 25 losses and a haul of nine international gold medals. Photo: Tim Clayton/Fairfax Syndication.

STEVE DENNIS

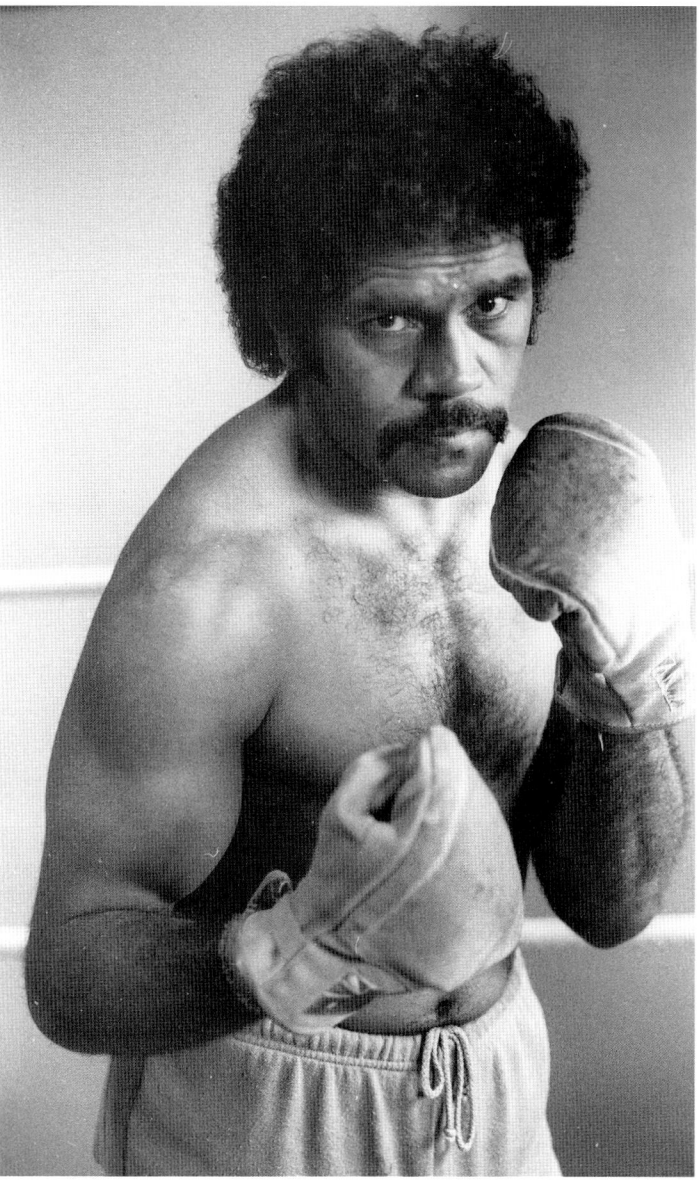

Steve was born in Walgett (NSW) in 1953. His professional boxing record was excellent: he won 36 of his 47 fights, drew two and lost 9. In 1976 he won the Australian professional welterweight title. After a brief retirement he won the title again in 1979. In December that year he lost the crown to **Lawrence Austin** over fifteen rounds. In 1980 he stopped **Hector Thompson** in what was to be Thompson's last fight. These bouts — and the **George Bracken** versus **Gary Cowburn** matches — demonstrated that Aboriginal fighters didn't 'go easy' on each other in the ring. In 1981 he moved up to the middleweight division and won the national title which he held until 1983. Since retirement he struggled to help sustain himself and his community at the impoverished Gingie Reserve, near Walgett, an area that remains bereft of any sporting facilities. Photo: Ern McQuillan Jr.

JOSPEH (JOE) DONOVAN

Since the 1960s Aboriginal people have turned increasingly to careers in amateur rather than professional boxing. Joe James Donovan is a notable role model. Born in Kempsey (NSW) in 1949, Joe had a phenomenal record: he was Australian light-flyweight champion in 1968; Australian flyweight titleholder in 1967 and 1969; and Australian bantamweight champion in 1971, 1973 and 1974. He also won ten state titles. He represented Australia at the Asian Games in 1967, winning the gold; he was in the national team at the Mexico Olympic Games in 1968, losing his third round bout in a disputed decision; and he fought for Australia at the Commonwealth Games in Christchurch in 1974. Joe won 150 of his 159 fights — one of the best records of any fighter in Australian boxing history. In 1994 he became only one of two Aboriginal men to be awarded a licence to judge amateur boxing. Photo: News Limited.

JEFFREY FRANCIS (JEFF) DYNEVOR

Aboriginal people became a strong presence in Australian sport in the 1960s: **Artie Beetson**, **Polly Farmer**, **Lionel Morgan**, **Lloyd McDermott**, **Evonne Goolagong-Cawley** and a host of professional boxers made an impact. In amateur boxing Jeff Dynevor (*right*) was one of the many outstanding athletes from Cherbourg Settlement (Qld). He was born in Nockatunga (near Dynevor Downs station in Qld) in 1938. Two Queensland boxers have won the bantamweight gold medal for Australia at a Commonwealth Games: **Robert Peden** in Victoria, Canada, in 1994 and Jeff Dynevor in Perth (WA) in 1962. Jeff beat Sam Abbey, a tough Ghanaian, in the final. Incredible as it may seem, this Cherbourg community of (then) 1800 people had three men in the 1962 Commonwealth Games boxing team: Jeff, **Adrian Blair** and Eddie Barney (the son of **Eddie Gilbert**). Jeff won the Australian amateur flyweight title in 1957 and held the national bantamweight championship from 1960 to 1962. Photo: Department of Aboriginal Affairs.

DANIEL GEALE

Daniel was born in 1981 in Launceston (Tas.). His mother is of the Palawa people. Starting out as a welterweight, he represented his country at the 2000 Sydney Olympic Games and later took out the gold medal at the 2002 Commonwealth Games in Manchester. Turning professional two years later, he won the IBO middleweight world championship in 2007, the IBF middleweight world title in 2011 and the unified WBA title in 2012. Daniel's professional boxing record stands at 36 fights, 31 wins (15 by KO) and five losses. A proud and gracious fighter who harks back to the more genteel eras, Geale climbed the ranks the hard way. He twice fought fellow Aboriginal middleweight champion **Anthony Mundine** for a win apiece. Geale trains young boxers and keeps fit that way. Photo: Steve Christo/Fairfax Syndication.

JACK HASSEN

Jack Friday was born at Palm Island (Qld) in 1926. In 1946 he had his first tent fight in Charters Towers under the name Jack Hassen. In a short career he attained world ranking when he beat Frenchman Pierre Montane. In 1949 he won the Australian lightweight title from Archie Kemp. Hassen punished him severely and, showing sympathy, asked the referee to stop the fight. Referee Joe Wallis motioned him to continue. Kemp died the next day, something that haunted Jack all his life. He never recovered his confidence. He held the title until 1951, completing his 36 fights with 29 wins and seven losses. A calm and serious man, he didn't want the fame and the fancy lights — his goal was to have a dairy farm. It was not to be as he lost the £20,000 he earned in three years. Jack was lionised by Aboriginal youth in Newtown and spent his declining years in Sydney's La Perouse community. Photo: News Limited.

ROLLO HINTON

Rollo Hinton was a much loved and respected man. Born in Singleton (NSW) in 1915, he had a very long career lasting from 1932 to 1943. He had an extraordinary 183 professional bouts of which he was successful in 83, drew 16, lost 81 and two were no contest results. Rollo was, albeit briefly, flyweight champion of Australia in 1937 and 1938. He beat Tiger Donnelly over fifteen rounds for the title in November 1937, defended it over the full distance against Donnelly in February 1938 and lost it to the same man in March 1938. He fought what have been called 'many serial battles', that is, multiple fights against the same opponents: Tiger Donnelly twelve times, and Jackie Ryan, an Aboriginal boxer, seven times. He fought excellent fighters, including Aboriginal boxers Maxie Richards and **Tommy Chapman**. Photo: *Australian Ring*/Christine Hinton.

JEREMIAH (JERRY) JEROME

The first Aboriginal man to win a national boxing title, Jerry began boxing at 33 and at 38 won the Australian middleweight title in 1912. Born at Jimbour Station, Dalby (Qld) in 1874, he was an outstanding horseman, successful professional runner and fine rifle shot. He fought too often and in poor condition: neither smoker nor drinker, he was addicted to food. The press made much of his appearance: 'this weirdly constructed native', 'as fat as a roly-poly', 'a half-tamed forest animal'. Adored by Queenslanders, he is well respected in boxing literature for his great fights at the Sydney Stadium. The Chief Protector of Aborigines hounded him, accusing 'this moneyed gentleman' of 'inciting Aborigines to refuse to work unless paid cash for it' at Taroom Settlement. He won 40 of his 64 fights, lost 23 and one was a no decision. He died at Cherbourg in 1943 where Jerome Street commemorates him. There is also a Jerome Street in Dalby. Photo: J C Davis Collection, Mitchell Library.

ANTHONY MUNDINE

One of the most controversial of Aboriginal sportsmen, Anthony (*on left,*) son of **Tony Mundine**, was born in Sydney in 1975. He has been described by some as the most polarising figure in Australian sports history. A dedicated Muslim convert, he and the media don't mix well on many issues. Anthony was a major figure for St George in rugby league. Between 1993 and 2000 he played 127 league games and had four appearances for New South Wales. People scoffed when he took to boxing, but as of 2017 he has had 55 fights for 47 victories. In that time he has held the WBA super-middleweight title twice between 2003 and 2008 as well as the IBO **middleweight title from 2009 to 2010 and the WBA** interim **super-welterweight ti**tle from 2011 to 2012. Every one of his title fights has been televised, a testament to his personality. Photo: Fairfax Syndication.

TONY MUNDINE, OAM

Tony has a unique record as the only Australian titleholder in four weight divisions. Born in Baryulgil (near Grafton, NSW) in 1951, a Bandjalung man, he came to Sydney looking for a rugby league career. But boxing captured him: he was Australian middleweight champion 1970–1975; Australian heavyweight titleholder 1972–1975 and 1977–1984; Commonwealth middleweight champion in 1972; Australian light-heavyweight champion 1975–1984; Commonwealth light-heavyweight titleholder in 1975; winner of the Australasian light-heavyweight title in 1980 and Australian cruiserweight champion 1981–1984. In 1974 Carlos Monzon defeated Tony in a world middleweight title bout. Tony won 80 of his 96 fights, drew one and lost 15. In his 80 wins, 65 were by knockouts — which remains the Australian record. He is one of the few great Aboriginal boxers whose life has been devoid of tragedy. He runs a successful gym in Sydney and has the joy of seeing his very talented son Anthony become a world boxing champion. Photo: Fairfax Photo Library/courtesy John Fairfax Holdings.

ROBERT PEDEN

One of the great boxers has been Robert Peden, born in Brisbane in 1973. He was Australian flyweight champion in 1991, bantamweight champion in 1992 and the featherweight titleholder in 1994. He represented Australia at the Barcelona Olympic Games in 1992, the World Titles in Finland in 1993 and the 1996 Atlanta Olympic Games. He won the bantamweight gold medal at the Commonwealth Games in Canada in 1994 (the same weight and medal as **Jeff Dynevor** in 1962). He is the only Australian ever to have won the King's Cup Trophy for the best boxer — in Bangkok in 1993. After the Atlanta Games he turned professional, boxing mainly in the United States. By 2007 he had won 25 of his 29 bouts, including two versions of the world super-featherweight championship (IBF and USBA). In 2012 he was inducted into the Australian Boxing Hall of Fame. Photo: Brian Peden.

RANDELL (RON) RICHARDS

Randell William (Ron) Richards was born at Purga Mission near Ipswich (Qld) in 1910. He was Australian middleweight champion in 1933 and 1936–1942; light-heavyweight titleholder 1937–1941; and heavyweight champion 1936–1938 and 1940–1941. Ron beat Gus Lesnevitch and lost twice to Archie Moore, both long-reigning world light-heavyweight champions. Many critics consider him the most talented fighter this country has produced. Former champion Vic Patrick had no doubt that he was the best fighter he ever saw. World War II made overseas fights impossible. Ron had too many fights, was badly managed and exploited and his life ended in tragedy. In 143 fights he won 105, drew ten, lost 27 and one was a no contest decision. Champion axeman **Leo Appo** once told Ron Richards's manager that if he had been given charge of the young Richards he would have made him the greatest axeman of all time. Photo: Michael Clarke.

BRIAN ROBERTS

According to Margaret Vincent, a former resident of 'the Block' in Redfern, she had two cousins 'who boxed a bit'. The 'bit' — a masterpiece of Aboriginal understatement — needs expansion. **Francis Roberts** was Australian amateur welterweight champion and boxed for Australia at the 1964 Olympic Games. Brother Brian Roberts, born in Kyogle (NSW) in 1953, held no less than three Australian professional titles: bantamweight, junior featherweight and featherweight. He was a contender for the Commonwealth titles in each of his three weight divisions and although he was defeated in all three of these major bouts, he emerged with acclaim. He fought some very good men including the widely acclaimed Azumah Nelson for the Commonwealth featherweight title in Accra, Ghana in 1981. Brian had 74 fights winning 38, drawing seven and losing 29. Photo: Ern McQuillan Jr.

FRANCIS (FRANK) ROBERTS

Frank was born in Cubawee (NSW) in 1945. He was the first Aboriginal boxer to be selected for an Olympics, at Tokyo in 1964. There he was accompanied by basketballer **Michael Ahmatt**. 'Honest Frank' as he was known, competed in the welterweight division and was the youngest boxer on the Australian boxing team. In 2000 he was given the honour of being a torch-bearer for the Sydney Olympics. He resided in Armidale (NSW). There he gave boxing lessons to local youths for close on 40 years, until his death from a heart attack in February 2011. Frank was given a state funeral, attended by over 400 people. 'A very beautiful man', said the Armidale mayor. Photo: Frank Roberts.

LIONEL ROSE, MBE

'From the Todd River in Alice to Redfern in Sydney he represented a hope that their own futures might rise beyond futility'. Such was the comment the night Lionel (*left*) beat bantamweight Fighting Harada in Tokyo in 1968 to become the first Aboriginal world boxing champion. In a time of turmoil this event gave Aboriginal people possibly their biggest morale boost ever. Born at Jackson's Track, Drouin (Vic.) in 1948, Lionel won the national amateur flyweight title in 1963. He turned professional and was Australian bantamweight champion from 1966 to 1969. After losing his world bantamweight title to Ruben Olivares in Los Angeles in 1969, he fought for the world junior lightweight title in 1975, losing a fifteen-round decision to Yoshiaki Numata. In 53 fights he won 42 and lost 11. Until Jeff Fenech, Rose had won more money than any other Australian fighter. He also spent, in his own words, '$100,000 in one year on wine, women and song'. Photo: Department of Aboriginal Affairs.

DAVE SANDS

The high-water mark of family sporting achievement belongs to the Ritchie brothers who fought under the name of Sands. Between Clem, Percy, George, Dave, Alfie and Russell they had 607 professional fights, won one Empire, one Australasian, four Australian and three state titles. Dave Sands, born at Burnt Bridge (NSW) in 1926, is considered, with Les Darcy and **Ron Richards**, as possibly the best boxer this country has produced. His record was outstanding: Australian middleweight champion 1946–1952; light-heavyweight holder 1946–1952; heavyweight champion 1950–1952 — in short, all three titles simultaneously. He was Australasian light-heavyweight as well as Empire middleweight champion. In 1950 and 1951 he was voted the most popular sportsman in Australia. He was killed in a truck accident, aged 26 and he is commemorated by plaques in Dungog, Kempsey and Sydney. Dave won 97 of his 110 bouts, drew one, lost 10 and two were no contests. Photo: News Limited.

BOBBY SINN

Bobby Sinn was born Robert Wills in Brisbane in 1932. He was one of Australia's major fighters in the 1950s. He was Queensland bantamweight champion in 1952 and featherweight titleholder in 1953. Bobby went on to win the Australian titles in both those divisions: he was bantamweight champion from 1953 to 1955 and then defeated Aboriginal Russell Sands for the featherweight title in 1955. He once had to forgo part of his purse to pay appearance money to the late world champion Jimmy Carruthers, a fight in which the champion-to-be was saved by the bell. He was inactive for several years, spending some time fighting in Sharman's tents. He had four fights in 1960 and 1961. Bobby had a total of 60 professional bouts, winning 38, drawing four and losing 18. Photo: Ern McQuillan Jr.

JAMES SWAN

Born in Alice Springs (NT) in 1974 and raised in the Northern Territory, James was one of Australia's most accomplished amateurs in the bantam and featherweight divisions. In all, he won nine Australian titles in the 54 kg division, and three Oceania gold medals. He fought at the Commonwealth Games in 1994 in Victoria, Canada and in 1998 at Kuala Lumpur, winning bronze medals on each occasion. He was selected for the 1996 Atlanta Olympics and for the Olympics in Sydney in 2000 and participated in a number of international contests. All of that adds up to a remarkable amateur career. He turned profession and in 2002 was Australian lightweight champion. Photo: Fairfax Photo Library/courtesy John Fairfax Holdings.

HECTOR THOMPSON

Hector was a world-class boxer with sufficient distinction to fight for two internationally recognised world titles. In 1973 he lost to Roberto Duran, one of the greatest fighters of the twentieth century, for the lightweight crown and in 1975 he lost (due to a cut eye) to the highly rated Antonio Cervantes for the junior welterweight championship. Both fights were held in Panama City. Born in Kempsey (NSW) in 1949 Hector had an outstanding record in the professional ring. He won the Commonwealth junior welterweight title in 1973, held the Australian junior welterweight title from 1971 to 1977, the Australian welterweight crown from 1977 to 1978 and was Australasian welterweight champion in 1973. He lost his Australian and Commonwealth junior welterweight titles to **Lawrence Austin**. He retired in 1978 and his comeback in 1980 was not successful, losing his last fight to **Steve Dennis**. In 87 fights he won 73, drew two and lost 12. Photo: News Limited.

GARY WILLIAMS

Gary Williams, brother of **Bobby Williams**, was born in Orange (NSW) in 1957. Unlike Bobby, Gary fought in both amateur and professional ranks. As an amateur he was Australian bantamweight champion in 1975 and the national featherweight titleholder in 1977 and 1979. To hold three national titles is an outstanding achievement in any sport. The brothers were products of the Orange Police Boys' Club. Gary represented Australia at the Commonwealth Games in Edmonton, Canada in 1978 where he lost in the quarter-finals. He had a huge tally of amateur fights — 216, of which he won 191 and lost 25, a remarkable record for any champion. Soon after he turned professional and won the Australian featherweight title in 1981. In the paid version of the sport, Williams had 40 bouts winning 32 and losing 8. Photo: Carl Sharpe.

R S (BOBBY) WILLIAMS

The 1975 national amateur boxing championships produced a unique feat: R S (Bobby) Williams won the featherweight title and brother **Gary Williams** the bantamweight in the previous contest on the same night. Bobby was born in Orange (NSW) in 1955. In 1972 he was advised that if he won a particular fight in Mudgee he would be selected for the Munich Olympics. He won only to be told he was too young to go. In 1990 he returned to the ring as a successful coach and trainer of Orana region boxers. Bobby won nine state titles, the national flyweight title in 1974, Australian Golden Gloves bantamweight championship in 1974, the featherweight crown in 1975 and was runner-up in the bantamweight division in 1976. Several Aboriginal amateur records are outstanding: **Joe Donovan** won 150 of his 155 bouts; Bobby won 155 and lost only 13 of his 168 fights. Photo: Carl Sharpe.

CHAPTER 8
CRICKET

Cricket evolved over centuries and spread with British colonial policies. Aboriginal people and cricket have had a rich and important relationship. But achievement in this sport now and in the immediate future is likely to be so much less than in other sports. Former Queensland fast bowler **Ian King** believes that cricket is a poor prospect for Aboriginals and Islanders. 'They love hitting, bowling and having a laugh', he says, values which were very much his own. For Aboriginals, cricket is essentially enjoyment, fun, running, moving, but it doesn't attract players the way rugby league, Australian football, soccer and even rugby union do. They don't appear to see in cricket the same career prospects, fame, money, social acceptance and celebrity status. The answer given by **Pastor Douglas Nicholls** in the 1930s still holds good for many Aboriginal youth. To the question, 'Why football?' he answered, 'cheaper than cricket, no pads or white trousers'.

We know much about the famous **1868 team**, particularly the feats of **Johnny Mullagh**, **Johnny Cuzens**, **Twopenny** and Bullocky. We have one outstanding book on that tour (*Cricket Walkabout* by John Mulvaney and Rex Harcourt) and two lesser ones. We know something about the men who battled the odds playing for Poonindie (SA), Coranderrk (Vic.), New Norcia (WA), Point McLeay (SA) and Deebing Creek (Qld); we know virtually nothing about the teams from Ballarat (Vic.) and Wallaga Lake (NSW). The stories of **Jack Marsh** and **Alec Henry** at the start of the last century and the achievements of those remarkable Queenslanders — **Mabel Campbell**, **Edna Crouch** and the legendary **Eddie Gilbert** and later **Faith Thomas**, **Ian King**, **Roger Brown**, **Jason Gillespie** — are in this book. Two notable players were Michael Mainhardt who played a few matches for Queensland and Sydney's Dan Christian who began a solid career in the shorter games in 2006 and was still a player in 2017.

Possibly the tragic ends of three famous men and the press mistreatment of another may have left Aboriginal people with

175

caution about making cricket a career. **Jack Marsh** had to disprove umpire contentions that he was a chucker [bowling with an illegal action], was hounded out of New South Wales cricket for 'reasons unknown' and suffered serious discrimination — not least his manner of death and the scarcely believable acquittal of his two White assailants who kicked him to death. Together with several other cricketers, **Alec Henry** was removed from Brisbane and Toowoomba to remote Yarrabah for 'getting above [their] station in life' and 'malingering'. Like Marsh, he was branded a chucker. The tragedy of **Eddie Gilbert** remains a blight on the administrators of Queensland Aboriginal people, cricket and mental asylums. The Queensland press treatment of **Ian King**'s indiscretions, even in the late 1960s, went way beyond that of anyone else's misdemeanours and quite beyond the usual sporting press glossing over or even covering up player behaviour.

There is one inglorious statistic, that of the eight or nine Aboriginal fast bowlers of real note, nearly 50 per cent who were branded as 'chuckers'. (Of the 3000-plus non-Aboriginal first-class bowlers, fewer than 0.5 per cent have been so labelled.) While the Aboriginal and Islander sample is small, it is simply improbable that these men were born 'genetic' throwers. The suspicion must remain that they were especially singled out — and for obvious reasons. **Faith Thomas** was also 'suspect'. Her bowling style, like that of **Marsh**, **Henry** and **Gilbert**, was off a very short run up with a very fast delivery. Faith explained: 'I was a fast bowler but, you see, being a blackfella, I conserved energy, didn't I, … and I'd only take about four steps and I'd take it off my shoulder …'

There are some happier stories. **Sam Anderson** scored over a hundred centuries in district cricket in northern New South

Bullocky, the wicketkeeper-batsman on the 1868 tour, played in 39 of the 47 matches scoring 589 runs at an average of 9.33. He also took 4 for 46. Photo: Daryl Richardson

Wales. The chief drawcard in Richmond cricket, he played for Queensland Country against the 'Metropolis' in 1906 and again in 1911. On 28 September 1928 thousands of fans went to Lismore (NSW) to watch two idols: **Sam** and Don Bradman playing for Kippax's team against Richmond-Tweed. Both scored ducks. **Anderson** was the man who caught the Don for nought. An excellent bowler and wicketkeeper — known as the 'Bungawalbyn Crack' and 'The Prince of Darkness' — he scored 77 in a district match at the age of 70. The general verdict was that it was 'only his colour that stood between him and the pinnacle of cricketing achievement'. (His grand-daughter was the esteemed author Ruby Langford Ginib).

In 1986 **Charles Perkins** resolved to send

A competitor in every sense, Kath Walker, later known as Oodgeroo Noonuccal, was one of Australia's leading activists and poets.
Photo: Doris Yuke Collection

'Every inch a cricketer': Sampson Barber of Coranderrk (Vic.) showing the contemporary cricket dress. His great-granddaughter, Merle Jackomos, was a keen historian of Cummera Mission. Photo: Merle and Alick Jackomos

an Aboriginal team to England to retrace the 1868 itinerary in 1988. **Mark Ella** and **Ian King** took charge of a seventeen-man team. The late and great writer and broadcaster John Arlott welcomed the team to the Channel Islands. 'I would have taken you for the usual Australian touring cricket team', he said, but for your perfect manners'! **John McGuire**, of equal distinction in cricket as in Australian football, was captain. Despite some early losses the team won 65 per cent of their matches. Apart from **McGuire**, the major figure was Michael Mainhardt, one of the most liked and respected men in Brisbane grade cricket. In 1980–1981 he played for Queensland against New Zealand and in 1982 played his only Sheffield Shield game, against Tasmania.

In that island state **Roger Brown** was a successful Shield cricketer for several years. He was also a fine soccer player. Cricketers of note seem to have arrived decades apart: **Gilbert** in the 1930s; none in the 1940s and 1950s apart from **Sam Anderson**; **King** in the 1960s and a national player who has no wish to be identified as Aboriginal; **John McGuire** and Michael Mainhardt in the 1980s; and **Jason Gillespie**, undoubtedly the most acclaimed and most successful of all, in the 1990s. He retired in 2008 and had a successful coaching career in Zimbabwe, Papua New Guinea and Yorkshire.

An Aboriginal cricket team toured New Zealand in 1988. The South Australian Cricket Association assisted Aboriginal juniors and Les Knox has spent a lifetime devoted to Aboriginal cricket including establishing a NSW Schools Aboriginal XI, a team of battlers and novices which trounced a visiting Bath (UK) Schools XI, complete with all the right gear. Albert Roberts captained the winning team — and then chose a new career as a member of the Australian under-19 Schoolboys rugby league team.

It remains to be seen whether Gillespie's achievements will inspire Aboriginal youth to take the game more seriously than **King** suggests is the case. At this time of writing, we have Ashleigh Gardner in the Australian women's team, and men like Scott Boland, D'Arcy Short, Brendan Doggett and Josh Lalor in the Big Bash League.

The Aboriginal cricket team to England, 1988:

In preparation the team played the Prime Minister's XI at Manly. *Back row, left to right*: Dennis Monaghan, Joe Marsh, Greg James, Paul Bagshaw, Michael Williams, Dwayne Breckenridge, Pius Gregory. *Middle row*: Michael Mainhard, Sean Appoo, Darrin Thompson, Bert Pearce, Laurie Marks, Donald Gardner, Les Knox. *Front row*: Neil Bulger, **Ian King** (coach), Bob Hawke (Prime Minister), **Mark Ella**, **John McGuire** (captain). *Absent*: Eddie Graham-Vanderbyl, Norm Fry.

Photo: Fairfax Photo Library/courtesy John Fairfax Holdings

1868 TEAM TO ENGLAND

The *Aborigines Protection Act of 1869* in Victoria began strict control of the black population. Had it been passed a year earlier the famous Aboriginal tour to England would not have taken place. The tour was a success in many ways and a disaster in others. The team played 47 matches, drawing 19, winning 14 and losing 14. King Cole died on tour, probably from tuberculosis, and Sundown and Jim Crow became so ill they had to be sent home. Only **Johnny Mullagh**, **Johnny Cuzens** and perhaps **Twopenny** had careers in cricket on returning to Australia.

Rear, *left to right*: Tarpot, Tommy Wills (captain and coach), **Johnny Mullagh**. *Front row*: King Cole (leg on chair); *standing, right*: Dick-a-Dick; seated *left to right*: Jellico, Peter, Red Cap, Harry Rose, Bullocky, **Johnny Cuzens**. [Charles Lawrence (co-captain), **Twopenny**, Tiger, Charley Dumas, Mosquito, Jim Crow, Shepherd and Sundown joined the others for the tour].

Photo: Australian National Library.

SAM ANDERSON

Sam Anderson was known as 'The Bungawalbyn Crack' and also as 'The Prince of Darkness'. Born in Deebing Creek Mission (Qld) in 1884, he was probably a Waka Waka man. He never made it to the top in cricket but he did score over 100 centuries in district cricket in northern New South Wales. The chief drawcard in Richmond cricket, he played for Queensland Country against the 'Metropolis' in 1906 and again in 1911. On 28 September 1928 thousands went to Lismore (NSW) to watch two idols: Sam and Don Bradman playing for Kippax's team against Richmond-Tweed. Both scored ducks. Sam's grand-daughter was the renowned Aboriginal writer Ruby Langford Ginibi. Maurice Ryan published a book on Sam entitled *Dusky Legend: Biography of Sam Anderson, Aboriginal Cricketer* in 2001. Photo: Michael Yabsley.

ROGER BROWN

Roger was born in Launceston (Tas.) in 1959. Until the arrival of **Jason Gillespie**, Roger had played more first-class cricket matches than any other Aboriginal cricketer: 31 for Tasmania between 1984 and 1987. An opening bowler, he took the same number of wickets as **Eddie Gilbert**, 87 in all at an average of 39.68. His batting average was 13.23. In this period Tasmania was very much the Cinderella side in Sheffield Shield cricket and Brown's wickets were gained against the strongest sides in the country. He toured Zimbabwe with the Australian under25 side in 1985–1986, and was also selected for the Prime Minister's XI. As is the case with so many Aboriginal achievers, he was an all-rounder: a talented footballer, he played soccer for Launceston Juventus. Photo: *Launceston Examiner*.

MABEL CAMPBELL

Mabel was born in Myora, Stradbroke Island (Qld) in 1908. Seen here with her cousin **Edna Crouch** (*left*), she married Sid Crouch, a cousin to rugby league star **Paddy Crouch**. Women's cricket started in Queensland in 1929 and was played exclusively in middle-class private schools. It was a remarkable feat for two Aboriginal women from state schools and from 'the other side of the social tracks' to gain state selection in such a 'silvertail' sport. Yet in the mid-1930s Mabel and cousin **Edna Crouch** (Paddy's sister) were playing for Wynnum Club and for Queensland. Mabel represented her state from 1934 to 1936, played against the visiting English side in 1934–1935 and topped the batting averages in the England versus Queensland matches. In the 1936 interstate carnival she scored 56 not out against the champions, Victoria. Photo: Thelma Crouch.

EDNA CROUCH

Edna was a member of a remarkable sporting family. She was a cousin of **Mabel Campbell**, sister to **Paddy Crouch**, aunt of state cricketer Thelma Crouch and Glen Crouch Jr (life member of the Brisbane Rugby League for his services as player and administrator). Born in Dunwich, Stradbroke Island (Qld) in 1910, she married Archie Newfong, rugby league player and Queensland middleweight boxing champion. Following Mabel's example, Edna played cricket for Queensland, in her case from 1934 to 1938. The press reported on a waterlogged match against England in the 1934–1935 season: 'Miss E. Crouch had surprising bowling averages'. She 'bowled a perfect length and her slow ball had many of the batswomen in trouble'. Cricket in this family went way back: in the 1890s there was a cricket team in the local Wynnum region competition that comprised nine Crouches, one related Campbell and one stranger! Photo: Thelma Crouch.

JOHNNY CUZENS

His birth name was Yellanach and he was born in Balmoral (Vic.) possibly in the mid 1840s. Known as Johnny Cuzens, this tiny man (5 feet 1 inch or 155 cm) was, with **Johnny Mullagh**, the star of the famous Aboriginal cricket team which toured England in 1868. There he played 46 of the 47 tour matches, scoring 1364 runs for an 18.94 average; he took 113 wickets for an 11.38 average. The god-figure of cricket, W G Grace, praised the 'all-round form' of Cuzens and Mullagh. In 1866 Johnny played for Victoria against Tasmania. After the English tour he and Mullagh were employed by the Melbourne Cricket Club as professionals. He played only six matches — 'his vitality had deserted him' and he returned to Framlingham reserve in western Victoria where he died in 1871, probably aged 26. Photo: Melbourne Cricket Club, MCG.

EDDIE GILBERT

Eddie bowled Sir Donald Bradman for a duck (in December 1931) in the fastest bowling spell Bradman said he had ever faced. He bowled at sizzling speeds off four or five shuffled paces. Born in Durundur near Woodford (Qld) in 1905, Eddie played 23 first-class matches for Queensland. In his career (1930–1935) he took 87 wickets at 28.97 average. In the December 1931 game he not only bowled Bradman but took 4 for 74 in an innings in which the great Stan McCabe scored 229 not out. In 1934–1935 he took a total of 9 for 178 against New South Wales and 5 for 77 against Victoria. Only one umpire ruled his delivery unfair. A 'controlled' Aboriginal person, he needed permission to play Shield cricket and travelled to Brisbane by train while team mates drove. Eddie spent 23 years in Goodna Psychiatric Hospital at Wolsten Park where again he experienced discrimination. Leading sportsmen, including Bradman, attended his large funeral at Cherbourg. Photo: Pat Mullins/Melbourne Cricket Club, MCG.

JASON GILLESPIE

When he took 7 for 37 against England at Leeds in 1997, Australians realised they had a great fast bowler, someone in the Lillee and Thomson mould. Jason was born in Sydney in 1975. His cricket career was one of triumph over immense obstacles: constant back problems, stress fractures in a body seemingly unsuited to his profession, a life-threatening nerve disease of the legs as a child, 'excruciating shyness, premature fatherhood and a miserable de facto relationship' according to sympathetic interviewer Daniel Williams. After a freak collision with Steve Waugh in Pakistan in 1999 he return to one-day cricket in 2000 with resilience and determination. In first-class cricket to the end of 2006, he played 71 Test matches for 259 wickets at 26.4 average and 97 one-day internationals for 97 wickets at 25.42. He scored two Test centuries and one Test double century. Photo: *AllSport Australia*.

ALBERT (ALEC) HENRY

Alec was one of three great Aboriginal fast bowlers to be picked on for 'throwing'. Born in Deebing Creek, near Ipswich (Qld) in 1880, Alec played seven first-class matches for Queensland from 1901–1904, taking 21 wickets at 32.04 average. His best average in grade cricket was 5.15 per wicket in 1902. Typical press comments were that he was 'a fiery, unpredictable fast bowler' whose 'pace was terrific and length splendid'; 'a genuine character, subject to moodiness'. An enthusiastic fielder, he often tired during matches. He was ill for most of his amazing sporting career. A winner of several major sprint races including Ipswich Gaslight events, he also played rugby union for Deebing Creek. He was removed to Barambah (renamed Cherbourg in 1931) 'for loafing, malingering and defying authority'. He was taken to the isolated Yarrabah mission near Cairns where he died of tuberculosis aged 29 — defiant at the rigid segregation system yet certainly victim to it. Photo: Jack Pollard.

IAN KING

Unlike his predecessors — **Alec Henry**, **Jack Marsh** and **Eddie Gilbert** — there was never any problem with Ian's beautiful fast bowling action. Born in Brisbane in 1945, this fine athlete played eight first-class matches for Queensland in 1969. He took 30 wickets at an average of 28.36 per wicket. Despite Ian's short career, writer Jack Pollard said 'he gave glimpses of rare talent, exceptional pace and splendid fielding ability'. An outstanding basketballer, he also boxed professionally under the name of Young Rainbow. He won 28 of his 32 welterweight bouts. Later he coached cricket clubs in Perth and the Western Australia under16 team. He was a key organiser as well as the coach of the Aboriginal team which toured England in 1988. Later in life he completed a Master of Health Sciences degree. Photo: *Courier-Mail*.

JACK MARSH

Two Aboriginal men are in cricket's 'legend' class: **Eddie Gilbert** and **Jack Marsh**. Born in the Clarence River District (NSW) in 1874, Jack and brother Larry excelled as sprinters. Jack was rated the fastest man in the state over 75 yards. In 1902 he took 58 wickets at 10 runs apiece in Sydney. As a specialist fast bowler he played six first-class matches for New South Wales in 1901–1903 despite attempts to brand him a 'chucker'. He took 34 wickets at a 21.47 average. His Aboriginality precluded him from an English tour. In 1902 the visiting Englishmen refused to play against him but the 1903–1904 side did: Marsh took 5 for 55. Banned from the Sydney Cricket Ground without any reason offered, he drifted into circus life. Then followed a life of petty crime. Two men were acquitted of kicking him to death in a street brawl in Orange in 1916: the judge's astonishing comment was that 'Marsh may have deserved it!' Photo: NSW Cricket Association.

JOHN McGUIRE

John McGuire was a rare all-rounder: a first grade cricketer and a first-division Australian footballer. Born in Northam (WA) in 1954, John played 85 Australian football games for East Perth from 1973 to 1979, overlapping for a while with his cousin **Barry Cable**, and 21 for Perth between 1980 and 1983. Cricket became his major sport and in first grade he played for Mt Lawley during which time he became that club's highest-ever run-maker, scoring over 6,000 runs at an average of over 500 per season. In all, he scored over 10,000 runs in grade cricket. In 1988 he captained the Aboriginal team which toured England in commemoration of the famed 1868 Aboriginal cricket tour. John has spent his working life in the Western Australian public service. Photo: John McGuire.

JOHNNY MULLAGH

His name was probably Muarrinim and he was born on Mullagh Station near Harrow in Western Victoria in 1841 or 1843. Known as 'Mullagh Johnny', then as Johnny Mullagh, he was described [with **Johnny Cuzens**] as 'constituting not only the backbone but some of the ribs as well' of the 1868 Aboriginal cricket tour to England. Mullagh played 43 of the 47 tour matches, scoring 1679 runs at an average of 22.68 and taking 237 wickets for an average of 8.97. Against Lord Harris's English XI in 1878 he didn't take any wickets for Victoria but top-scored with 36 out of 156 in the Colony's second innings, a feat which inspired the crowd to collect £50 for him! After a short spell as a professional with the Melbourne Cricket Club he continued with the Harrow Club in the Murray Cup until 1890. A memorial obelisk was sponsored by the *Hamilton Spectator* and erected to this 'virtuous, exemplary man' at the Johnny Mullagh Park in Harrow. Photo: Mechanic's Institute, Harrow, Victoria.

NEW NORCIA TEAM

A Spanish Benedictine monk, Dom Rosendo Salvado, introduced the game to the people he described as 'these poor natives, so hideous to look at'. Daisy Bates, an early anthropologist, wrote about the hundreds of spectators who flocked to see the Aboriginal players from New Norcia mission (WA). Nicknamed 'The Invincibles' and coached only by a local grazier, H S Lefroy, the team walked 120 km each way for matches in Perth and Fremantle. When the *Aborigines Act 1905* was passed, rigid control became the norm — and that was the end of the cricket. Historian Bob Reece has written a book on the team: *The Invincibles: New Norcia's Aboriginal Cricketers. 1879–1906*

THE 1879 NEW NORCIA TEAM

Standing at rear, Patrick Yapo, John Walley, Benedict Caper, Anthony Nelabut, Alec Wegnola (or Wanola) (captain); *sitting front row*, Paul Jater, John Blurton, H S Lefroy (coach), Frederick Yrbel, Joseph Nogolot; *sitting lower front right*, Felix Jackimara.

Photo: John Mulvaney and Rex Harcourt.

FAITH THOMAS

Faith Thomas is a significant figure in Aboriginal and Islander sport as she was the first woman to be selected for any national side, thus representing the breakthrough for Aboriginal women. Born Faith Coulthard at Nepabunna Mission (SA) in 1933, her mother was an Adnyamathana tribal woman from the Flinders Ranges. As a child she was sent to Colebrook Children's Home in Quorn (SA). After attending university for a year — where she played squash and hockey — she became a nurse. A fast bowler using a short run up, she was chosen for South Australia against England and New Zealand. Faith was often referred to as 'Dusty Miller' — in praise of her resemblance to Australian bowling legend Keith Miller. In 1958 she was chosen for two Tests against England: one match was abandoned and the second was played at St Kilda Oval. While nursing in the Territory she played hockey for Alice Springs. Photo: Faith Thomas.

TWOPENNY (MURRUMGUNARRIMIN)

Twopenny's name may have been Jarrawuk, Bynyarra or Murrumgunarrimin. He was most likely the only New South Welshman in the 1868 cricket team, born at Ulladulla in about 1847. Despite controversy about his bowling action he headed the tour bowling averages with 35 wickets at 6.9 apiece. On return he played one club season for Newtown (NSW) in 1869 and 1870. Employed as a professional practice bowler at the Domain, the man described by the Melbourne *Argus* as 'the fastest bowler and hardest hitter of the lot' was chosen to play in his one and only first-class match — the thirteenth inter-colonial game between Victoria and New South Wales in 1870. He made 8 and 0 in a game and took 0 for 56 in a game won handsomely by Victoria. He died in 1883 in West Maitland. The Aboriginal community believe he is buried at an Aboriginal-owned park called Tobwabba in Forster (NSW). Photo: Daryl Richardson.

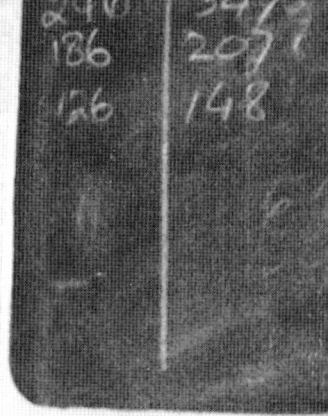

CHAPTER 9
DARTS

The modern numbered dart board dates to 1896. Some people don't regard this popular pub game as a sport, but we do. The internet and televised darts coverage have done a great deal to make this sport both entertaining and popular.

Kyle Anderson, an engaging personality and always adorned in Aboriginal motif clothing, has attracted a good deal of attention here and in Europe. In 2017 **Kyle** became the first Aboriginal to win a World Series of Darts title.

Australia has competed in every world darts championship since 1976 and every Asia-Pacific Cup since 1980. The Cup is a mixed event (men and women), a trophy won seven times thus far by Australia. Ease of access no doubt explains the astonishingly high Aboriginal participation. **Horrie Seden**, **Ivy Hampton**, **Eileen Foster**, **Charmaine Barney** and **Kyle Anderson** are in this Hall of Fame. **Ivy** and **Eileen** are both in the Australian Darts Hall of Fame.

Harena Williamson and Beau Anderson holding their World Youth Cup in Durban, South Africa, in October 1999. Both are from Perth.
Photo: Phil Wyatt

Barry Rowan, then a junior from the Northern Territory, was runner-up in the World Youth Cup in 1986. Marlon Johns from Western Australia won the Australian Junior Singles in 1987 and was runner-up in 1988; he was runner-up in the under-18 World championship. Ian Brown of Queensland won the national Junior Singles in 1988 and was runner-up the following year. Both young men represented Australia in the World Junior Championships in London. All three went on to play senior darts for their states. In 1999 two Queenslanders, Greg Major from Woorabinda and Tony Blackman from Gladstone, became the first Aboriginal players to win the Australian Pairs in the national championships. The culmination of all this came in October 1999 in Durban, South Africa, venue of the inaugural Youth World Cup, won by Australia. Harena Williamson, aged 17, won the gold in the girls' event; Beau Anderson (**Kyle**'s brother) aged 16, won the bronze in the boys'; together they won the gold in the mixed doubles and the overall World Cup. Both are Nyungar from Perth.

In 2017 the first all-Aboriginal team to play in an international competition (in New Zealand) hailed from Rockhampton in central Queensland.

The controlling body likes to think of darts as an integrating sport. We agree. Darts is the one sport that doesn't need lessons in race relations. Every state has had Aboriginal and Islander members of their representative teams.

Ian Brown
Photo: NT Darts Association

KYLE ANDERSON

Kyle was born in Subiaco, Perth in 1987. He started playing darts at 6 and was already competing in tournaments by the age of 9. Anderson's older brother Beau had started playing a few years prior, and they teamed together to win the Australian junior boys championship in 2000. Kyle turned professional in 2012 — the first Aboriginal player to do so. After qualifying for the 2014 world championship, Anderson became only the seventh player to throw a nine-dart finish in the history of the event (the equivalent of a perfect 147 break in snooker). He moved to the UK, and won the Auckland Darts (three dart) Masters in 2017. Kyle then set a new world record for the highest ever average in darts history of 134.84 for a match. He has ranked as high as 22nd in the world. Photo: Emma Morley/Kyle Anderson.

CHARMAINE BARNEY

Charmaine was a talented and respected darts champion. She was born in Brisbane in 1965 and represented Queensland from 1986–1992. Her great year was 1991 when she was runner-up in the Australian ladies singles, won the Pacific Master's ladies singles, was selected for Australia in the World Darts Championships in Holland in 1991 where she was runner-up in the World Singles, and was invited to play in the Winmau 18th World Darts Championships in London. Charmaine represented Australia in the 1992 Pacific Cup VII held in Melbourne: she won the gold in the ladies singles, silver in the ladies doubles and teams event. Charmaine was runner-up to **Eileen Foster** in the All Aboriginal event in Canberra in 1987. Many darts officials considered her a truly great player and her seedings in various world tournaments confirmed her status. Charmaine retired for active competition in 1993. Photo: Charmaine Barney.

CHAPTER 9
DARTS

The modern numbered dart board dates to 1896. Some people don't regard this popular pub game as a sport, but we do. The internet and televised darts coverage have done a great deal to make this sport both entertaining and popular.

Kyle Anderson, an engaging personality and always adorned in Aboriginal motif clothing, has attracted a good deal of attention here and in Europe. In 2017 **Kyle** became the first Aboriginal to win a World Series of Darts title.

Australia has competed in every world darts championship since 1976 and every Asia-Pacific Cup since 1980. The Cup is a mixed event (men and women), a trophy won seven times thus far by Australia. Ease of access no doubt explains the astonishingly high Aboriginal participation. **Horrie Seden**, **Ivy Hampton**, **Eileen Foster**, **Charmaine Barney** and **Kyle Anderson** are in this Hall of Fame. **Ivy** and **Eileen** are both in the Australian Darts Hall of Fame.

Harena Williamson and Beau Anderson holding their World Youth Cup in Durban, South Africa, in October 1999. Both are from Perth.
Photo: Phil Wyatt

195

Barry Rowan, then a junior from the Northern Territory, was runner-up in the World Youth Cup in 1986. Marlon Johns from Western Australia won the Australian Junior Singles in 1987 and was runner-up in 1988; he was runner-up in the under-18 World championship. Ian Brown of Queensland won the national Junior Singles in 1988 and was runner-up the following year. Both young men represented Australia in the World Junior Championships in London. All three went on to play senior darts for their states. In 1999 two Queenslanders, Greg Major from Woorabinda and Tony Blackman from Gladstone, became the first Aboriginal players to win the Australian Pairs in the national championships. The culmination of all this came in October 1999 in Durban, South Africa, venue of the inaugural Youth World Cup, won by Australia. Harena Williamson, aged 17, won the gold in the girls' event; Beau Anderson (**Kyle**'s brother) aged 16, won the bronze in the boys'; together they won the gold in the mixed doubles and the overall World Cup. Both are Nyungar from Perth.

In 2017 the first all-Aboriginal team to play in an international competition (in New Zealand) hailed from Rockhampton in central Queensland.

The controlling body likes to think of darts as an integrating sport. We agree. Darts is the one sport that doesn't need lessons in race relations. Every state has had Aboriginal and Islander members of their representative teams.

Ian Brown
Photo: NT Darts Association

KYLE ANDERSON

Kyle was born in Subiaco, Perth in 1987. He started playing darts at 6 and was already competing in tournaments by the age of 9. Anderson's older brother Beau had started playing a few years prior, and they teamed together to win the Australian junior boys championship in 2000. Kyle turned professional in 2012 — the first Aboriginal player to do so. After qualifying for the 2014 world championship, Anderson became only the seventh player to throw a nine-dart finish in the history of the event (the equivalent of a perfect 147 break in snooker). He moved to the UK, and won the Auckland Darts (three dart) Masters in 2017. Kyle then set a new world record for the highest ever average in darts history of 134.84 for a match. He has ranked as high as 22nd in the world. Photo: Emma Morley/Kyle Anderson.

CHARMAINE BARNEY

Charmaine was a talented and respected darts champion. She was born in Brisbane in 1965 and represented Queensland from 1986–1992. Her great year was 1991 when she was runner-up in the Australian ladies singles, won the Pacific Master's ladies singles, was selected for Australia in the World Darts Championships in Holland in 1991 where she was runner-up in the World Singles, and was invited to play in the Winmau 18th World Darts Championships in London. Charmaine represented Australia in the 1992 Pacific Cup VII held in Melbourne: she won the gold in the ladies singles, silver in the ladies doubles and teams event. Charmaine was runner-up to **Eileen Foster** in the All Aboriginal event in Canberra in 1987. Many darts officials considered her a truly great player and her seedings in various world tournaments confirmed her status. Charmaine retired for active competition in 1993. Photo: Charmaine Barney.

EILEEN FOSTER (WILSON)

Eileen Foster was formerly known as Eileen Wilson. Like her younger sister **Ivy Hampton**, she was born at McLaren Station in the Northern Territory in 1941 and began playing darts in Alice Springs. In the mid-1980s **Charlie Perkins** promoted a national Aboriginal championship in Canberra. Eileen won the women's title, beating a young **Charmaine Barney** in the final. It was to be the only such tournament: there was no need for it since darts has shown itself to be the most accessible and the most democratic of all sports. Eileen was runner-up in the Puma Pacific Masters in Perth in 1983 and runner up in the Australian Masters' ladies doubles in Canberra. She was selected for Australia to play in the first major competition for 'soft point darts', a new electronic version of this indoor sport. She and Michelle Mainsbridge of New South Wales were runners-up in this international competition held in Chicago. Photo: Eileen Foster.

IVY HAMPTON

The most tolerant of sports for Aboriginals and Islanders has been darts, a game in which they have excelled out of all proportion to their numbers. Access has been easy, even in the often segregated hotel bars in the Territory. Ivy was a star among many. She was born at McLaren Station near Tennant Creek (NT) in 1936. She was a member of the winning Australian team in the first (ten-nation) Pacific Cup held in Newcastle in 1980, the event in which she won the Pacific Cup singles and pairs titles. Ivy also represented Australia in England in the esteemed tournament, the Winmau World Ladies' Masters. Her preference for hospital work among her own people in Alice Springs led her to reject a professional darts career. Her sister **Eileen Foster** also played darts for Australia. Photo: Department of Aboriginal Affairs.

HORRIE SEDEN

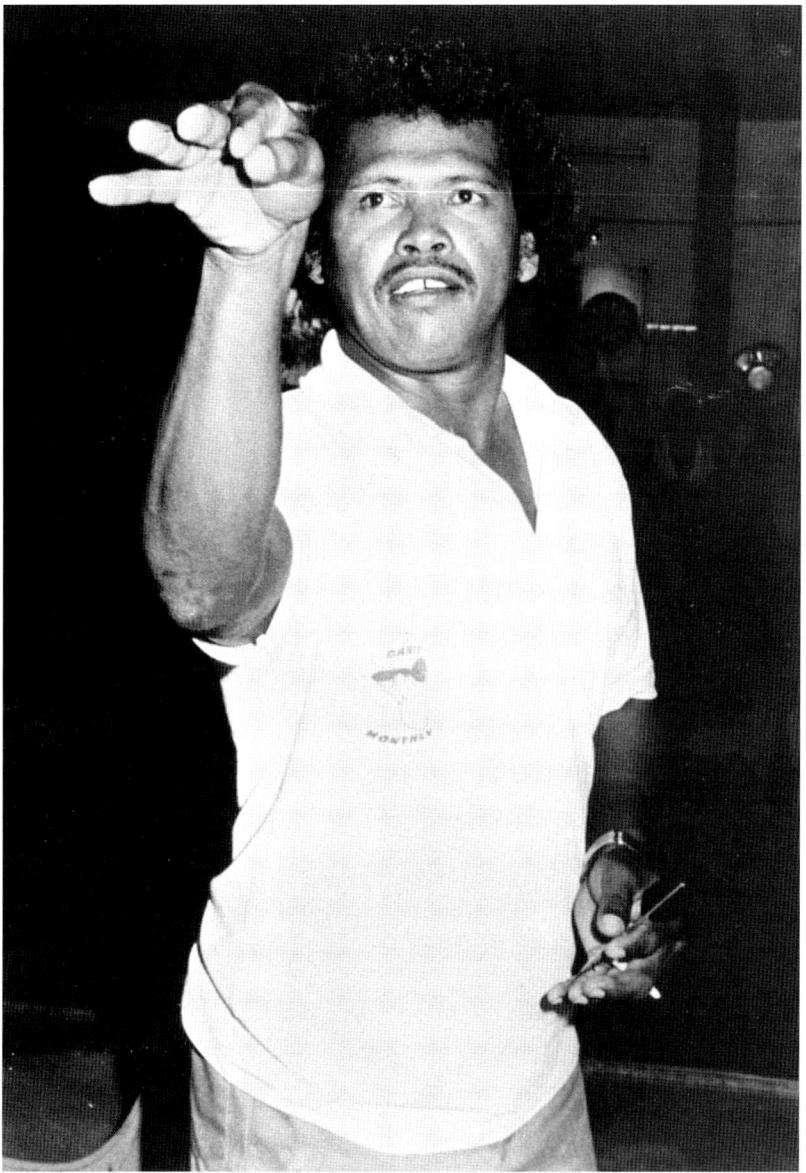

There is an astonishingly high Aboriginal participation in the sport of darts, more so than in any other sport. Role models are important and there could be no better example than the man described by Peter McMenamin, president of the Darts Federation of Australia, as 'a gentleman's gentleman, a fantastic little fellow'. Horrie — a Darwin-based Thursday Islander — was born in Cairns (Qld) in 1946. He has had an outstanding representative career: for Australia in World Cup V in Brisbane, World Cup VI in Denmark and in the Winmau World Masters from 1985 to 1990. Horrie has been runner-up and winner of the Australian singles title and winner of the Australian Grandmaster championship. Horrie was certainly an inspiration for Marlon Johns and Ian Brown, two Aboriginal lads who won the Australian junior singles titles in 1987 and 1988 respectively. Photo: *NT News*.

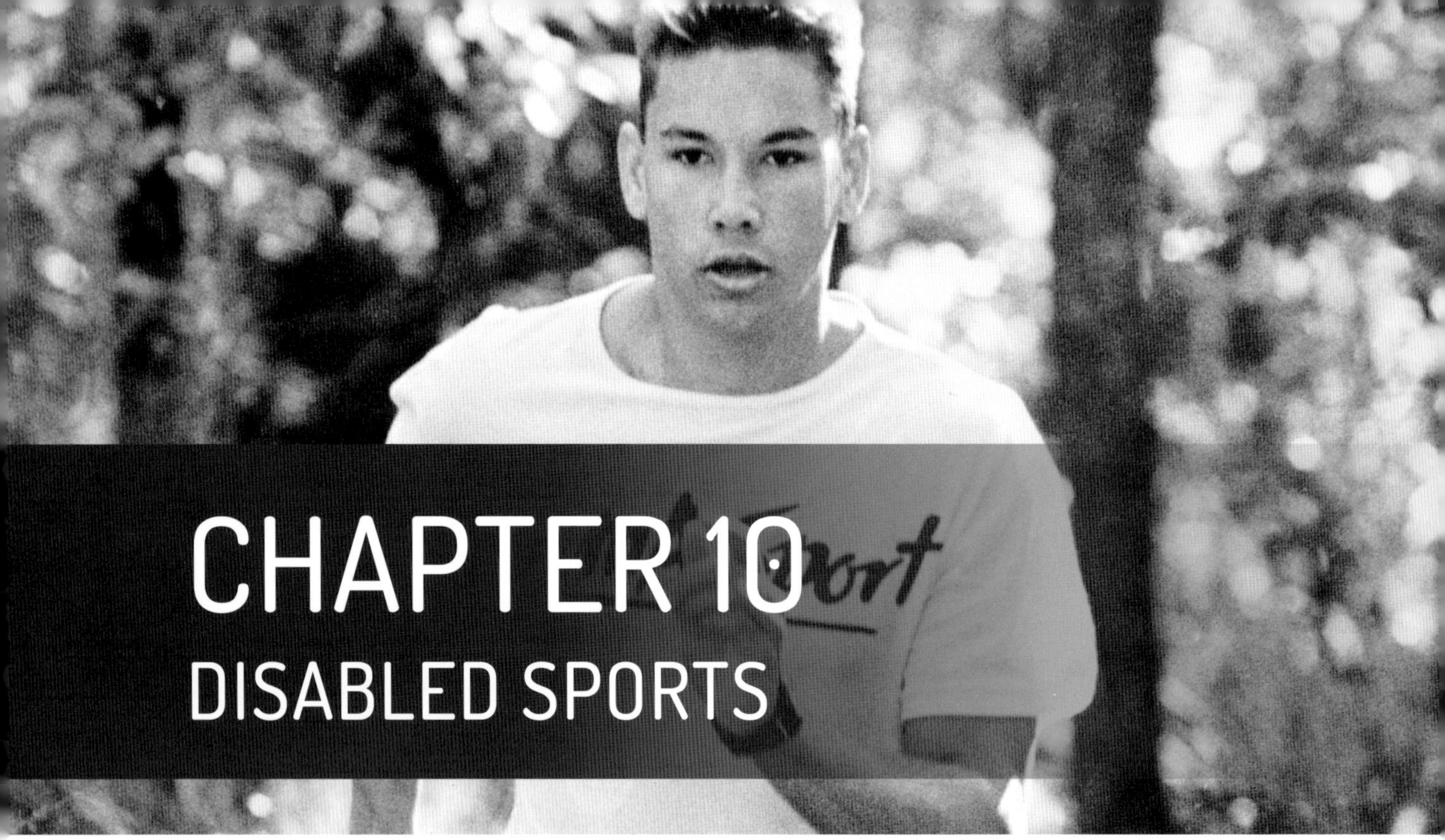

CHAPTER 10
DISABLED SPORTS

Some 40 years ago disability sport was considered too awkward to portray on television. In the 1970s, the ABC televised a documentary that was considered brave. It warned that viewers could find some scenes distressing. This sports category has come a long way indeed, and is now well received and acclaimed.

Disabled sports competitions began in the 1920s. Following World War II, Dr Ludwig Guttmann at Stoke Mandeville Hospital in the United Kingdom suggested a major competition for war patients in particular. That resulted in the first organised international competition in Rome in 1960. The Paralympics are now synonymous with the Stoke Mandeville Games.

Disability or disabled sport is sometime called parasport or adaptive sport. There are some nineteen divisions, ranging from archery to wheelchair forms of basketball, boccia (a game related to lawn bowls), fencing, rugby, and tennis. Wheelchair rugby is hardly a delicate sport — renowned for its

Kayla Clarke — raised in Ipswich (Qld) — represented Australia in the 2012 London Olympics as an all-round swimmer. She won a medal in a world Paralympian event in 2009. Kayla has an intellectual disability.
Photo: Australian Paralympic Committee

fast action, violent clashes and no-holds-barred attitudes.

Disabilities of many kinds are recognised: sight loss, muscle impairment, limb dysfunction, intellectual disability and cerebral palsy as well as wheelchair-bound competitors and amputees. Often there are several categories within a particular sport. Especial sports have been developed, such as goalball — a form of indoor soccer for the sight-impaired.

Torita Blake (Issac): Torita is from the Kamilaroi nation, Mount Gravatt (Qld). She (unofficially) broke the T38 (vision impaired and cerebral palsy) 800 m world record in February 2015 as a 17-year-old. She competed at the 2012 London and 2016 Rio Olympic Games.
Photo: Australian Paralympic Committee

Tahlia Rotumah is from the Minjungbal nation, and is also of South Sea Island descent. She won silver medals in the 100 m and 200 m sprints at the 2006 Far East and South Pacific Games held in Kuala Lumpur.
At 16 she competed in the 2008 Summer Paralympics in Beijing.
Photo: Australian Paralympic Committee

BEN AUSTIN, OAM

Ben has a remarkable record in international swimming competition. An above-elbow amputee as a result of birth complications, he swims in the S8 (physical disability) classification. Born in Wellington (NSW) in 1980, Ben has participated in three Paralympics (2000, 2004, 2008) for a total of three gold, four silver and three bronze medals. In two Commonwealth Games, he has won two gold medals. He has also swum in World Championships, competing in freestyle, butterfly and breaststroke events, as well as in medley relays. His finest achievements were winning the 50 m and 100 m freestyle at the Manchester Commonwealth Games in 2002, the 100 m freestyle in Athens in 2004 in world record time and his gold in the 4 × 100m relay in Beijing in 2008. Ben has been honoured by the Australian Paralympic Committee and by the Queensland Government, and was awarded an OAM for services to disabled sport. Photo: Simon Alekna/Fairfax Syndication.

DISABLED SPORTS

TRACY LEE BARRELL, OAM

Tracy Lee was born in 1974 as a congenital amputee, possibly the result of medication taken by her mother during pregnancy. She has no legs and only one arm, using a skateboard to move from a young age. Tracy declined the use of prosthetic limbs. (She was once denied a disability card by the government because they considered her mobile enough.) When 14, her mother enrolled her in the NSW Amputee Sporting Association. Later she was classified as an S4 swimmer. A Paralympic swimmer, she won two gold medals at the 1992 Barcelona Olympic Games: the women's 4 x 50 m freestyle S1-6 event and the women's 50 m butterfly S3-4 event. Following retirement in 1994, Tracy dedicated herself to the promotion of disability sport and to Aboriginal achievement. Tracy has also played sitting volleyball in international competitions. Photo: Troy Howe/Fairfax Syndication.

RAYMOND (RAY) BARRETT

Raymond Barrett was born in 1952. His family are Wiradjuri people from Blakney and Pudman Creeks, New South Wales. As a youth he was an archer, but after being hit by a car in 1965, aged 13, he relied on a wheelchair. He trained as a printer and technician. Ray broke several athletics records in shot putt, discus, sprints and long-distance wheelchair racing and won three medals at the Third Commonwealth Paraplegic Games in Edinburgh. At the 1972 Summer Paralympics in Heidelberg, Germany, he won a bronze medal in the 100 m wheelchair dash, and was fifth in the slalom event. In the 1974 Fourth Commonwealth Paraplegic Games in Dunedin, New Zealand, Ray won gold, silver and bronze medals and set world records on all three occasions in the wheelchair dash, and a bronze medal in wheelchair basketball. In the same year, at the International Stoke Mandeville Games, England, he won a gold and two bronze medals. Photo: Australian Paralympic Committee.

DONNA BURNS

Donna was born in Echuca (Vic.) in 1973. At a young age she moved to Melbourne where she attended a school for disabled children. Donna has an intellectual disability. At school she showed an interest in both netball and basketball. She achieved a notable double by playing for Victoria in both disabled netball and basketball. Chosen for the national basketball team, she travelled to Europe and played seven internationals in the warm-up to the Barcelona Paralympics in 1992. Opponents included the United Kingdom, Spain and Brazil. At Barcelona she scored 128 of the team's 273 points on the way to the gold medal in basketball. This made her the star player. Donna won the Disabled Sportswoman of the Year at the National Aboriginal Sports Awards in 1993. Photo: Sally Duncan.

KEVIN COOMBS, OAM

Kevin is the most distinguished of the many able and disabled Aboriginal and Islander athletes. Born in Swan Hill (Vic.) in 1941, a gunshot wound left him a paraplegic at the age of 11. This didn't stop his ability and determination. He went on to represent Australia in wheelchair basketball at the Paralympics in 1960, 1968, 1972, 1980 and 1984. There can be few athletes anywhere in the world who have been selected for their country over such an extended period. He participated in the Commonwealth Wheelchair Games in Dunedin and in the Silver Jubilee Games in England in 1977, and he represented Australia in Germany and England, at the World Championships in Canada, and at World Challenge in Los Angeles. His achievements have been a beacon for a number of Aboriginal disabled athletes including Peter Kirby, Marjorie Patrick, Karl Feifar, Donna Burns and Beverley Champion. Photo: Kevin Coombs.

KARL FEIFAR

Karl ranks as one of Australia's foremost disabled athletes. He lost a leg below the knee as a child. Born in Subiaco (WA) in 1973, Karl's great year was 1990: in the World Championships for the Disabled, held in Holland, he won three gold and two silver medals and set world records in the pentathlon and long jump. He also won the shot putt, javelin and discus. Karl went on to the 1992 Paralympics in Barcelona where he won a gold medal in the 4 x 100 m relay and a silver in the long jump. He withdrew from competition in 1993. His 1990 triumphs became the model for Kalgoorlie's Beverley Champion, athlete and swimmer, who was named National Disabled Sportswoman of the Year in 1999. Photo: West Australian Newspapers Ltd.

PETER KIRBY

Born in Bega (South East NSW) in 1964, Peter was the son of a Wiradjuri father and mother. At 13, he lost his right hand and forearm from touching a fallen high-voltage power line. Before the accident, he excelled as a schoolboy athlete. The Eden community, where Peter grew up, helped finance his training and competition expenses. As an arm amputee athlete in the 1984 New York and Stoke Mandeville Paralympics, Peter won one gold in the men's 4 x 100 m relay A49 event, silver in the men's 4 x 400 m relay A49, and three bronze medals — in the men's 100 m A6, men's 400 m A6 and men's long jump A6 events. While Kevin Coombs was the first Aboriginal Paralympian in 1960, Peter was the first Aboriginal Paralympian to win a gold medal. Photo: Bill Brown, ABC South East NSW.

WARREN LAWTON

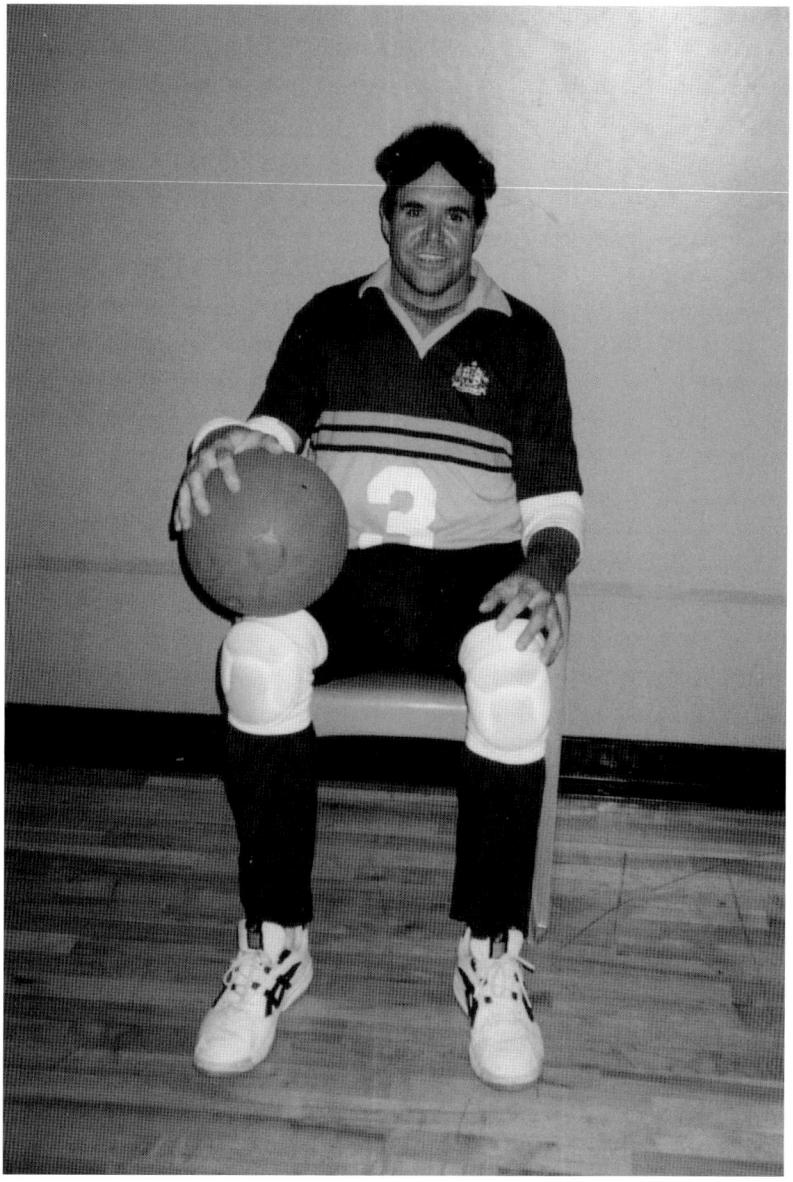

Born in 1966 in Augathella (Qld), Warren was a Paralympic athletics and goalball competitor with a visual impairment. Born with the sight problem, Warren first competed at the Summer Paralympics in New York in 1984, in three athletic events, winning a bronze medal in the men's high jump B3. He won another bronze in the high jump at the 1986 World Championships for the Disabled, in Gothenburg, Sweden. Warren took part in two athletics events at the 1988 Seoul Games. From athletics Warren turned to goalball, a special event for the visually impaired, a sport invented in 1946. Warren was in the Olympic goalball team in Barcelona in 1992 and again in Sydney in 2000. Later he turned to coaching. Warren has been recognised by awards from several organisations, including a NAIDOC Sportsman of the Year award. Photo: Warren Lawton.

AMANDA REID (FOWLER)

Born in 1996, Amanda is a Guringai woman from Sydney who grew up in Blaxland (NSW). She has cerebral palsy and an intellectual disability. At the 2012 London Summer Paralympic Games she competed in the S14 100 m breaststroke event. Remarkably for any athlete, she changed sports and turned to cycling. In her first international in that sport, she won a silver medal in the Women's C2 500 m Time Trial at the 2016 UCI Para-cycling Track World Championships in Montichiari, Italy. At the 2016 Summer Paralympics in Rio, she won a silver medal in the women's 500 m Time Trial (C13). In Los Angeles in 2017, Amanda won gold in the women's 500 m time trial C2 and women's 3 km individual pursuit C2 and a silver in the women's scratch race (C13). Photo: Australian Paralympic Committee.

CHAPTER 11
HOCKEY

There was a strong traditional form of the game in many societies, even dating back to ancient Egypt. No one is sure of modern hockey's origins but we do know that a similar game, called shinty, was played in Scotland. Pre-settlement, Torres Strait Islanders played a game called kokan, similar to field hockey.

In the Northern Territory, Joe Daby and Joseph Kelly had good records in the 1970s and 1980s respectively. But it was Steve Larkin who took most of the early honours. He played for the Northern Territory under-21 side for four years, for the senior team for seven years and was in the Australian Universities side for three years. He became the Territory's senior coach in 1990. And then came Baedon Choppy, the first Aboriginal man to play for the national Kookaburras, followed soon after by the dynamic pair of **Des Abbott** and **Joel Carroll**. **Lorelle Morrissey**, **Nova Peris**, **Brooke Peris** and **Mariah Williams** were to follow as Australian representatives.

The game is attracting more Aboriginal and Islander players, especially in the wake of the spectacular achievements to date. Hockey Australia runs a national Indigenous Program aimed at encouraging the game, especially in the remote regions of Western Australia, Queensland and New South Wales.

Terry Elms played hockey for the Northern Territory from 1980 to 1985 and again in 1992. She also coached and umpired junior hockey.
Photo: Pip Marsh

DESMOND (DES) ABBOTT

Born in Darwin in 1986, Des was a star performer in the Kookaburra field hockey squad. At midfield and as a powerful striker he is considered most dangerous in the circle. In 2007 Des toured Europe with an Australian Institute of Sport team. He made his international debut for Australia in the team which won the Champions Trophy series in Rotterdam. By the end of 2013, when he retired, he had played 111 internationals, scoring 61 goals. Australia won the bronze medal at the Beijing Olympics with Des prominent in the 6–2 demolition of the Netherlands for the medal. He was in the final list of nominees for the International Hockey Federation's Young Men's Player of the Year Award in 2008. His local team is the Vodafone Territory Stingers which he captained. Des is a nephew of Dottie Daby, a renowned Northern Territory basketball and hockey player. Photo: Chris Scott/Newspix.

JOEL CARROLL

The Northern Territory has a proud list of hockey champions: **Phynea Clark**, **Des Abbott**, **Steve Larkin**, **Nova Peris**, **Brooke Peris**, and Joel. A cousin of **Des Abbott**, and a nephew of Joe Daby, one of the Territory's best-ever hockey players, Joel was born in 1986 in Darwin. He was a member of Australia's under-21 team. A strong striker, he could play in any number of forward positions. Joel made his Test debut in 2009. He was in the winning gold-medal team at the 2010 New Delhi Commonwealth Games and in both winning teams at the 2010 and the 2012 Men's Hockey Champions Trophy. He was a member of the 2012 Olympic team in London that won the bronze medal. Joel played a total of 98 games for Australia between 2009 and 2015. Photo: Australian Sports Commission Image Library.

BAEDON CHOPPY

Born in Mackay (Qld) in 1976, Baedon Choppy followed his parents into field hockey. After selection for Queensland he rose to vice-captain of the national under-21 side. A talented striker, he was selected in the national Kookaburras side to play in Malaysia in 1996, followed by Olympic representation at Atlanta. He scored four goals in the Games, including the winning goal for the bronze medal. After Atlanta he played in the 18th Champions Trophy Tournament in Madras and the 19th Tournament in Adelaide in 1997. In that year he was again vice-captain of the national junior team which won the gold medal at the World Championships in England. His outstanding play there gained him selection in the Junior World XI. In 1997 he was National Aboriginal and Torres Strait Islander Sportsman of the Year. In 1998 he played in the World Cup in Utrecht. Baedon played 57 games for Australia and scored 29 international goals between 1996 and 1999. Photo: Sport: The Library.

PHYNEA CLARK

The Northern Territory has produced some outstanding women field hockey players: **Rose Damaso, Louisa Collins, Terry Elms, Nova Peris, Brooke Peris** and **Phynea Clark**. Born in Darwin in 1968, **Phynea** has the distinction of representing two states in both senior and junior hockey, a feat rare in Australian sporting history. She represented the Northern Territory under-21 and seniors from 1984–1985 to 1991. **Phynea** moved to Victoria and played under-21 and seniors for that state between 1987 and 1988. A member of the Australian under-21 team in 1986, Phynea toured New Zealand in 1987. Photo: Pip Marsh.

STEVE LARKIN

Son of Fred Larkin, a Wynnum-Manly rugby league player and Irene, a Northern Territory netball and basketball representative, Steve was destined to excel. Born in Lismore (NSW) in 1960, a Kungaran Nation man, Steve played 40 games in national under-21 hockey (1977–1981) and 75 in the Australian championships (1979–1988). He was in the Australian Universities team (1982–1984) which included a one-off match against NZ Universities, and competed in at least nine first grade premiership finals. Steve coached the NT senior men's team in 2002 and 2003, played over 250 first grade games in Darwin and Brisbane and also coached first-grade men's, women's and university teams to success. Once president of the Darwin Hockey Association, Steve has worked with the Australian Medical Association as a senior executive in the Commonwealth government and was AIATSIS Principal from 2004 to 2008. He is now Pro Vice-Chancellor at Newcastle University. Photo: Charles Darwin University.

LORELLE MORRISSEY

Though Born in Mildura (Vic.) in 1973, Lorelle is a Bundjalung woman from the Tweed Coast in northern New South Wales. In 1991, at 17, she was in the Australian under-18; under-21; and the Australian Open teams, all at the same time. In 1992 she played in the under-21 Junior World Cup in Spain where they won the silver medal. Lorelle was in the Australian Open squad for the Barcelona Olympics; and made her Open test debut in 1992 playing a three test series against Great Britain, becoming the first Aboriginal woman to play test hockey for Australia. Lorelle played in a further test series against Korea in 1993. Lorelle played for the Queensland Scorchers before retiring from Queensland and international representative hockey in 1994. She then moved to Canberra where she played for a number of years, winning the McKay medal in two consecutive years. Continuing to play hockey at Master's level, Lorelle once again represented Queensland and Australia in the over-35 and over-40 teams. In 2000, Lorelle was named in the Queensland Team of the Century. In 2018 Lorelle continues to play and coach for Kingscliff her home club, in the Tweed Border competition as well as playing for Capri in the Gold Coast competition. Photo: Lorelle Morrissey.

BROOKE PERIS

Born in Darwin in 1993, Brooke is a niece of **Nova Peris**. She became a member of the Australia women's national field hockey team, and was selected to represent Australia at the 2016 Rio Olympics. Brooke left her close-knit and sports-loving Darwin community to secure her place in the national side: she was in the 2017 squad, having played no less than 106 games for Australia. That an aunt and niece should notch up 197 international appearances in one sport is a truly remarkable statistic. Not a surprise, her idols and role models have been **Nova Peris**, **Des Abbott** and **Joel Carroll**. Brooke was Northern Territory Sportsperson of the Year in 2014. Photo: Hockey Australia.

NOVA PERIS, OAM

Nova Peris is one of Australia's most capped international players in any sport. Born in Darwin in 1971, Nova was a boundary umpire in Australian football, then played hockey for Australia in the Junior World Cup in New Zealand in 1992. As Nova Peris she defied convention: a mother at 19, holding a full-time job with Telstra, she set out to be a role model for Aboriginal people by continuing to shine at the top level of international competition. As a midfielder Nova played 91 internationals for Australia and was a member of the Australian team which won the Champions Trophy — in effect, the world title — in Amsterdam in 1993, in Dublin in 1994 and in Mar del Plata (Argentine) in 1995. Nova Peris turned from hockey to athletics in 1996. In 1998 at the Kuala Lumpur Commonwealth Games, she won a gold medal in the 200 m sprint, thus becoming the first Australian to win a gold in two sports at two of the world's most important international games. Photo: Nova Peris.

MARIAH WILLIAMS

Born in 1995, Mariah hails from Parkes (NSW). Her two sports were touch football and hockey, which she began playing at 4 and is the game that brought her national attention. Her record is remarkable given that she had four knee surgeries before the age of 21. Mariah made her Hockeyroo debut in 2013 against Korea. The highlights of Mariah's career to date have included the World League semi-finals in Antwerp, Belgium in 2015 and the World League final in Rosario, Argentine in the same year. She competed in the Champion's Trophy 2016 and was selected for the 2016 Olympic Games in Rio where the national team finished in sixth place. As at the end of 2017, Mariah had played 56 games for Australia. Photo: Hockey Australia.

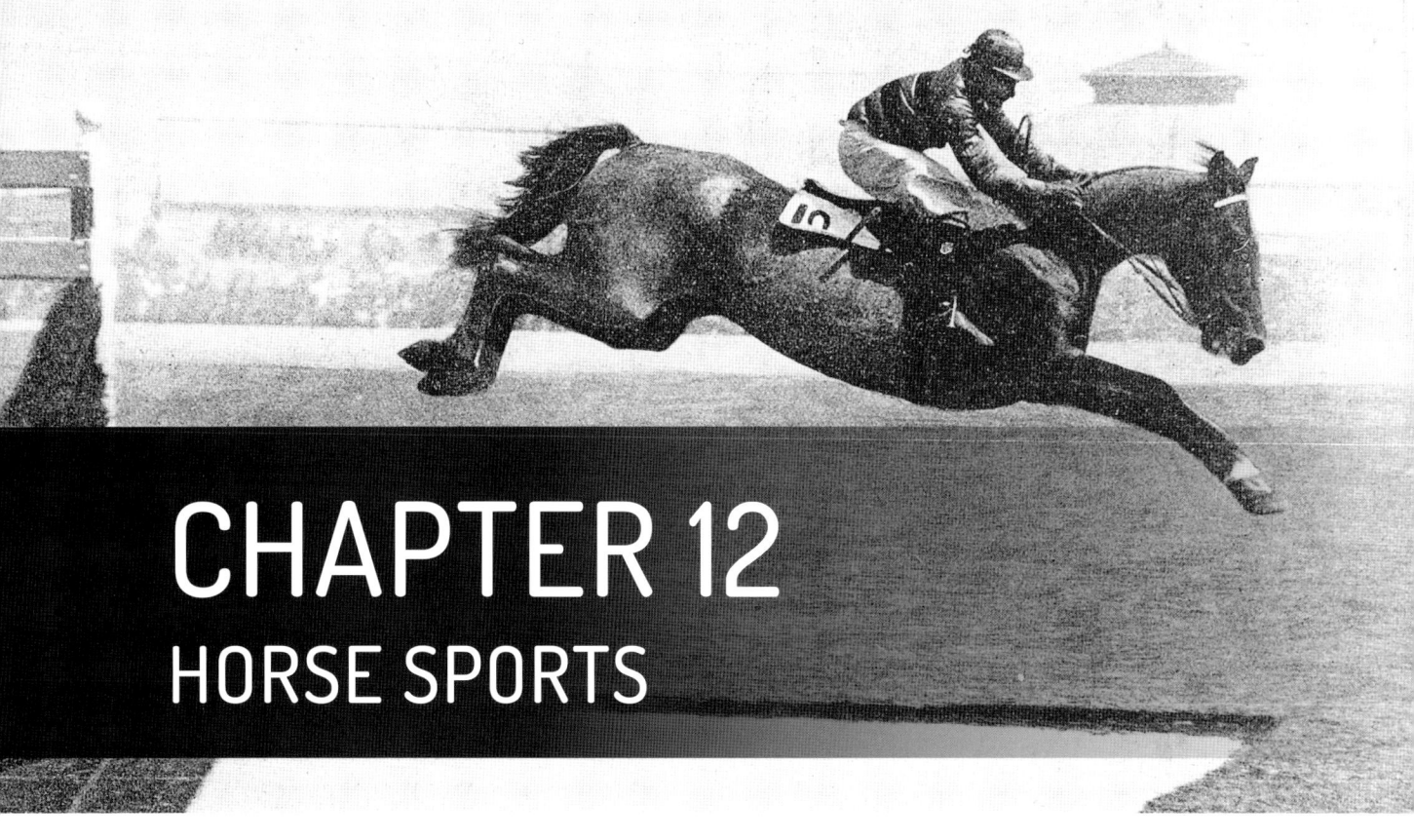

CHAPTER 12
HORSE SPORTS

In the nineteenth century Aboriginal people developed a strong relationship with horses as stockmen on cattle and sheep stations. They became the backbone of the pastoral industry — and later, in the 1960s — the agents of both a work boycott (at Vesteys cattle-station in the Northern Territory) and a legal campaign for better wages through inclusion in cattle-station wage awards from which they had always been excluded on racial grounds.

The history of Aboriginal people in the cattle industry is a long one, and not a pretty one. The details of their treatment emerged in the wage tribunal hearings of 1966. The Arbitration Court of the time ruled that Aboriginal people were to be worthy of equal wages for equal work (over a five-year period). The romantic bush ballads and legends of our outback history were hardly noble.

Stations in the north were bought and sold with both cattle and Aboriginal people included in the purchase. Wages were mostly in the form of rations even though cattlemen were heavily subsidised by the government for both capital works and for operational costs in 'maintaining Blacks' on their properties. That there were friendly relations on some stations didn't alter the fact that Aboriginal people, as virtual serfs, came with the property and 'belonged' to the owners. In many instances the women were treated as sexual chattels and one facet of the child removal practices arose from the embarrassments of unwanted progeny ('yellow fellas') sired by owners and staff.

Sexual exploitation was the order of the day. It was common practice among drovers — the stockmen who drove animals to better grazing or to abattoirs — to dress young Aboriginal women in men's clothing and pretend that they were their 'work assistants' rather than their sexual servants. In 1934 South Australia passed an interesting law: 'It is an offence for any Aboriginal woman to be found dressed in male attire and in the company of any male person other than Aboriginal and both are guilty of an offence.' Ted Egan's song 'The Drover's Boy' is a pointed and poignant portrait of those events.

The Aboriginal relationship with horses played out in another context. An important arm of the Australian Imperial Force in World War I was the Anzac Mounted Infantry, the Remount Unit. One of its two squadrons was commanded by Captain A B ('Banjo') Paterson, Australia's iconic poet. His unit included the Aboriginal rider Joe White who served in the Middle East with the famed 'Queensland Black Watch' of the 11th Light Horse Regiment. Other Aboriginal horse troopers were David Mullett of Victoria, Jim Hubbard from western New South Wales and Harry Hawkins, Walter Crouchy and Leslie Franks from Queensland. Yet another was the father of rugby league star **Frank Fisher**, Frank Fisher Senior, celebrated on national television in October 2017, the 100th anniversary of the famous (and successful) cavalry attack on the Ottoman Turks in the Battle of Beersheba (in today's Israel).

Earlier these men were considered 'too dark for the Light Horse' and it was only in mid-1917 that they were able to enjoy equal pay and conditions including the right to drink in the Army's wet canteens. On discharge they all reverted to the status of second-class citizens, ineligible for returned servicemen's benefits and land allotments for those who served and survived.

Jerry Jerome of boxing fame was a renowned horse-breaker in his day. His tasks included training war transport horses known as whalers. Some cattlemen encouraged their Aboriginal men to go to town to bush rodeos, even helping them participate in all but the drinking events. Many excelled at these roughriding shows. Equestrianism is quite different in that it is smooth rather than rough and an expensive sport. It has a different ethos, arena and cast of characters. Only three Aboriginals made it in the showring. Horseracing should have offered Aboriginal people opportunity but didn't (apart from the few jockeys discussed below).

At the turn of the last century 'the great half-caste rider' **Billy Waite** was considered equal to the legendary rider and entrepreneur Lance Skuthorpe. Another working colleague of Skuthorpe's was 'a very good-looking aborigine' named Queensland Harry. Rated as a great roughrider and much pampered by Skuthorpe, he was dressed by the rodeo impresario in the best suits, bedecked in showy jewellery and always introduced into the ring as 'A Prince of the Great Never-Never'.

Yet another of Skuthorpe's troupe was Wild Harry (Harry Phillips), later known as Mudgee or Old Mudgee. With his wife and children (Freddie and Rosie), he was well cared for by Skuthorpe, albeit in some peculiar but effective ways. One of Skuthorpe's 'new' routines consisted of presenting the scrubbed-up kids to the audiences in this way:

> These children are full-blooded aborigines, the last of a dying race. This boy is a prince and this girl a princess, and they belong to a race that once owned this country ... The day is not far distant when these people will be as rare as diamonds. Yet today they stand before you barefoot, with eyes worth a million and teeth superior to the finest pearls. The eyes and teeth are all they have ... Look closely at their white teeth, and remember that the way to make them smile is to put something in the hats they take with them.

We don't know what happened to Freddie and Rosie but Old Mudgee was still trying out broncos in his eighties.

Wild Harry or Old Mudgee: whatever the name, Harry Phillips was one of the great Aboriginal horsemen.
Photo: Ann Weldon

In 1921 Billy Tindall, a 'full blood from Goondiwindi' (Qld), defeated 28 competitors to win the Australian cattle-throwing championship. In the same year Jack Bond also won an Australian tying and throwing championship at Moree (NSW). As did so many Aboriginal riders, he attempted to conquer the outlaw horse Bobs. For many years he worked at Auburn and Hawkewood stations, the work places of the great **Alec Hayden**. In the 1920s Jack Murray was an esteemed bareback rider in Thorpe McConville's Wild West Show. **Jack 'Sonny Carbine' Watson**, "a half-caste from Gatton", won the very rich prize of £100 in a Sydney buckjumping event in 1924.

In 1937 the roughriding authorities organised a series of Test matches between Australia, Canada and the United States. The three-man Australian team included cousins **Alec Hayden** and **Jimmy Williams**. That two Queensland Blackfellas were in such a team, at that time, was indeed remarkable. Queensland, as we have seen, was the most authoritarian of all domains, yet that state allowed for some spectacular Aboriginal and Islander sporting achievements.

A remarkable roughrider born in Western Australia was **Fred Wilson**, also known as 'Mulga Fred'. He rode in south-eastern Australia and came to prominence between 1911 and the 1930s. In the West, Simon Gentle was an expert rodeo man, winning several competitions and having the distinction of being paid the same wages as other riders. Bert Clark of South Australia rode against American and New Zealand teams. In the late 1940s Wally Mailman of Augathella (Qld) was prominent in regional events. He rode for Australia against a New Zealand team, winning a trophy donated by Joyce Frame of Chinchilla. Wally, who died in 2000, was joined by his brothers and two other Queensland Aboriginal families — **Lindsay Black** and his brothers from Springsure and Ritchie Fraser and his brothers from Winton — in making their sport more professional. The Mailman, Black and Fraser families were among the mainstays of the now-regular touring rodeo shows.

One of the leading post-war buckjumpers was **Johnny Cadell**, described in some detail below. ('Saddle bronc riding' began to replace the term buckjumping in the 1960s and 1970s.) Other roughriders of note in the 1950s were King Costello and Tommy Dodd.

The magazine *Hoofs and Horns* has featured Aboriginal roughriders from time to time, often referring to them by a single name such as 'Cliff', 'Mick', 'Scobie'. Biographical details were absent. [Colin wrote two essays for that magazine, on roughriders, equestrians and on jockeys (July and December

Donald Fraser, shown here, and brother Richie (from the Winton area of Queensland) were not only great roughriders but singers and guitarists. Photo: Jenny Hicks

1996). There the human stories take precedence over the equine stories.]

There have been Aboriginal women in the roughriding and in the horse industry, but not many. Such occupations were reasonably common in the 1940s and 1950s but liberation of various kinds in the 1960s have put an end to those activities.

It was marvellous to have two 'men of colour' in the forefront of equestrianism or showring riding: Rowley Doctor — said by his surviving widow to be of Māori descent — and Paul Joseph Coe, known in the ring as **Jimmy Callaghan**, very much of Aboriginal descent. (It is most likely that Doctor — thought to have been born in Glenelg (SA) but for whom there are no birth records — was Aboriginal.) The two won a number of important and rich pairs events at the Royal Easter Shows.

Horseracing, whether in the United States or Australia, has a history of racist attitudes and practices. Land owners turned over the job of training horses to black slaves or servants. While a few men became the toast of the American turf, like Jimmy Winkfield and Isaac Murphy, in Australia the 'blackboys' remained the strappers, groomers and stable hands. In the United States native horsemen were assigned ludicrous names like Cato, Pompey and Caesar. Here they suffered the indignity of names like Hitler, Mussolini and Stalin. The cattlemen we knew, those who 'baptised' these men with such names, considered themselves 'good employers', moral men who looked after their human flocks. This was colonial overlordship at its very worst. Often they were given the names of the stations for which they worked — which is what happened to young '**Peter St Albans**' who was named after James Wilson's stud farm and to **Jimmy Williams** in Queensland.

The careers of four great jockeys, **Darby McCarthy**, **Frankie Reys**, **Merv Maynard** and **Leigh-Anne Goodwin** are described below. Darby was aggressive about his Aboriginal identity; Frankie suppressed it until his death; Merv was the proud son of Fred Maynard, an esteemed Aboriginal activist in the 1920s; Leigh-Anne was proudly Aboriginal. The reason for both extremes lay not in the personalities of the riders but in a sport that has a reputation for its attitudes and practices. (John Maynard has written an important work on *Aboriginal Stars of the Turf.*)

Following McCarthy, two young Aboriginal men started with promise: Lyell Appo in Queensland and Glen Pickwick in Sydney. Though competent, neither is considered to be in McCarthy's class. Appo turned to boxing and in 1993 became Australian strawweight champion. Norman Rose rode particularly well for a while, on a mare named Nook. He then became a superb strapper, working with trainer Kevin Burns. Harry Fuller from Warren (NSW) is listed in the *Guinness Book of Records* as having won the most races on the same horse, an animal named The Grey Ghost.

Leigh-Anne Goodwin achieved that in Queensland, as described in her biography below.

Lyall Appo was not only a fine jockey but an outstanding boxer. He won the Australian strawwieight title in 1993.
Photo: Lyall Apppo

Rowley Doctor, said to be Māori but more likely of Aboriginal descent, was one of the great showring riders of the twentieth century. He won numerous pairs events with Jimmy Callaghan.
Photo: Royal Agriculture Society of NSW

Bert Clark, born at Nepabunna in South Australia, rode rodeo against United States and New Zealand team. He is shown here with Premier John Bannon at the inaugural National Aboriginal and Torres Strait Islander Sports Awards. Photo: Christine Clark

In the 1940s, Wally Mailman of Augathella in Queensland was prominent in regional events. He rode for Australia in an international against New Zealand. He died in January 2000 aged 76. Wally was the father of renowed actor Deborah Mailman.
Photo: Jenny Hicks

Queensland jockey Norm Rose was a much respected horseman. Here he is shown riding the sprinter Nook in 1974. Together they had a number of wins.
Photo: John Fairfax Group

LINDSAY BLACK

Born at Springsure (Qld) in 1930 Lindsay Black — probably a Yumba Burin man — had parents devoted to competitive riding. Racial bullying was a feature of his youth. Early experience mustering cattle led to his starting out on big jumpers at the age of 14. Lindsay went on to become the first Aboriginal roughrider to win the world buckjumping championships. He won a number of Queensland's major competitions. Lindsay and his brothers, particularly Frankie, together with Ritchie Fraser and his brothers from Winton, were to become involved in an important enterprise. In 1946 the Australian Roughriders' Association (ARRA) was formed to make their sport more professional. The Mailman, Black, Fraser and Parter families were among the mainstays of the now-regular touring rodeo shows. Since the formation of the professional associations, only Lindsay has won national titles (two, in 1956 and 1957). Photo: David Mansel/Stockmans' Hall of Fame.

JOHNNY CADELL

Johnny was born in the shade of a coolibah tree near Adelaide River (NT) in 1920. His father was of both Aboriginal and Malaysian blood and his mother was of Aboriginal descent. People said Johnny was born to ride. A stockman at Mataranka Station in the 1930s and 1940s, he began a long and successful roughriding career. His working life included a 12-year stint at Dalhousie Station, on the Northern Territory and South Australia border, followed by a spell in Adelaide where he worked for R M Williams training polo ponies, as well as other duties. His ride on the wonderfully named 'The Tantanoola Ghost' led to his being compared with the best in Australia. Johnny was buckjumping champion of South Australia from 1948 to 1951, winning at the Marrabel Rodeo. He was runner-up in the Australian championship in 1950. Later he appeared in a movie and a television series. Photo: *Hoofs and Horns*.

JIMMY CALLAGHAN

Jimmy was born Paul Joseph Coe in Cowra (NSW) in 1900. His early life was not untypical of the Aboriginal experience. Despite two brothers serving in the First World War and having family, he was deemed an orphan and sent to Bomaderry Children's Home near Nowra. From there he was 'stationed out', that is, sent to work on properties for rations. He began a show-ring riding career and either took or was given the name Callaghan. In 1922 he won the Mark Foy's Pizza High Jump on the legendary Thumbs Up, an eccentric and erratic horse. He won the same event in 1925 on Young Highlander and the Vice-Regal High Jump in the same year. Callaghan jumped 7 feet 6 inches (2.28 m) on Thumbs Up in Brisbane in 1925 and won several pairs events with the champion rider, Rowley Doctor, said to be Māori but most likely of Aboriginal descent. Callaghan also had a successful roughriding career, as did his brother Leo. Photo: Royal Agricultural Society of NSW.

LEIGH-ANNE GOODWIN

The first and only Aboriginal female jockey to ride a winner in a city event, **Leigh-Anne Goodwin** was born in Dirranbandi (Qld) in 1969 and completed her apprenticeship in Roma (Qld). A single mother, she rode to finance the purchase of land and to build a small house for herself and young son. Leigh-Anne had limited opportunities and was constantly looking for a book of rides in country meetings. She did well and in more than 600 rides in eight years of riding she achieved almost a hundred wins. She was also an Aboriginal youth worker. In September 1998 her dream came true when she won a city event on 33 to 1 outsider Getelion at Eagle Farm. In November 1998 Leigh-Anne asked family and friends to make her a promise: if ever she fell, they were not to leave her on a life-support system. On 5 December 1998, at a Roma meeting, Bachelor King snapped a leg and fell, causing Leigh-Anne grievous injuries. The life support was turned off soon after. Alan Peach/*Sydney Morning Herald*.

ALEC HAYDEN

Alec was the most successful and the most respected of many brilliant Aboriginal roughriders. Born at Piggot Camp near Chinchilla (Qld) in 1909, he is still revered in the rodeo world. Alec won the Australian buckjumping championship in 1936 at Warwick on Nightly, in 1938 on Arrawidgee and in 1939 on an impressively named horse, Knickerbocker Buckeroo. He won the national bullock-riding title in 1941. Alec represented Queensland against New South Wales in 1937, and then came a noteworthy family feat when he and his cousin **Jimmy Williams** represented Australia in a tri-Test series against Canada and the USA. Alec conquered all, from north Queensland down to Victoria and in his period was regarded as the country's leading rider. Jack Frame, a doyen among the roughriders, told us that 'he was the greatest rider of them all'. Alec was thrown and crushed to death by a blind weaner while cattle-drafting at Auburn Station. He was only 34. Photo: Frank Hayden.

BILLY JONAS

William James Albert (Billy) Jonas, pictured here with rodeo clown Old Tom Crawford, was an outstanding member of Thorp McConville's famous buckriding show, 'Wild Australia'. The show became prominent in the first decade of the twentieth century with Jack Morissey and Billy Jonas the stars of the show. Billy went to England in June 1911 to ride in the coronation procession of King George V, held at Westminster Abbey, and returned with a Cockney wife. Billy's grandson, Bill Jonas, a Worimi man from the Karuah River area of New South Wales was for a time the principal of AIATSIS and a Commissioner on the Human Rights Commission. A geographer, Bill was the first Aboriginal man to gain a doctorate. Photo: Bill Jonas.

MERV MAYNARD

Born in Sydney in 1932, Merv Maynard's was the son of Fred Maynard, a legendary early Aboriginal activist. Merv began riding in 1946 aged 14. The dominant rider of the Newcastle region during the 1950s, he rode in the 1952 Melbourne Cup and in three successive Caulfield Cups. His record of cup victories across country NSW is unprecedented with more than 1500 winners between 1948 and 1994. The 'Darby Munro of the Bush' was rated as one of Australia's top riders in a period regarded as the golden age of Australian jockeys. A trailblazer, at his peak he rode winners in New Zealand in 1958 and in Singapore and Malaysia between 1960 and 1964. As an apprentice Merv rode the winner (Salamanca) in the first Queen's Cup (formerly the King's Cup) at Randwick. When Queen Elizabeth visited in 1992 she opened the new grandstand at Randwick and asked to meet the jockey who had won the first Queen's Cup 40 years earlier. Merv was honoured to meet the monarch. Photo: John Maynard.

RICHARD (DARBY) McCARTHY

He was the 'genius rider', wrote critic Bert Lillye; he was the 'man who had sweet hands and a perfect seat', according to writer Max Presnell. The man who had to show exceptional talent in the face of much discrimination was born in Cunnamulla (Qld) in 1944. Even at the age of 17 he announced: 'If I'm going to be a success it is important that I be known as an Aboriginal success'. His major victories included the Newcastle Gold Cup in 1962, the Stradbroke Handicap in 1963, 1964 and 1966, the Brisbane Cup in 1966 and the Doomben One Hundred Thousand in 1968. His greatest feat was winning the AJC Derby and AJC Epsom in successive races at Randwick in 1969. Darby McCarthy rode extensively in Ireland, France, Germany and New Zealand. In 1978 he made a comeback in New Caledonia and in 1983 began coaching young riders. Photo: Fairfax Photo Library/courtesy John Fairfax Holdings.

FRANKIE REYS

In 1973, aged 41, Frankie won the Melbourne Cup on Gala Supreme. That season he was second in the Caulfield Cup. Frankie was born in Cairns (Qld) in 1932, the seventh in a family of fourteen. His first ride in Gordonvale, at 17, was a winner; his last ride, at Flemington on his birthday in 1976, was also a winner. In between he rode 948 winners, 915 seconds and 863 thirds, many in country events. On six occasions he rode four winners in a day; on three race days, he rode five winners on the card. He won the VRC Oaks in 1962 and was joint winner of the Australian Cup in 1969. At Flemington alone he won the Melbourne Cup, the Oaks, two Bagot Handicaps, the Manifold Stakes, Craiglee Stakes, Maribyrnong Plate and two Craven 'A' Stakes. He was president of the Victorian Jockeys Association for ten years. In his Melbourne Cup speech, tears flowed and silence reigned 'for one of racing's most courageous and best-loved fighters'. Photo: *Herald & Weekly Times*.

PETER ST ALBANS

Peter St Albans, born in 1863, later took the name of his foster father and died as Peter Bowden. At 13 he was employed at the St Albans stud owned by James Wilson. Some say he 'was an abandoned half-caste', others that he was an illegitimate son of one of the Wilsons. In 1876 the shrewd Wilson put 'the mysterious 13-year-old midget jockey' on Briseis, which duly won the AJC Doncaster in Sydney. Two days later the pair won the All Aged Stakes over one mile. Peter, who was not even apprenticed, won the 1876 Melbourne Cup on Briseis, carrying the extremely light weight handicap of 6 stone 4 pounds (40 kg). As the telegrams came through, the Sydney crowds cheered and celebrated for 'little St Albans and the filly'. He also won the 1880 VRC St Leger, the 1881 Sires' Produce Stakes, the Ascot Vale Stakes and the Geelong Cup. From 1880 he had small success as a trainer until his sudden death in 1898. Painting: sketch for portrait of Briseis by Frederick Woodhouse held by Racing Museum of Victoria.

BILLY WAITE

Of all the roughriders between 1900 and 1920, Billy Waite was probably the best of them. Banjo Paterson and Jack Dempsey of the Anzac Mounted Infantry, the riders Rowley Doctor and Lance Skuthorpe were unanimous about his outstanding ability, both in the Light Horse and in civilian life. In a pre-war contest to establish supremacy, he rode against Lance Skuthorpe with each rider offering three horses to his opponent. Billy successfully rode all three of Skuthorpe's animals. A champion whip-cracker, several legends attach to him: that he illegally shortened stirrups and that he held a horse's ear in his teeth while the animal was saddled. He travelled to England and rode at Wembley in 1911 and then to the United States where he became a citizen and rode for the Barnum and Bailey Circus. It seems he died there by his own hand. Photo: courtesy of Joy Baines and Peter Bridge, Hesperian Press.

JACK ('SONNY CARBINE') WATSON

Jack was once described in the roughriding literature as 'a half-caste from Gatton', a small town in south-east Queensland. He worked for Lance Skuthorpe's Wild Australian travelling rodeo show. A most gifted show team member, Jack worked with Lance Sr on and off for twenty years. Jack won the very rich prize of £100 in a Sydney buckjumping event in 1924. In the same year Watson won the world buckjumping championship in Sydney in three days of rugged, tense competition. The late sportswriter Jack Pollard commented that 'by then he had absorbed so many of Lance's ideas that expert spectators told each other he must be Skuthorpe's son'. Watson accompanied Violet and Lance Skuthorpe on a six-month tour of the United States in 1938 and he probably remained there. Photo: Jenny Hicks.

JIMMY WILLIAMS

Jimmy was born in the Beaudesert region of southern Queensland, probably in 1908, with no birth registration. The grandparents and parents of James Frederick Stanley Williams worked on a property owned by a Williams — hence the name. In 1937 Jimmy achieved two things: he married a cousin, May Himstedt, 'by permission of the Chief Protector of Aboriginals', and he was selected, with his cousin **Alec Hayden**, to represent Australia in a roughriding Test match. That two of a three-man team should be Aboriginal cousins from remote Queensland was quite remarkable, especially as one of them was 'a controlled Aborigine' under the state's repressive laws. At the Royal Easter showground, the 'Manly Ferry' International Buckjumping Contest (first prize £50) was followed by the International Bulldogging Contest (first prize £36) with both events contested by three-man teams from America, Canada and Australia. Photo: Beryl Wandrey.

FRED WILSON ('MULGA FRED')

Fred Wilson — aka Fred Clark and 'Mulga Fred' — was born in Port Hedland (WA) circa 1874. Droving brought him East in 1905 where he joined professional rodeo troupes and worked as a horse breaker. He became an outstanding buckjumper, won Victorian titles and was considered one of the best roughriders of his era. He rode for the mandatory ten seconds in 1948, aged 74. Fred was a master buckjumper until the 1930s, performing exhibitions thereafter. He also threw boomerangs and whipped cigarettes from volunteers' lips before large crowds. He was reputedly the model for the famous 1920s and 1930s racially-based Pelaco fitted-shirt advertisements. In these pictorials, Mulga Fred declared in supposed pidgin English: 'Mine Tinkit They Fit'. Historian Richard Broome has an Australian *Dictionary of Biography* entry on 'Mulga Fred' and an article in *Aboriginal History*, vol. 22, 1998. Photo: James McColl, the Warracknabeal Historical Society.

CHAPTER 13
NETBALL

Netball was introduced into England in 1895 by the United States as the indoor form of basketball. This seven-a-side game is played essentially by women and is popular in some 60 countries. (Men do play the game). Top-line international competition is limited to 16 countries, most of them Commonwealth nations. The contest between Australia and New Zealand (the Constellation Cup) is fierce and attracts large numbers of live and television viewers. Some Cup matches have had close on 15,000 spectators.

In the current world rankings, Australia is first followed (in order) by New Zealand, England, Jamaica, South Africa, Malawi, Wales, Fiji, Uganda and Northern Ireland.

Stacey Campton, a Gunggari woman from south-west Queensland, is the manager of the Ngarara Willim Centre at RMIT University in Melbourne. She is an international netball umpire of great standing and mentors and coaches young umpires.
Photo: Stacey Campton

NICOLE CUSACK

Nicole Cusack was an outstanding all-round athlete. Born in Surry Hills (NSW) in 1966, she competed in the Australian swimming championships in 1979 and 1980. In 1987 and 1988 Nicole played basketball for the Bankstown Bruins premiership team. Her major sport is netball, playing for the NSW under-17, under-19 and under-21 teams, and for the NSW Open team from 1986 to 1995. A member of the Australian under-21 team, she graduated to the senior side and was a regular member of the national team from 1989 to 1999. Nicole was chosen for the South African tour and the 9th World Championships in Birmingham in 1995. She was a member of the winning World championship team. Nicole retired in 1999 having played 52 Tests — an achievement that placed her ninth in the Australian record book for the number of representative netball games played. Photo: Fairfax Photo Library: courtesy of John Fairfax Holdings.

MARCIA ELLA, OAM

Sister to the three rugby union **Ella brothers**, Marcia Ella — born in La Perouse (NSW) in 1963 — was the first Aboriginal netball international. She began her representative career as a member of the New South Wales under-21 team. From 1984 to 1987 she was a regular member of the NSW Open side. Marcia first played for Australia in the under-21 team in 1984, then moved up to the Australian Open team in 1986 and 1987, including a tour to England in 1986 and the World Championships in Scotland in 1987, the year the national team came second. This was the start of Australia's ascendancy in the sport. Marcia spent many years in the Department of Community Services in Lismore (NSW) and is now a member of the Aboriginal Justice Advisory Committee. Photo: Marcia Ella.

SHARON FINNAN, OAM

Few athletes have the chance to be members of a world championship winning team. **Nicole Cusack** and **Sharon Finnan** are two who have this distinction. Sharon has had a long career in netball. Born in Surry Hills (NSW) in 1967, her first success was in the NSW under-21 side in 1987. She was elevated to the NSW Open team in 1988 while still a junior and in that year she was a member of the Australian under-21 team which won the World Cup. As a member of the 1990 Australian Open team she participated in the Commonwealth Games in Auckland, the Johnson and Johnson Cup, and in the Test series against England and against New Zealand. She was chosen for the Australian team which won the World Championships in 1991, played in the World Championships in Christchurch in 1999 and was in the Australian squad in 1994 and again in 2000. By January 2000, Sharon had played fifteen matches for Australia. Photo: Sharon Finnan.

BIANCA FRANKLIN (GITEAU)

Bianca, an older sister to **Lance Franklin**, was born in the town of Dowerin, north of Perth, in 1984. A child in a sports-dedicated family, she began playing netball at the age of 8. At 15 she represented Western Australia in the under-17 team. Bianca's team in the Western Australia state league was the Flames, whom she helped win their first national championship in 27 years. At 19 she won a scholarship to the Institute of Sport and played for the Canberra A team, the Darters, where she was goal attack and goal shooter. Bianca was a member of the Australian under-21 squad from 2003 to 2005, and represented her state in junior and senior teams. She married Matt Giteau, a star rugby union player who had over 100 games for the Wallabies. Photo: Michael Clayton-Jones/Fairfax Syndication.

ANDREA MASON

Although born a 'Sandgroper' in Subiaco (WA) in 1968, Andrea Mason enjoyed her entire sporting career as a 'Croweater' in South Australia. Several South Australian Nunga women have played netball for South Australia including Doris Keeler, Bonnie Jones and Margot Walker. But the star was Andrea, a fine all-rounder. She was in the South Australian under-21 netball team at the age of 15, a most unusual achievement. She was in that under-age side in 1983 and again in 1985. A great achievement was her selection for the Young Australians in 1985. Andrea graduated to play in the South Australian senior team in 1986 and 1989 and was nominated for the Australian squad in 1987. She was in company with **Marcia Ella** but she didn't play in any internationals. Andrea also represented South Australia in track and field athletics. In 1986 Andrea was voted South Australian Sportsperson of the Year, together with Lois Agius and Wilbur Wilson. Photo: Department of Aboriginal Affairs.

CHAPTER 14
POWERLIFTING

Like weightlifting, powerlifting is a sport that involves a test of strength. It consists of three attempts at three kinds of lift: squat, bench press and deadlift. Powerlifting developed from a sport known as 'odd lifts'. The sport is universal and has been a Paralympic sport (bench press only) since 1984. It can be performed equipped or un-equipped, that is, with a supportive bench shirt or squat/deadlift suit or briefs. In some of the sport's federations knee wraps are allowed in the equipped version but not in the unequipped division. It has participants in both genders and it caters for all ages.

BERNIE DEVINE

Born in Adelaide in 1959, Bernie was Northern Territory titleholder in the 52–56 kg and under 60 kg class. He won the Australian 52 kg title in 1981, the 60 kg title in 1987, and then the 67.5 kg event in 1988. Chosen to represent Australia, Bernie came seventh in the World Championships in Norway in 1987 and represented Australia again at the World Titles in 1988. Thereafter he won the national Masters' titles in 1989 and 1991. Even as a 'senior', he remained in world class, winning a bronze medal in the 1992–1993 World Championships in Canada. In 1996, in the 60 kg class, he lifted a total of 495 kg and qualified for the world championships. Photo: Bernie Devine.

JOANNE (JODI) EDWARDS

An unusual set of sports for an unusual woman: such was the relationship of Jodi to powerlifting, weightlifting and outdoor soccer. Born in Sydney in 1967, Jodi was both NSW and Australian powerlifting champion in the 63 and 67.5 kg divisions in 1989, 1990 and 1991. In 1990 she placed second in the World Championships in France and won the division in that tournament in Bendigo in 1991. She was second in the world titles in England in 1992. Jodi then turned to weightlifting, a separate sport. She won the NSW 60 kg division in 1993, the Australian title in the 50 kg event in the same year and travelled to Colorado for a challenge cup in preparation for the world titles in 1993. A knee injury, followed by surgery, then motherhood, ended her career. Jodie represented southern NSW against the ACT in outdoor soccer and played for Illawarra soccer team for four years. She was an Aboriginal sports development officer with the NSW government. Photo: Jodi Edwards.

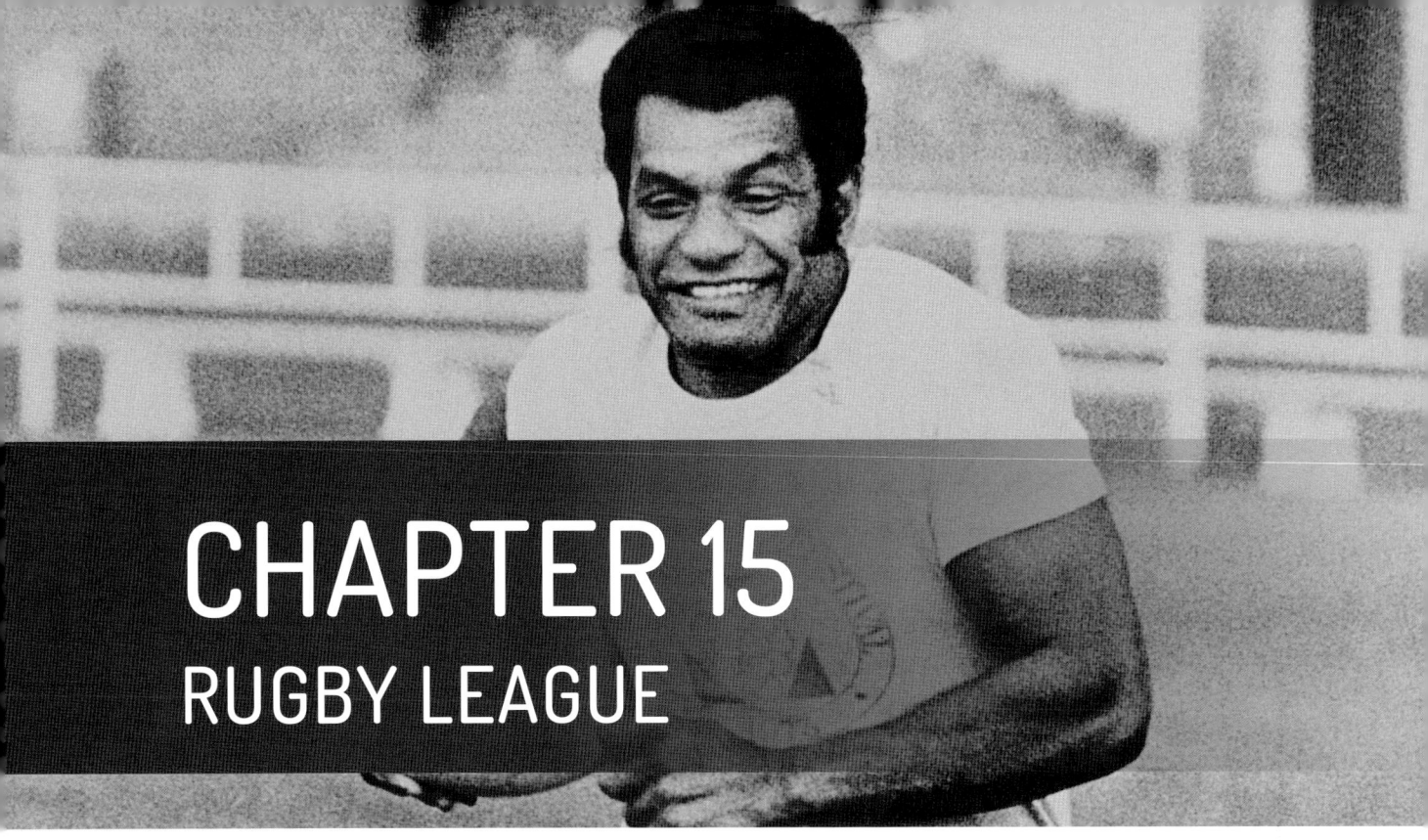

CHAPTER 15
RUGBY LEAGUE

Rugby league became an independent professional breakaway from rugby union in 1908. Darts and this code of rugby have generally been kinder to Aboriginal and Torres Strait Islanders than any other sport. This 'working class' rugby game — played almost solely in Queensland and New South Wales — has required little from its players in the way of class, income, schooling, clothing or equipment. Especially since the 1980s and 1990s, it has offered financial and status rewards for the elusive, the creative, the fast, the tough and the exciting.

It wasn't always so. The present-day celebration of Black achievers masks some dismal history. The first 'dusky' players (to use the language of the time) were George Green and Paul Tranquille between 1909 and 1922. George, who may well have been of Islander descent, played sixteen games for Eastern Suburbs between 1908 and 1913 and then joined North Sydney's 'shoremen' in 1918 as their hooker. (Historian Andrew Moore has written about two George Greens in that era and he contends that 'our' **George Green** may not have had any Aboriginal or Islander connection. We have accepted his descent history.) He was in North's only premiership sides in 1921 and 1922. George went on to lecture, to awaken interest in the sport in North Sydney and to coach Norths. Moore believes there was no racism involved at this time: in 1923 the NSW Rugby league recognised Green's pioneer status and arranged a testimonial match in his honour. Paul Tranquille, the New South Wales 220 yard sprint champion, was another 'public favourite' who played for Norths in the early 1920s. In 1925 the first Aboriginal footballer to tour abroad in any code was Glen (Paddy) Crouch of Queensland. He was a member of a successful state side that toured New Zealand.

There was to be a long break between this pioneering period and full Aboriginal and Islander access to the game. New South Wales government policy was to move Aboriginals from towns back to remote missions and to declare all youth wards of the state. Most Aboriginal children were excluded from the state public school system: the policy of 'exclusion-on-demand' meant that principals could and did exempt any or all Aboriginal children from attending before they reached the compulsory school-attendance age — on the grounds that White parents objected to their presence in the classroom! There was also social exclusion — a refusal by local White teams to have Aboriginals in their sides. These factors made Aboriginal participation almost impossible.

That there were any players in the 1930s, 1940s and early 1950s is remarkable. However, six men of note emerged in the game that its fervid supporters claim is tougher, more spectacular and more intellectually satisfying than rugby union. A regular member of the famous Cherbourg teams, **Frank Fisher** played five-eighth for Wide Bay against the visiting British teams in 1932 and 1936. So impressed was the English captain, the legendary Gus Risman, that he wrote to Fisher suggesting that he come to England for a career. Fisher, then a 'controlled' Aboriginal under the restrictive Queensland special legislation, applied to the Sub-Department of Health and Home Affairs for permission to apply for a passport. This was refused, allegedly on the ground that one sports star from Cherbourg — namely, cricketer **Eddie Gilbert** — was enough!

A happier story, though only marginally so, is that of Arthur ('Stokel' or 'Stoker') Currie. In 1937 he played for the NSW Country side that beat Sydney City, a rare victory in that series. He was a member of the top-ranking Tweed Heads All Blacks side which was created because local teams wouldn't include Aboriginal players. The famous **Redfern All Blacks** and the Moree Boomerangs were formed in these eras of rejection, exclusion and segregation.

John Simon was fast, strong and an adept kicker who played 192 games for Illawarra, Sydney City, Parramatta and Auckland between 1990 and 1999. He played in four State of Origin games and in one Test for Australia.
Photo: Fairfax Photo Library/
Courtesy John Fairfax Holdings

Stoker's grandson **Tony Currie** is a celebrated international.

The brothers **Lin** and **Dick Johnson** hailed from Currabubula near Tamworth (NSW). Both played fullback: Lin for Canterbury Bankstown and Dick for South Sydney, Cessnock, Western Suburbs and finally Canterbury. In 1941 the brothers were opposing fullbacks in the City versus Country fixture. Walter Mussing, an immensely popular South Sea Islander, played 37 games for St George immediately after World War II. **Wally McArthur**, who was born in the Northern Territory and removed as a child to an assimilation home in Adelaide, began his sporting life as a junior sprinter. Alleging that a colour bar was hindering him, he went to England and there had a remarkable rugby league career amassing a total of 165 games for four different clubs between 1953 and 1959.

RUGBY LEAGUE

Vern and Frank Daisy were two of a great family of footballers in the Foley Shield competition in north Queensland. Ricky Page's book, *Indigenous Heroes of the North West and Gulf Region* (2015) feature these two Kalkadoon men on the cover.
Photo: Tony Irelandes

In chapter 1 we described the 1960s as the 'decade of opportunity'. Certainly this was the case in a few sports: **Evonne Goolagong-Cawley** in tennis; **Polly Farmer** in Australian football; **Lionel Rose** in boxing; **John Kinsella** in wrestling; **Cheryl Mullett** in badminton; and **Michael Ahmatt** in basketball. But it was in league that Aboriginal people really found their niche. **Lionel Morgan** became the first Aboriginal to play for Australia in 1960. The uncompromising Newtown and New South Wales prop **Bruce Olive** played at this time. **Artie Beetson** says that the first time he encountered racial sledging on the field was from Bruce. He yelled back to Bruce: 'you're two shades darker than midnight than I am!' **Ron Saddler** captained and coached New South Wales and toured with the Kangaroos. **Eric Simms** broke all kicking records, played for New South Wales and eight World Cup matches for Australia. Other notables were Kevin Yow Yeh, Eric Pitt, Bruce 'Larpa' Stewart (the uncle of the Ella brothers), Eric Robinson and **Kevin Longbottom**.

The 'daddy' of them all was **Arthur (Artie) Beetson** who came from Roma in Queensland in 1966. Regarded as possibly the greatest ball-playing forward of all time, he played 28 matches for his country, as captain on two occasions. He led Eastern Suburbs to two premierships and was the undoubted hero of the first State of Origin match in 1980. He once said: 'I consider myself an Australian first, a Queenslander second and part-Aboriginal third'. Yet in his post-career as player and as a state and national selector, he gave every appearance of being Aboriginal first. His influence and the amount of time he has put into the game have helped develop Aboriginal players enormously.

In the Beetson era of the 1960s, two South Sydney players came to the fore: **Eric Simms** and **Kevin Longbottom**. In the early 1970s **George Ambrum** played two Tests for Australia in a period that saw a huge increase in the number of first grade players. The trickle was now a full-flowing stream with spectacular performances from Ray Blacklock, Eric Ferguson, **Larry Corowa** (who was the glamour player of the time), Ross Gigg, David Grant (**Artie Beetson**'s cousin), Percy Knight, Terry Wickey and Mark Wright.

The State of Origin series which began in 1980 provided for greater involvement of Queenslanders and eventually led to the presence of three teams in the Sydney competition. The stars, in the real sense of that overused word, were **Sam Backo**, **Tony Currie**, **Colin Scott**, **Dale Shearer**, **Mal Meninga**, **Sam Thaiday**, **Justin Hodges**, **Greg Inglis** and **Jonathan Thurston**.

The extremely shy and reluctant Ewan McGrady from Toomelah Reserve in northern New South Wales starred for Canterbury–Bankstown and won the Rothmans Medal in 1991.
Photo: Fairfax Photo Library/
Courtesy John Fairfax Holdings

Rhys Wesser is of Aboriginal and South Sea Islander heritage. He played 218 first-grade games for Penrith and Souths, and another four State of Origin games for Queensland as a slashing runner at fullback and on the wing.
Photo: Gregg Porteus/Newspix

The Queensland versus New South Wales rivalry was also the spur to some outstanding southern players: **Mal Cochrane**, **Steve Ella** (a cousin of the famous rugby union trio), **John ('Chicka') Ferguson**, **Ron Gibbs**, **Cliff Lyons** and **Ricky Walford**.

Since the 1980s the number of Aboriginal and Islander players has increased to the point where they now constitute over ten per cent of the Sydney first grade players. Given that Aboriginal and Islander people constitute less than three per cent of the New South Wales and Queensland populations this is indeed an amazing over-representation. The only comparable figures are in Australian football and by way of sharp contrast, darts! One match doesn't make a statistical truth but the 1987 grand final between Canberra and Manly was both freakish and normal in that there were seven Aboriginal and Islander players on the field!

During the last twenty years league has become a particularly fertile field for Aboriginal and Islander players. They now comprise 12 per cent of the entire player roster. Round 13 of 2016 featured twelve Aboriginal players: seven from the Gold Coast (Ash Taylor, James Roberts, Greg Bird, Josh Hoffman, Ryan James, Nathan Peats and Nathan Davis) and five from South Sydney (Cody Walker, **Greg Inglis**, Kyle Turner, Alex Johnston and Dane Nielsen). That represented a staggering 42 per cent of the starting line up at kick off! Since 2008 there have been eleven games featuring a total of ten Aboriginal players. The 2015 grand final between the Brisbane Broncos and the North Queensland Cowboys had the unique distinction of having **Justin Hodges** and **Jonathan Thurston** as opposing captains.

Craig Salvatori played 94 games for Eastern Suburbs between 1986 and 1993 and two Tests for Australia in 1991. Photo: Fairfax Photo Library/courtesy John Fairfax Holdings

Ray Blacklock (*left*), and Eric Ferguson. Ray, an uncle of **Nathan Blacklock**, was in Newtown's 1981 grand final against Parramatta. In that match, **John ('Chicka') Ferguson** was on the opposite wing to Ray. Photo: Newtown RLFC

The 1990s brought about a veritable flood of great Aboriginal and Islander talents some of whom will undoubtedly become members of this Hall of Fame: **Nathan Blacklock**, Owen Craigie, Ashley Gordon, Jeff Hardy, Lee Hookey, Ken and Kevin McGuiness, Ewan McGrady, Chris McKenna, **Anthony Mundine**, Ken Nagas, **David Peachey**, **Wendell Sailor**, Craig Salvatori, Rod Silva, John Simon, **Matt Sing**, **Gorden Tallis**, Darrell Trindall, **Steve Renouf**, **Andrew Walker (2)**, Craig Wing and not least, the incomparable **Laurie Daley**, later to become the NSW State of Origin coach from 2012 to 2017.

This magnificent parade doesn't mean that all is honey and light. In 1999 a Canterbury player racially vilified **Anthony Mundine**. His startling defence was that he wasn't racially abusing Mundine but another player nearby, Aboriginal Robbie Simpson! Despite efforts to keep the matter 'in house' and dealt with 'inside' — which is typical of football officialdom in all codes — Mundine insisted on pursuing the matter. He had the satisfaction of seeing the Australian Rugby League fine the offender $10,000 despite Canterbury's indignation that it was all 'unfair and unAustralian'! The NRL, which doesn't have the same formal code of conduct as introduced by the Australian Football League, has, in effect, introduced an important precedent by this heavy sentence.

The array of Aboriginal talent has been quite remarkable. **Preston Campbell** had much input into the creation of the Indigenous All Stars team in 2008. **Nathan Blacklock**, **Matt Bowen**, **Scott Prince** and **Timana Tahu** excited both fans and sports writers. **Tahu** and **Andrew Walker (2)** joined **Wendell Sailor** in achieving the rare feat of playing both union and league for Australia. The Aboriginal team of the century covering all players from 1908 to 2007 comprises 17 players, all of whom are members of this Hall of Fame.

The current crop of outstanding Aboriginal and Islander players includes: Dane Gagai (4 Tests, 7 State of Origin games), Will Chambers (6 Tests, 6 State, plus 23 Rugby State), Wade Graham (5 Tests, 4 State), Andrew Fifita (7 Tests, 10 State), Blake Ferguson (7 Tests, 7 State), Greg Bird (17 Tests, 18 State), Jack Bird (5 State), Nathan Peats (3 State), Ryan James, Tyrone Peachey, Latrell Mitchell, Ash Taylor, and Aidan Sezer.

There is, perhaps, one slightly sour note. When Aboriginal activist Michael Anderson sought to establish a separate league of Aboriginal *nations* teams some years ago, the proposal was met with indignation at such an 'outrageous' idea. Reactions included the inevitable claims that this would be a South African form of apartheid and was out of the question. One suspects that the reaction had more to do with the prospect of regular teams losing their Aboriginal star players than with ideological concerns about apartheid. Anderson's notion was no different to the ideas behind the **Redfern All Blacks** way back in the 1930s or with the Dreamtime team in the early twenty-first century: voluntary separatism — which is hardly imposed segregation.

A much brighter note is the emergence of women in rugby league. In February 2017 the Indigenous Women's All Stars — coached by **Dean Widders** — beat a World All Stars in a significant match. That Aboriginal side included **Bo de la Cruz**, already a member of the Hall of Fame for her prowess in touch football. The inaugural women's Test game began against New Zealand in 1995. **Katrina Fanning**, a member of that side, went on to play 24 Tests for the national Jillaroos team.

The year 2017 was to be the end of **Jonathan Thurston**'s international careers.

Jamie Soward was a bit of an enigma – often considered under-involved as a play-maker, he proved the pundits wrong by guiding St George to the 2010 Premiership. In his 231 club games, 3 State, and 2 Country matches, Soward amassed a staggering 1428 points.
Photo: NRL Media

He began league life playing for Canterbury who let him go because they considered him too small. Canterbury was the side that wrote to us in 1987 to say that they had never had Aboriginals in their sides and were unlikely to recruit any. They forgot the Johnson brothers in the 1930s and 1940s. They also forgot that they had on their books the man who is today acclaimed the best ever player in league football history: **Jonathan Thurston**.

TEAMS

There is a longish history of all-Aboriginal teams. The remarkable annual competition, the NSW Rugby League Knockout, has had some scholarly attention, particularly from Heidi Norman. But the story of the **Redfern All Blacks** needs to be told.

The Tweed Heads All Blacks arose solely as a result of Aboriginal exclusion from White teams in 1930. Efforts 'to admit the dusky athletes to the white fold' in 1931 failed, 'the Noes having it by 17 votes to 15, with the result that the Whites will have to struggle on as best they can'. A legendary member was Arthur (Stoker, sometimes Stokel) Currie, grandfather of **Tony Currie**. Stoker played for the NSW Country side that beat Sydney City in 1937, a rare feat.

The famous Cherbourg teams of the 1920s and 1930s won many local league trophies in southern Queensland. **Frank Fisher**, grandfather of **Cathy Freeman**, was a central figure in their successes. Invited to play professionally in England, the Aboriginal administration refused him permission to apply for a passport. Evan Whitton, esteemed journalist and rugby critic, who grew up in neighbouring Murgon, wrote of Cherbourg football in 1977:

> Most visible was their football team. They trained every day, and worked up a talent for ensemble playing … Over the years they offered the people in the district an entertainment that, in form and style, was as close to the Bolshoi Ballet as probably they would ever want to see, which is an attitude I would be inclined to share.

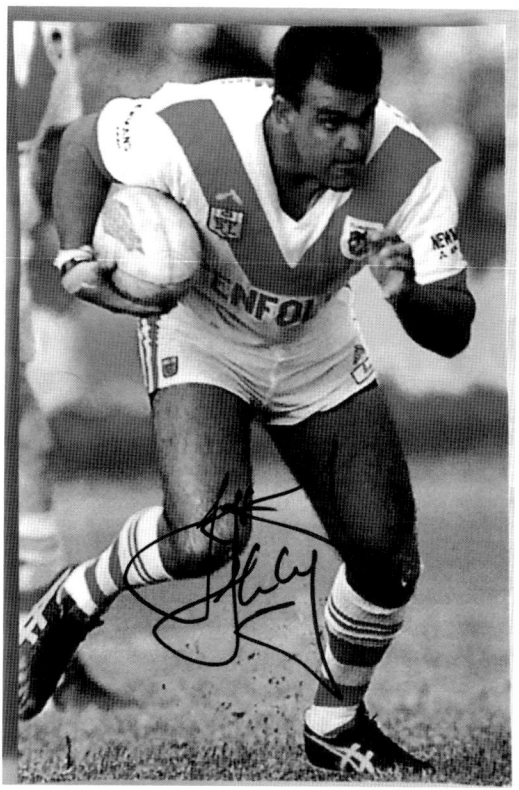

Jeff Hardy played 246 games for Illawarra and St George as a rock-solid and creative second-rower. He also played four seasons in the UK. Hardy is now the driving force in Aboriginal Oztag in Australia. Photo: Jeff Hardy.

The Cherbourg team

Cherbourg was the leading side in the South Burnett district in the 1920s.

Back row: William Porteous Semple (Superintendent); *Second row left to right*: Frank Fisher, Colin Sheridan, Percy Bond, William Hegarty, Norman Bird, Livingston Chambers, Dick Dalton; *Front row left to right*: Fred Martin, Adam Cobbo, Hughie Ross, Bob McGowan, Felix Sanders, Joe Hegarty (with dog), Clive Duncan, Willy (Galumba) Fisher.

Photo: Ken Edwards

GEORGE AMBRUM

Until the end of the 1960s there were only fifteen Aboriginal or Islanders in senior football. Social, legal and political restrictions made it difficult for Aboriginal youth to 'get away' from the control of officialdom. A very talented group, they included **Artie Beetson**, **Lionel Morgan**, **Ron Saddler**, **Eric Simms** and **George Ambrum**, all of whom represented Australia. George was an Islander descended from Ambrym Island in the New Hebrides. He was born in Cairns (Qld) in 1943. He was one of the first Aboriginal or Islander players to have a career in English rugby league, playing 28 games for Bradford Northern in 1967–1968. An imposing winger, he played 172 games for the North Sydney Bears between 1964 and 1974. His great accolade came in the first of two Tests he played for Australia against New Zealand in 1972: Man of the Match. His brother John also played for Norths from 1964 to 1967. Photo: *Rugby League Week*.

SAM BACKO

The descendants of those brought, kidnapped or 'blackbirded' to work in the Queensland sugar cane fields in the 1890s are still struggling for recognition of their separate identity. The original Pakoa family from Vanuatu became the Backo family and one of its famous sons, Sam, was born in Ingham (Qld) in 1961. He is rated as one of the greats among rugby league forwards. Injuries limited his career to eight years from 1983 to 1990. He played 105 games for the Canberra Raiders, including the loss to Manly in the 1987 grand final. This massive and unstoppable prop was at his best in the Test series against England: he became the first (and only) forward to score tries in all three Tests. Sam played 20 games for Brisbane Broncos and eighteen for Leeds in England. He played seven State of Origin games for Queensland and six Tests for Australia. His mother was Evelyn Scott, former chair of the Council for Aboriginal Reconciliation. Photo: Ian Collis.

GEORGE AMBRUM

Until the end of the 1960s there were only fifteen Aboriginal or Islanders in senior football. Social, legal and political restrictions made it difficult for Aboriginal youth to 'get away' from the control of officialdom. A very talented group, they included **Artie Beetson**, **Lionel Morgan**, **Ron Saddler**, **Eric Simms** and **George Ambrum**, all of whom represented Australia. George was an Islander descended from Ambrym Island in the New Hebrides. He was born in Cairns (Qld) in 1943. He was one of the first Aboriginal or Islander players to have a career in English rugby league, playing 28 games for Bradford Northern in 1967–1968. An imposing winger, he played 172 games for the North Sydney Bears between 1964 and 1974. His great accolade came in the first of two Tests he played for Australia against New Zealand in 1972: Man of the Match. His brother John also played for Norths from 1964 to 1967. Photo: *Rugby League Week*.

SAM BACKO

The descendants of those brought, kidnapped or 'blackbirded' to work in the Queensland sugar cane fields in the 1890s are still struggling for recognition of their separate identity. The original Pakoa family from Vanuatu became the Backo family and one of its famous sons, Sam, was born in Ingham (Qld) in 1961. He is rated as one of the greats among rugby league forwards. Injuries limited his career to eight years from 1983 to 1990. He played 105 games for the Canberra Raiders, including the loss to Manly in the 1987 grand final. This massive and unstoppable prop was at his best in the Test series against England: he became the first (and only) forward to score tries in all three Tests. Sam played 20 games for Brisbane Broncos and eighteen for Leeds in England. He played seven State of Origin games for Queensland and six Tests for Australia. His mother was Evelyn Scott, former chair of the Council for Aboriginal Reconciliation. Photo: Ian Collis.

ARTHUR (ARTIE) BEETSON, OAM

Roma (Qld) was his birthplace in 1945. At 16 Artie Beetson knew he wanted to be a professional footballer. Starting as a centre this giant of rugby league played front-row forward for Balmain (74 games), Parramatta (16), Eastern Suburbs (132), Hull Kingston Rovers in Britain (12). He represented New South Wales 17 times and Queensland 3 times. 'Thanks a million, Artie', cried the Brisbane press and fans as he captained Queensland's victorious side in the first State of Origin match in July 1980. Between 1966 and 1980 the man described by the British as the best forward in football played fourteen Tests and 14 World Cups for Australia and was the first Aboriginal player to captain the national team. He coached Queensland under-19, Easts, Cronulla, the Queensland State of Origin team and became a national and New South Wales selector. In 1999 he coached the first-ever Aboriginal Test side that beat Papua New Guinea in two internationals. Photo: *Rugby League Week*.

NATHAN BLACKLOCK

The 'try-scoring machine' was born in Tingha (NSW) in 1976, and is from the Anaiwan language group. Nathan is a nephew of Ray Blacklock who played on the wing for Newtown Jets in the 1981 grand final. The tiny town of Tingha also produced **Preston Campbell** and Owen Craigie. Blacklock's speed and finishing ability on the wing led to 121 tries from a mere 142 games mostly for St George. Nathan was the NRL's top try-scorer for three consecutive seasons (1999–2001). A stint with Hull FC (UK) saw him rack up 33 more tries in 47 starts. Representative honours were two Test matches for Australia, two Country Origins for NSW. A switch of codes saw Blacklock play five Super Rugby games for the NSW Waratahs in 2003. Photo: NRL Media.

MATT BOWEN

Although born in Cairns (Qld) in 1982, Matt grew up and was schooled in the remote community of Hopevale. Bowen's family language is Guugu Timidhirr. The diminutive full-back moved to Townsville and was signed on by the North Queensland Cowboys. His electric speed and yawning side-step and dummying helped him to score 130 tries in his 270 first grade games. Always exciting to watch, Matt attracted an almost cult following amongst the young kids. Bowen played one Test match and ten State of Origins, too few in the eyes of many fans. Since retirement in 2013, he played a further two seasons with Wigan (UK). He continued his involvement in Aboriginal communities and sport as an ambassador and community engagement officer. Photo: NRL Photos.

PRESTON CAMPBELL

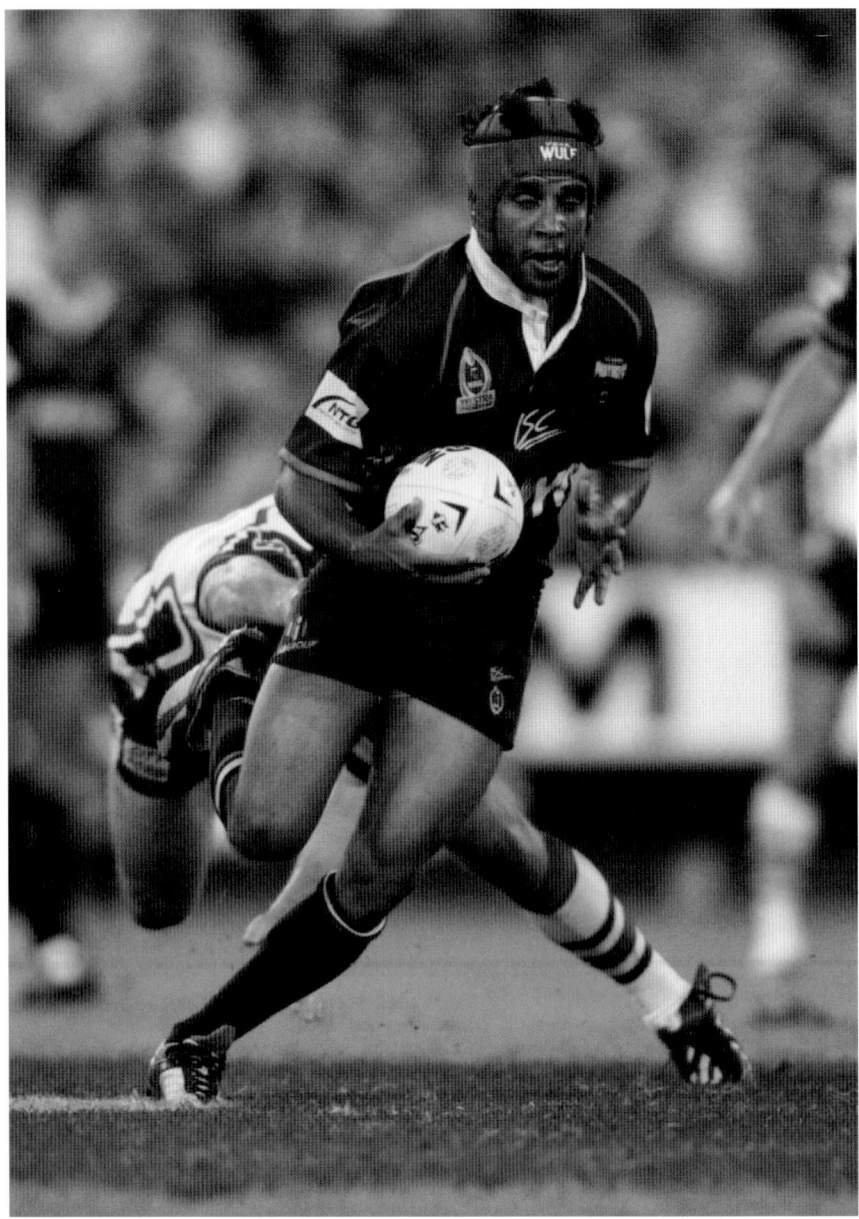

One of the smallest halves to play at the top level of rugby league, Preston's elusiveness and speed at half-back and five-eighth created many try-scoring opportunities. Born in Inverell (NSW) in 1977, he grew up in the small town of Tingha a cousin of fellow Hall-of-Famers **Nathan Blacklock** and **Greg Inglis**. Preston had 267 games for the Gold Coast, Cronulla and Penrith, amassing 903 points. Although he was never selected for Tests or Origin, he played three Country Origin matches, was Dally M Player of the Year (2001), and played in a premiership with Penrith (2003). A tireless worker for Aboriginal well-being, he was awarded the Ken Stephens Medal for his efforts in providing awareness in mental health, cultural identity and Closing-the-Gap programs. Photo: NRL Photos.

MAL COCHRANE

Mal Cochrane went straight from Taree High School to play for Manly. Born in 1961, he spent his childhood at Purfleet, the Aboriginal community on the outskirts of Taree (NSW). He played for the Australian Schoolboys under-19 team in 1978 and captained that side in 1979. Mal won the Dally M Hooker of the Year in 1986 and again in 1987. He holds the premiership record for the most points in a season by a hooker (172 in 1986). Mal won the prestigious Rothman's Medal in 1986 and was chosen as a member of an Aboriginal 'Honour' side in 1987, announced on the day of the Manly versus Canberra grand final. He was in the winning team. Mal played 118 games for Manly between 1982 and 1990, scoring 410 points. In 1996 he coached the Australian Aboriginal team on its tour of Great Britain. Mal has devoted himself to youth work through sport at Purfleet and in 1999 was the major figure in establishing an Aboriginal Test team. Photo: *Rugby League Week*.

LARRY COROWA, MBE

Larry Corowa was the glamour boy of league in the late 1970s. Born in Tweed Heads (NSW) in 1957 he was 19 when he scored five tries for Monaro against the visiting British side. In 1978 he scored 24 tries for Balmain, for whom he played 96 games between 1978 and 1983. In a late comeback he played two games for the Gold Coast in 1991. Larry played five matches for NSW and toured with the 1978 Kangaroos which included two Tests for Australia. Larry was considered the fastest man in football — and so he was: in 1978 he won a special match-race against Steve Proudlock, the winner of that year's Stawell Easter Gift. Larry will long be remembered for his speed, elusiveness, dexterity, skill and humour. The *National Times* declared that Larry and the three **Ella brothers** constituted 'the four black footballers who may well reform most of the principles that Australia has laid down for its black sportsmen'. Photo: Ian Collis.

GLEN (PADDY) CROUCH

The first Aboriginal footballer in any code to tour abroad was Paddy. Born in Dunwich, Stradbroke Island (Qld) in 1904 he began his career as a union player, switching to rugby league in 1922. He played wing and centre for Coorparoo from 1922 to 1927. In 1925 he played all eleven games for the Queensland side touring New Zealand. Glen Crouch captained the Brisbane team which toured north Queensland in 192 — and won a cigarette case for being the best back on tour. A career in league administration led to Life Membership of the Wynnum Fisherman's Club, Wynnum-Manly Football Club and Queensland Rugby League. Paddy's family was very much involved in sport: his sister was **Edna Crouch** and his cousin **Mabel Campbell**; his niece Thelma Crouch played cricket for Queensland and his son Glen was awarded Life Membership of both the Seagulls and the Brisbane Rugby League for his services as a player and administrator. Photo: Thelma Crouch.

ANTHONY (TONY) CURRIE

Currie is synonymous with championship quality football. In 1937 Arthur 'Stoker' Currie played for the Tweed Heads All Blacks, created because local teams excluded Aboriginals. Stoker played rugby league for NSW Country in the side that beat Sydney City. His nephew Alan Currie was the Brisbane Rothmans Medal winner in 1978. Grandson Anthony (Tony) Currie won the Sydney Rothmans Medal in 1982. Born in Brisbane in 1962, Tony had an illustrious career as a winger and centre. He played 74 games for Wests (Qld), nine for Redcliffe (Qld), 65 for Leeds in the UK, 38 for Canterbury and 36 for Brisbane in the Winfield Cup. Tony had an impressive record: fifteen State of Origin games for Queensland and seven Tests for Australia. His career spanned the years 1981 to 1993. His last match for Wests in the 1993 Brisbane grand final was both memorable and unmemorable: he played a brilliant defensive game, made the first try, was knocked unconscious and has no memory of the game. Photo: *Rugby League Week*.

LAURIE DALEY, AM

Laurie Daley was one of the world's best players. Born in Junee (NSW) in 1969, he has achieved immense stature in this football code. By the end of 2000 he had played 244 games for the Canberra Raiders, five World Cup games, 23 matches for New South Wales, 26 Tests for Australia and five Super league Tests. Laurie was captain of three consecutive winning NSW State of Origin teams, in 1992, 1993 and 1994. In 1995 he won the Dally M award and was *Rugby League Week* Player of the Year. He was Super league Player of the Year in 1997. In 1992 the experts voted Laurie the best five-eighth in the world. The statistics don't really reflect his superlative play and football brain. From 2012 to 2017 he coached the NSW State of Origin side. A statue of Laurie is located at the entrance to Bruce Stadium in Canberra. Photo: Fairfax Photo Library/courtesy John Fairfax Holdings.

STEVE ELLA

Five members of the Ella clan are in this Hall of Fame. Steve Ella was the rugby league star. Born in Mt Pritchard (NSW) in 1960, this cousin of the rugby union **Ella brothers** played full-back, centre, wing, half-back and five-eighth for Parramatta in the heyday years of the Eels (who won the premiership four times between 1981 and 1986). A 'freakish attacking centre', 'a superbly gifted player with abundant pace, great anticipation and remarkable ball skills', Steve played 156 games for this great team between 1981 and 1987 including five grand finals. He toured with the 1982 Kangaroos, played 23 games for Wigan in the UK, eight matches for NSW and three Tests for Australia. In a career spanning ten years, often beset by injuries he retired in 1989, having scored 544 points and achieved a club record of 23 tries for Parramatta in the 1982 season. Photo: *Rugby League Week*.

KATRINA FANNING

Playing for the Junee (NSW) Diesel's (**Laurie Daley**'s junior club), Katrina was a hard-running forward who played in the front row in the world's first women's rugby league test match in 1993. Born in 1973, and raised in Junee, Fanning went on to be capped 24 times as a Jillaroo, including the 2000 and 2003 World Cups. She captained New South Wales and Country New South Wales. Katrina has also played rugby union (as a second rower) for the ACT Brumbies, futsal for the national Aboriginal team (as goalie), and handball for the ACT side that contained fellow Hall-of Famers **Delma Smith** and **Jo Lesiputty**. She has worked tirelessly as a public servant and volunteer in Aboriginal homelessness, domestic violence and multicultural services. In 2014, Katrina was awarded ACT Women of the Year for her advocacy for Aboriginal people. Photo: Katrina Fanning.

JOHN ('CHICKA') FERGUSON

John Ferguson was a rugby league star who will long remain in the memory. Almost all critics regard him as deserving of far more international selection. Born in Sydney in 1954, his career began in 1980 and ended in 1990. In that time he was a scintillating winger for Newtown in 73 games, for Eastern Suburbs in 32, for Canberra in 94 and for Wigan in the UK in 25 matches. The English press considered him 'eerie'. In 1988 this fast and most elusive winger was Canberra's leading try-scorer. His representative selections don't do justice to his talents: he played eight games for NSW and three Tests for Australia against New Zealand. Few fans and reporters will ever forget his marvellous try that sent the 1989 grand final into extra time, or his performance in his last match for Canberra in the 1990 grand final against Penrith. Photo: *Rugby League Week*.

FRANK ('BIG SHOT') FISHER

Frank Fisher was the grandfather of **Cathy Freeman**. Born in Townsville (Qld) in 1905 his family was 'transported', as were so many Aboriginals in Queensland, to 'another place' — Cherbourg. A handy cricketer and an excellent sprinter, he preferred 'the intensity of rugby league'. Frank played for Cherbourg and for Wide Bay against the visiting British side in 1932 and 1936. He so impressed the famous English captain that A J (Gus) Risman invited Frank to play in England. As a controlled Aboriginal he had to apply to the Aboriginal administration for permission to apply for a passport. This was refused — on the ground that one star from Cherbourg (**Eddie Gilbert**) was enough! A big man, he weighed a solid 95 kg as a five-eighth. Frank was still playing class football at 40. His nickname derives from admonishing a late-for-practice hero: you might be the champ, he said, 'but I'm the big shot here and I run this football team'. He was also known as King Fisher. Photo: Lillian Gray.

RON GIBBS

Ron is a Barkindji man who was born in Brewarrina (NSW) in 1960. He played his junior football in Bourke before being picked up by Easts (Sydney Roosters) in 1983. Gibbs moved to Manly, earning himself the nickname 'Rambo' for his kamikaze-style running and tackling. Equally at home in the second row or centre, Gibbs was a slashing wide runner who hit the ball (and his opponents) with everything he had. 'Rambo' played 152 NRL games for Easts, Manly, Gold Coast and Wests, and a further 41 matches for Castleford (UK). He represented NSW Country Origin twice, and won the 1987 premiership with Manly. Gibbs initiated and ran a sevens tournament in Bourke, and coaches able and disabled Aboriginal football teams. Photo: *Rugby League Week*.

GEORGE GREEN

Our research indicates that George Green was the first man of Aboriginal or Islander descent to play professional rugby league in Australia. Born in Grafton (NSW) in 1886 or 1888, his father was a mariner of Afro-Caribbean origin. First knowledge of him comes with his 22 appearances for Eastern Suburbs from 1909 to 1911. He moved to North Sydney, for whom he played a total of 92 games between 1912 and 1916 and between 1918 and 1922. It is most likely that he spent 1917 with Newtown. George was the major tactician for the 'Shoremen' as Norths were then called. 'One of Nature's gentlemen ... a tower of strength in the rucks, was the press verdict of the man who played hooker in North Sydney's two and only premiership sides, the glory teams of 1921 and 1922. George continued as a coach and strategist for Norths after his retirement from play. Photo: North Sydney Football Club.

JUSTIN HODGES

Born in Cairns (Qld) in 1982, Justin signed as a centre for the Brisbane Broncos in early 2000. A great admirer of **Steve Renouf**, Hodges' style was more like a forward: a great fend, basketball-like overhead passes, and the ability to stand and off-load in a tackle. For a big man he was not short of pace. A move to the Sydney Roosters saw him play in two grand finals before returning to Brisbane to play out the final eleven years of his career. Together with **Jonathan Thurston** in the same backline, he illustrated why Queensland rugby league was simply the best. Justin played 13 tests for Australia, 24 State of Origins, 251 NRL matches, including 4 grand finals. He was Dally M Centre of the Year in 2007. Photo: NRL Media.

GREG INGLIS

Of Dungutti heritage, Greg was born in Kempsey (NSW) in 1987. Although raised in Macksville, playing his junior football for Bowraville and Newcastle, Inglis represented Queensland in 30 State of Origin matches. A strong and powerful runner with a great side-step, he is equally at home at full-back, centre or on the wing. To date, Greg has represented his country on 39 occasions, and played 242 NRL games (139 tries) for Melbourne Storm and South Sydney. Inglis was a member of the Melbourne Storm's four grand final teams (2006–2009), as well as South's 2014 premiership side. He won a Clive Churchill Medal (2007), four Dally M awards, and was the Golden Boot Best Player in the World (2009). He and **Jonathan Thurston** came to represent sporting achievement on the football fields. Photo: NRL Media.

ALLEN (DICK) JOHNSON

In the late 1930s and early 1940s most New South Wales Aboriginal people had to live on reserves. They were treated as wards of the state, unable to travel freely and almost all Aboriginal youth were excluded from the state schooling system. The Johnson brothers were an aberration in rugby league. Allen, younger brother of **Lin Johnson**, was born in Currabubula (NSW) in 1916. He played 29 games for South Sydney (1938–1939) including the losing 1939 grand final match; he played country football in Cessnock (1940–1942); then seventeen games for Western Suburbs (1943 and 1945). His longest spell was with Canterbury for whom he played 38 games between 1946 and 1948 including the losing 1947 grand final match. Dick played for Country in 1941 and 1942 and for City in 1945 — a rare feat. He played eleven games for NSW in 1939, 1941 and 1945. The magazines described him as 'a sure handler, long kicker, with excellent judgement'. Photo: Ian Collis.

LINDSAY (LIN) JOHNSON

After Paul Tranquille and **George Green** in the 1920s the Johnsons were the first senior players in NSW rugby league. Lindsay Johnson, brother of **Allen (Dick) Johnson**, was born in Currabubula (NSW) in 1913. Lin came to football via the North Newcastle team and then played 91 games at full-back for Canterbury between 1939 and 1946, kicking 150 goals. He kicked the winning goal in Canterbury's defeat of St George in the 1942 grand final. Lin kicked four goals that day; the Dragons' three goals were kicked by a famous name in Australian history, fast bowler Ray Lindwall. As he took the final kick, Lin slipped in the mud, the ball barely scraping over the bar for what has been described as the worst winning goal in football history. Lin represented New South Wales twice in 1940 and played for City against Country in 1941 and 1942. In the 1941 Country versus City match, **Dick** and Lin were the opposing full-backs. Photo: Ian Collis.

JULIE LANDY-ARIEL (YOUNG)

Julie's family is originally from Katherine (NT). Though she was born in Sydney (NSW) in 1985, Julie was raised by the Awabakal people in the Lake Macquarie region. Landy-Ariel is a dual international — representing at Oztag in 2011 against New Zealand. She was in the Jillaroos team, as hooker, from 2012 to 2014, including the 2013 victorious World Cup side. Julie has a long history of refereeing in the Newcastle rugby league, and now co-runs a training facility in Sydney with her husband Nick Landy-Ariel (see Kickboxing and Martial Arts). Julie's younger sister Emma also represented Australia in the 2013 Jillaroos World cup side and the 2016 ANZAC test match against New Zealand. Her sister-in-law **Bec Young** is also a dual international. Photo: Nick and Julie Landy-Ariel.

DAVID LIDDIARD, OAM

David is a Ngarabal man. Born in Penrith (NSW) in 1961, Liddiard was a speedy winger and full-back for Parramatta. He was Dally M Rookie of the Year in 1983, and a member of the premiership-winning team the following year. He later moved to Penrith, where he had been a junior, briefly linking up with his younger brother Glen. Liddiard played 131 NRL games for 39 tries. David founded the National Aboriginal Sporting Chance Academy (NASCA) in 1995, which helped promote Aboriginal education, health and employment, as well as bringing high-profile athletes to remote communities. Of all the sports champions, Liddiard has been outstanding in his community development work, and was finally rewarded with an Order of Australia medal in 2014. Photo: Robert Pearce/Fairfax Syndication.

KEVIN ('LUMMY') LONGBOTTOM

'Lummy' was a large barrel-chested man who played full-back for South Sydney between 1961 and 1969. His career began with Kensington United. For Souths, he starred alongside such luminaries as John Sattler, Ron Coote, Bob McCarthy, Elwin Waters, and **Eric Simms**. Kevin was born in Sydney in 1939. If he wasn't scoring tries, or scything his bulky frame through opposition's defences, he was kicking goals from near-impossible angles and distances. In the days of heavy leather balls, Kevin regularly kicked goals from 50 to 55 m out. He played 105 matches for Souths, including the 1967 grand final win over Canterbury. Kevin was a fine golfer and caddied for many leading tour professionals. He died of cancer at the young age of 47 at La Perouse (NSW). John Ellicott has written a long essay on Kevin in his 2014 book, *Uncommon Heroes*. Photo: *Rugby League Week*.

CLIFF LYONS

Cliff Lyons was born in Narrandera (NSW) in 1961. He began his rugby league career in 1984 as five-eighth for North Sydney. He played 23 games for the Bears, 24 for Leeds, six for Sheffield in the UK, then 309 games for Manly-Warringah. Only 28 men have played 300 or more games: two are Aboriginal — **Scott Prince** and Cliff, who is 7th on the list. A key figure in the Manly attack, he won the Clive Churchill Medal as Best Player in the 1987 grand final. He won the coveted Dally M Award for Best Player of the Year twice, in 1990 and 1994. Cliff was in the Aboriginal team that played for the Pacific Cup in Tonga in 1990. Given his talents and awards it is surprising that he played only six matches for New South Wales and six Tests for Australia. In 1999 he played for the Aboriginal side in two Tests against Papua New Guinea. Photo: *Rugby League Week*.

WALLY McARTHUR

Wally McArthur was born in Borroloola (NT) in 1933 and given the name McArthur after the local river. He was removed from there to the 'half-caste' institution in Alice Springs where he befriended **Charles Perkins**, from there to Mulgoa Mission near Penrith and from there to St Francis's Home in Adelaide, an institution which didn't believe in sport. A brilliant sprinter, he ran well at the national athletics championships in Hobart in 1951. Believing his colour was against him for an amateur career, he turned professional and won ten events. He switched sports and began a successful rugby league career in England where, as the 'Black Flash', he played a total of 165 games on the wing for Rochdale, Blackpool, Salford and Workington Town between 1953 and 1959, scoring 611 points. He was chosen for the Rest of World versus England, a game in which he scored four tries. Photo: *News & Sunday Mail*.

MAL MENINGA, AM

'A colossus in the code' of rugby league: 'simply the best' — words that summarise the man who displayed fine leadership qualities and who never boasted or swaggered on or off the field. Born in Bundaberg (Qld) in 1960, this 110 kg South Sea Island descendant has achieved more than any other rugby league player in the history of the sport. Between 1978 and 1994 he played 41 games for Queensland, 46 Tests for Australia, 23 as captain. He is the only man chosen for four Kangaroo tours; he is Australia's second-most capped player and is the highest points scorer in all Tests and State of Origin matches. As wing or centre he amassed an astonishing total of 465 matches for 2667 points made up of 140 games for Souths (Qld), 166 for Canberra, including four grand finals and two as captain of the winning side (1989 and 1990) and 31 games for St Helens in the United Kingdom. He became coach of the Canberra Raiders, the Queensland State of Origin and the national Kangaroos. Photo: *Rugby League Week*.

LIONEL MORGAN

Between 1960 and 2017 some 36 Aboriginal or Islander people had played rugby league for Australia. It was perhaps appropriate that the first international should hail from an area which excluded Aboriginal people from local teams in the 1930s, leading to the creation of teams like the Tweed Heads All Blacks. Lionel Morgan was born in Tweed Heads (NSW) in 1938. Between 1956 and 1958 he played for Tweed Heads, by then an 'open' team, then moved to Brisbane's Wynnum-Manly team for whom he played 130 games. This quiet and unassuming man was an outstanding winger. He represented Brisbane in 22 matches and Queensland on fourteen occasions. The pinnacle of his career was selection for Australia in two Tests against France in 1960 and one World Cup match in England in the same year. His son Bradley played 300 games for Wynnum-Manly, 100 of them in first division. Photo: Lionel Morgan.

NARWAN FOOTBALL CLUB

The Narwan football team had to fight vigorously to gain a place in local competition: the White community in Armidale (NSW) condemned the formation of the team as a form of South African-style apartheid. Through the efforts of the local Catholic priest, Dave Perrett, Narwan gained entry in 1977 and achieved great things for rugby league and for the Aboriginal community. This is the team that won the Caltex Shield in 1980.

Back row, left to right: Robert Kelly, Gary Davison, Mitch Morris, Mary Quinlan, Clarrie Moran, Eric Kelly, Derek Moran, Brian Dennison, Michael Quinlan, Jim Widders. *Front row*: Richard Smith, Pritchard Moran, Alistair Moran, Dempsey Kelly, Sylvester Cook, Lewis Kelly.

Photo: *Armidale Express*.

BRUCE OLIVE

Artie Beetson recalled that the first time he encountered racial sledging on the football field: it was from none other than fellow Aboriginal player, Bruce Olive. Born in 1930, in Casino (NSW), this uncompromising and tough prop forward began his rugby league career with Wests in Wollongong between 1958 and 1963 and then moved to Newtown, then into the Sydney senior league between 1964 and 1967. Bruce was one of the early Aboriginal stars in an era when few were in top football. His Aboriginal opponents at the time included **Artie Beetson**, **George Ambrum**, John Ambrum, **Kevin Longbottom**, Eric Pitt, Eric Robinson and Kevin Yow Yeh. He played 73 games for Newtown and in three City versus Country matches. His representative career began in 1958. Between 1958 and 1962 he played in eight matches for New South Wales against Queensland and in two matches against touring sides. Beetson talks respectfully of his toughness and his footballing skills. Photo: Ian Collis.

DAVID PEACHEY

David is a Wiradjuri man who was born in Dubbo (NSW) in 1974. Signed by the Cronulla Sharks, Peachey made an immediate impact — dazzling opponents with his broken running, audacious chip-and-chase runs, and a loping turn of speed. He was Dally M full-back of the year in 1999. He represented Australia in Super League and NSW Origin three times. 'Peach' racked up an impressive 266 games for Cronulla, South Sydney and Widnes (UK), scoring 127 tries along the way. Named NAIDOC Sportsperson of the Year (2003), David set up his own foundation (2004) and has been a true ambassador for the Aboriginal community through the NRL, NASCA, and a host of awareness programs and festivals. Photo: NRL Media.

SCOTT PRINCE

A nephew of Vern Daisy of the Kalkadoon people, Scott was born in Mt Isa (Qld) in 1980. His brother Stephen represented Australia in touch football. Scott was taken on by the North Queensland Cowboys in 1998. The clever and often brilliant half-back notched up a total of 300 games for the Cowboys, Broncos, Tigers, and Titans, as well as four Test matches and five State of Origins. Scott was a prolific goal-kicker, amassing 1054 points (67 tries, 389 goals, 8 field goals) along the way. He captained the Wests Tigers to their first premiership in 2005. Scott was named Dally M half-back of the year in 2010, and Rugby League Internal half-back of the year in 2008 and 2010. Prince now works in the Aboriginal community and is co-author of three childrens books. Photo: Simon Alekna/Fairfax Syndication.

REDFERN ALL BLACKS

The oldest Aboriginal rugby league team, the Redfern All Blacks — sometimes called the RABs or plain 'Redfern' — may have had its roots in the Depression of the 1930s, but its birthdate is most generally given as 1944. At that time, the NSW Aborigines Welfare Board was detaching young Sydney men from their families and sending them to outback towns as indentured but unpaid apprentices. It was also a time of 'assimilation', a breaking up of Aboriginal population clusters. The team began as a way of holding on to Aboriginality, to space, and a place in mainstream society. The cultural and social importance of the team was boosted when, in the early 1960s, the Foundation for Aboriginal Affairs, an essentially non-Aboriginal body in Sydney, gave its strong support for the Club's continuation.

The Redfern All Blacks in 1945: *left to right*: Dick Lord (ball boy), Lal Hinton (captain), Merv (Boomenulla) Williams, Vestey Jarrett, Ray (Sugar) Williams, Jack McLaren, Jackie Simms, Isaac (Ike) Bates, Cec Stewart, Alan Duren, Babs Vincent, Laurie (Divebomber) Perry, Colin Saunders, Eric (Nugget) Mumbler.

Photo: Ike Bates.

STEVE RENOUF

Several critics rated Steve Renouf as the player of the 1990s. Described as having 'extra-special abilities' and as 'a world-beater', this modest athlete was born in Wondai (Qld) in 1970. One of twelve children, his late father Charlie was a pro runner and tent boxer. His mother Nerida spent most of her life in the dormitory system on Aboriginal settlements and missions. A brilliant rugby league centre, he has shone for the Brisbane Broncos, for Queensland and Australia. Beginning his career in 1988, by the end of the 1999 season he had played 183 games for Brisbane, 13 for his State of Origin side, 11 Tests for Australia, in one World Cup Final and in one World Cup Challenge match. He was the top try-scorer of the year in 1994. In 1999 he decided to quit representative rugby and signed for Wigan in England for the 2000 season for whom he played 59 games. Photo: Fairfax Photo Library/courtesy John Fairfax Holdings.

REDFERN ALL BLACKS

The oldest Aboriginal rugby league team, the Redfern All Blacks — sometimes called the RABs or plain 'Redfern' — may have had its roots in the Depression of the 1930s, but its birthdate is most generally given as 1944. At that time, the NSW Aborigines Welfare Board was detaching young Sydney men from their families and sending them to outback towns as indentured but unpaid apprentices. It was also a time of 'assimilation', a breaking up of Aboriginal population clusters. The team began as a way of holding on to Aboriginality, to space, and a place in mainstream society. The cultural and social importance of the team was boosted when, in the early 1960s, the Foundation for Aboriginal Affairs, an essentially non-Aboriginal body in Sydney, gave its strong support for the Club's continuation.

The Redfern All Blacks in 1945: *left to right*: Dick Lord (ball boy), Lal Hinton (captain), Merv (Boomenulla) Williams, Vestey Jarrett, Ray (Sugar) Williams, Jack McLaren, Jackie Simms, Isaac (Ike) Bates, Cec Stewart, Alan Duren, Babs Vincent, Laurie (Divebomber) Perry, Colin Saunders, Eric (Nugget) Mumbler.

Photo: Ike Bates.

STEVE RENOUF

Several critics rated Steve Renouf as the player of the 1990s. Described as having 'extra-special abilities' and as 'a world-beater', this modest athlete was born in Wondai (Qld) in 1970. One of twelve children, his late father Charlie was a pro runner and tent boxer. His mother Nerida spent most of her life in the dormitory system on Aboriginal settlements and missions. A brilliant rugby league centre, he has shone for the Brisbane Broncos, for Queensland and Australia. Beginning his career in 1988, by the end of the 1999 season he had played 183 games for Brisbane, 13 for his State of Origin side, 11 Tests for Australia, in one World Cup Final and in one World Cup Challenge match. He was the top try-scorer of the year in 1994. In 1999 he decided to quit representative rugby and signed for Wigan in England for the 2000 season for whom he played 59 games. Photo: Fairfax Photo Library/courtesy John Fairfax Holdings.

RON SADDLER

Ron Saddler has an enviable but somewhat overlooked record in rugby league. Born in Murwillumbah (NSW) in 1942 he began his career with Murwillumbah Brothers in 1963 and soon moved to Eastern Suburbs in the Sydney competition. He played 118 games for the Roosters, scoring 92 points. Ron, always described as a reliable defender, played four City versus Country matches in the seconds and then achieved what was remarkable for an Aboriginal player in the early 1960s when he captained the NSW Colts against France in 1964. In 1967–1968 Ron played six representative games for New South Wales captaining the side on one occasion-five against Queensland and one against a touring side. It is likely that he was the first Aboriginal player to be appointed a captain of any side in any sport. In the 1967–1968 Kangaroo tour of Europe he played twelve matches for Australia but no Test matches. Photo: News Limited.

WENDELL SAILOR

Queensland seems to have an endless supply of Aboriginal and Islander rugby league champions. Born in Sarina (Qld) in 1974, Wendell Sailor represented Queensland under-19s in 1993, then joined the Brisbane Broncos in that year. This tall, strong, speedy and attacking winger played 189 games for Brisbane and 33 for St George, amassing 510 points. He played 17 matches and three Tri-series games for Queensland between 1996 and 1999, 21 Tests for Australia, five Super League Tests and twelve tour matches. Hardly a conventional player, one could always expect the unexpected from him. In 2001 he switched to rugby union. He had 47 games for the Queensland Reds, 8 for New South Wales and 37 for the Wallabies — an incredible record! He is one of three Aboriginal/Islander dual national representatives (together with **Andrew Walker (2)** and **Timana Tahu**). Photo: courtesy John Fairfax Holdings.

COLIN SCOTT

Born in Charters Towers (Qld) in 1960, Colin Scott built an impressive rugby league record. He played full-back, initially for Townsville Souths and East Brisbane, then moved to Wynnum-Manly for whom he played 131 games. Colin had a brief spell with Castleford in the United Kingdom in 1986. By the time Brisbane Broncos joined the Sydney competition his career was coming to an end: he played 14 games for the Brisbane Broncos before retiring. In a career which began in 1978 and ended in 1988 he went on three tours with Queensland (1983, 1984 and 1987), played one Test for Australia against New Zealand in 1983 and 27 games for Queensland including 18 State of Origin matches. On retirement he began a successful coaching career in Townsville. Photo: *Rugby League Week*.

DALE SHEARER

Dale Shearer had an amazing record in rugby league. Born in St George (Qld) in 1965 he began his career in 1983. In 1984 his Mackay side won the Foley Shield for the first time in two decades. At 18 he played his first game for Queensland. By 1986 he was in the national side. Always versatile, he has played 209 first grade games — as full-back, five-eighth, winger and centre for seven teams over eleven years from 1985 to 1995: with 86 games for Manly-Warringah, 27 for the Brisbane Broncos, 33 for Gold Coast, 3 for South Queensland, 14 for Widnes in the UK, 26 matches for Queensland (scoring 66 points) and 20 Tests for Australia (for 60 points). He was in Manly's 1987 premiership side. He ended that season by kicking the winning goal to clinch the State of Origin series for Queensland against New South Wales. Photo: *Rugby League Week*.

ERIC SIMMS

Eric Simms helped change the rules of rugby league. His ability to score field goals, then worth two points, caused administrators to reduce the value to one point. Born near Newcastle (NSW) in 1945, he was the brilliant full-back and superlative kicker for South Sydney from 1965 to 1975, during which time he played 206 senior games. Eric played in five consecutive grand finals from 1967 to 1971, four of them in the victorious side. He was the season's leading points scorer from 1967 to 1970. In 1969 he broke the long-standing record for most points in a season — 265, a record that lasted until broken by Michael Cronin in 1978. He played only one game for New South Wales but was selected for Australia in eight World Cup matches in 1968 and 1970. Given his skills and his reputation it is surprising that he was never chosen for a Test. Photo: *Rugby League Week*.

MATT SING

Although he grew up in the small mining town of Dysart (Qld), Matthew Charles (Matt) was born in Winton (Qld) in 1975. A small but powerful man, he began his first grade career as a winger at Penrith, then moved to the Sydney Roosters, and to the North Queensland Cowboys in 2002. He had a final stint with Hull FC in the United Kingdom, all of which enabled him to amass a total of 323 first grade games and 176 tries. From 1995, this compact athletic speedster, with a great swerve and an amazing ability to break a tackle, represented Queensland 24 times, and was capped for Australia on 15 occasions. In 2000, Sing was awarded the Australia Sports Medal for his contribution to international rugby league. Photo: Fairfax Photo Library/courtesy John Fairfax Holdings.

TIMANA TAHU

Of Barkindji heritage, Timana was born in Melbourne in 1980. He grew up in Bourke (NSW) before moving to Newcastle where he was recruited by the Knights. A strong centre and winger with quick hands, a great step and fend, Tahu was always hard to stop in broken play. He was a key member of Newcastle's 2001 premiership side, represented Australia five times and played in 12 State of Origins for NSW. His finishing ability is reflected in 121 tries in 196 first grade matches. A switch to rugby union was natural for a man of his size and speed. After 20 matches for the NSW Waratahs and four Tests for the Wallabies, he returned to rugby league. Tahu has been an outspoken opponent of racism in sport and continues to work in Aboriginal health. He now lives and coaches in Texas, having played Pro Rugby for Denver. Photo: NRL Media.

GORDEN TALLIS

This remarkable, tough, uncompromising player has brought a new excitement and dimension to the role of the forward in rugby league. Gorden Tallis was born in Townsville (Qld) in 1973. He began with Townsville Centrals and then moved to St George in 1992; he played 54 games for the Dragons until 1995. He sat out 1996 because of a dispute about his transfer to the Brisbane Broncos. He started with the latter in 1997 and by the end of 1999 he played 161 games for Brisbane Broncos by 2003. Gorden had 20 Queensland representative games, seven State of Origin and three Super league Tri-series. By the end of 1999 he had played 16 Tests for Australia and three Super League Tests. He won the Clive Churchill Medal in 1998, and was in Brisbane's Super League grand final win in 1997 and their National Rugby League grand final victory in 1998. Photo: Fairfax Photo Library/courtesy John Fairfax Holdings.

SAM THAIDAY

Of Torres Strait Islander heritage, Sam was born in Sydney (NSW) in 1985. His family moved to Townsville (Qld) where he played his junior rugby league. Signed to the Brisbane Broncos in 2002, making his first debut the following year. 'Slammin' Sam's mobility, bullocking wide running and one-on-one tackling earned him a second-row position for the 2006 State of Origin series. From that year onwards, Thaiday played 279 games for Brisbane (winning grand finalist in 2006), 34 Tests for Australia, and 29 State of Origins for Queensland. Other accolades include the Rugby League International Second-rower of the Year and the Ken Stephens Medal (both 2011). In his latter years Sam also played prop and hooker, and captained the Broncos on 46 occasions. Photo: NRL Media.

JONATHAN THURSTON

Considered by many to be the greatest player the modern game has produced, Thurston's talent, skills, vision and humility make him *the* role model for all that is great in sport. Born in Brisbane in 1983, Jonathan had trouble securing an NRL contract because of his slight stature! He only played 29 games for Canterbury before signing with the North Queensland Cowboys in 2005. Thus began the most stellar of careers: 38 Test matches, 37 State of Origin games, 299 NRL games, 2056 points, three grand finals, 11 Dally M awards, three Provan-Summons Medals, the Clive Churchill Medal, Rugby League International Half-back and Five-eighth of the Year, and RLPA Player of the Year on four occasions. Jonathan's humility, compassion and awareness for the community has had him named Queensland's Australian of the Year (2018), and awarded the Australian Human Rights Medal in 2017. Photo: Melissa Adams/Fairfax Syndication.

RICKY WALFORD

Ricky Walford may not have reached the giddy heights of several of the great Aboriginal rugby league players but in so many ways he represents the ideal player on the field. Handsome, athletic, always fair, his career spanned fifteen years, 1982 to 1986: he began with Eastern Suburbs (13 games), moved to North Sydney (10 games) and found a home with St George from 1985 onwards playing no less than 207 games for the Dragons. His representative career doesn't reflect his sterling performances in almost every match he played. Ricky, born in Walgett (NSW) in 1963, played in two City firsts and two Country Origin games and one State of Origin match in 1990. In all he played 235 matches, scoring 990 points. Ricky has spent much time working with Aboriginal youth in rural New South Wales. Photo: *Rugby League Week*.

DEAN WIDDERS

Dean's family is of the Anaiwan language group. His grandmother was one of the Stolen Generation. Widders was born in Armidale (NSW), playing his junior football as a lock-forward for **Narwan**. Brought to the Sydney Roosters in 1996, he began a first grade career that spanned 219 games (including 59 tries) quite an achievement for a big forward. Dean's quick hands, and canny ability to stand and deliver passes, saw him often stand in the five-eighth role. He had one NSW Country cap. Since retiring, Dean has coached the **Redfern All Blacks**, was an ambassador for and director of NASCA, and is currently an ambassador and Player Welfare education officer for the NRL. Widders was awarded the Ken Stephens Medal in 2004 for his work with youth in the local community. Photo: NRL Media.

REBECCA (BEC) YOUNG (ANDERSON)

Born in 1981 and raised in Newcastle (NSW), Bec is from the Worimi people of the Port Stephens region. She played rugby union from school age, and played her first game for Australia in the 2006 Women's Rugby Union World Cup — playing 5 Tests as an inside-centre. In 2007, she married Michael Young (former Newcastle Knight's full-back and hooker), which began her passion for rugby league. Young's debut as a Jillaroo was in 2011, playing 8 tests — as a front-rower and lock. She is a tireless forward who controls the ruck, and tackles like a demon for the full 80 minutes. Bec has been in 4 Indigenous All Stars teams — captaining the triumphant 2017 side. Rebecca runs a Traditional Owners company that helps inform and protect local Worimi sites. Photo: NRL Media.

CHAPTER 16
RUGBY UNION

Aboriginal connections with 15-a-side rugby union are fewer than in most other stadium sports. On the face of it, it is surprising that there is any connection. Several key factors limit Aboriginal involvement: well-to-do private schools are essentially the feeder system to senior rugby; there is class prejudice in an allegedly classless society; the nature, location and composition of clubs has made access difficult; and until 1995 rugby union was a wholly amateur game.

Rugby is said to have been invented in 1823. Seventy years later the first Aboriginal representative player was **Frank Ivory** who played for Queensland colony in 1893. The famed sports newspaper, the *Referee*, was impressed, saying that his performance was 'characterised by a fine judgment of distance and effective tackling'. In 1894 he played twice against New South Wales, in both games switching from centre to full-back. The *Referee* concluded:

The success which marked every game played by Frank Ivory is very gratifying to me, the more so because I honestly did not think he was capable of sustaining the heavy knocks, bruises and blows which it was his lot in the position of full-back. That he was game I knew, but I was quite unprepared for the brilliancy which characterised his play generally.

There is sufficient evidence to say that the 15,000 crowd gave him a rough time because he was black.

For many years it was generally believed that the first Aboriginal man to represent Australia was **Lloyd McDermott** in 1962. But research has shown that at least one of two interesting players in the 1930s was Aboriginal: **Cec Ramalli**. The other was John Howard, about whom we can find little.

In the 1930s there was a team known as Bretts-Windsor Timber Mill, a firm which gave employment to out-of-work rugby league players, and which was expelled from competition because it paid its players to play and paying players money in rugby union was then a 'hanging offence'. John Howard played for Queensland in 1937 and in 1938 for Australia in the second Test against the All Blacks. Shortly before he died, the late Joe French, former president of the Australian Rugby Union, told us that Howard was Aboriginal: 'a reasonably dark half-caste' was his phrasing. Perhaps a clue is that he was called 'Blondie'. It seems he attended St Joseph's College in Brisbane; and there is some record of his having died in a prisoner-of-war camp in Malaya.

Ramallie Nashie Deen came from Bombay. Settling in Queensland he changed his name to Nashie Deen Ramalli and married Adeline Doyle, a resident at the Aboriginal reserve that was later to become Toomelah at Boggabilla. Their son Cecil played his rugby at Sydney's Hurlstone Agricultural School. He played two Tests against New Zealand. He and John Howard were in the same 1938 second Test side. Cecil survived the infamous Fall of Singapore to the Japanese in February 1942, unduly harsh treatment as a prisoner of war on the Thai-Burma railroad and he was in Nagasaki when an atomic bomb obliterated that city. After the war he became a great coach and did much for junior rugby on Sydney's North Shore.

The man who has done so much to foster Aboriginal rugby is **Lloyd McDermott** through his Lloyd McDermott Rugby Development Team. It would take another fifteen years before the explosion of the three Ella brothers. **Glen**, **Mark** and **Gary Ella** were three of seven brothers sharing one bedroom in a La Perouse house — with one tap and one power point. They attended Marrickville High School in Sydney where they decided to play rugby and were fortunate to have the deputy principal Geoff Mould as their coach. They also had a successful role model in their older brother Rodney. Another key mentor was their uncle Bruce 'Larpa' Stewart who played rugby league for Easts in the late 1960s.

The three brothers scored 25 of the 103 tries scored by the Australian Schoolboys' side in 1977–1978, described as 'the greatest Australian rugby side, pound-for-pound and point-for-point ever to tour the United Kingdom'. John Reason, rugby's very sophisticated critic and author, wrote:

> Undoubtedly the stars of the team are the three Ella brothers, Glen, Gary and Mark. They are absolute magic as handlers and runners. Their impromptu work at close quarters, both in the use of the ball and in working round opponents was something completely beyond the experience of the England boys.

Everyone reached for new superlatives to describe the Ellas: 'thrilling footballers'; 'creators of the most spectacular tries in Australian rugby'; 'an indefinable something that urges crowds through the gate'; 'a supernatural ability to anticipate each other'. 'Bloody unfair that one team should have all three of them' said the Gordon team's coach on their 41 to 3 loss to Randwick in 1980.

Following on the Ellas, Damian Kelly, David Ross, Barry Lea and Scott Bligh played for Australian Schoolboy teams. **Lloyd Walker** played eight Tests and **Jim Williams** played 14 games for Australia. Commonwealth Games representatives at Kuala Lumpur in 1998 included Shane Drahm and Brendan Williams in sevens rugby, a side which included **Jim Williams**.

In the early years of rugby league, there was a fair amount of dual representation in league and union. But since the end of World War II, 24 men and one woman can boast of being dual internationals. Four of them are Aboriginal or Islander: **Wendell Sailor**, **Timana Tahu**, **Andrew Walker (2)** and **Bec Young**.

The outstanding player of more recent times has been **Kurtley Beale**. By the end of the 2017 season he had played 110 games for New South Wales and 71 games for the Wallabies national side. Despite some uneven seasons Kurtley has become one of the most capped national representatives in the game of rugby.

Women have now come into their own in Australian Rules football, rugby league and rugby union sevens. Teams and competitions are promoted and given media attention. As could be expected, Aboriginal women are well represented in both national and international sevens rugby. Recent players of note have been Mahalia Murphy, Taleena Simon and Tanisha Stanton.

John Howard of Brisbane played two Tests against New Zealand in 1938. It is believed that he was of Aboriginal descent.
Photo: Norman Byrne

Bruce ('Larpa') Stewart played rugby league for Easts in the late 1960s. He was a strong influence on his nephews, the Ella brothers. Photo: Fairfax Photo Library/courtesy John Fairfax Holdings

KURTLEY BEALE

Kurtley Beale was born in Blacktown (NSW) in 1989. A remarkable rugby talent, and a controversial one, by the end of 2017 Kurtley had played 71 Tests for Australia (scoring 143 points), 16 Bledisloe Cup games against New Zealand, 12 IRB Cup matches and in 28 World Championship games. A scholarship boy at St Joseph's in Sydney, Kurtley was in the Australian Schoolboys' side from 2004 to 2006. As full-back, fly-half or on the wing, and a remarkably good goal-kicker, he has played 110 games for the NSW Waratahs, and had spells with the Melbourne Rebels (2011–2013) and English club Wasps (2016). In 2011 he received the John Eales Medal, awarded to Australian rugby's best player of the year. Despite a series of personal problems and some off-field matters, he made it back into the international arena. Photo: Tim Clayton/Fairfax Syndication.

GARY ELLA

The youngest of three legendary brothers, Gary Albert Ella was born in La Perouse (NSW) in 1960. Together with his twin brothers **Mark** and **Glen** he was a major figure in the 1977–1978 Australian Schoolboys' team, considered the best team ever to play rugby union in Britain. The British press was not alone in extolling the three brothers as 'absolute magic in handling and running'. At outside centre, Gary was beautifully balanced, an efficient tackler, with superb footwork and 'smart hands'. Following several knee operations he was recalled to Randwick to notch up his 100th game for the Greens. Gary played his last two matches against Auckland and Canterbury in 1988 — at inside centre for the first time. He played in seven grand finals for Randwick, in 26 matches for NSW and six tests for Australia. Following a career with ATSIC in Bourke and then with NSW Aboriginal Affairs, he has had a long coaching career. Photo: Bret Harris.

GLEN ELLA

Glen Ella, twin brother of **Mark**, was born in La Perouse (NSW) in 1959. As members of the triumphant Australian Schoolboys' tour to Britain in 1977–1978, the Ella brothers contributed 25 of the team's 103 tour tries. Coach Geoff Mould believed Glen's best position was at full-back: 'he can see a try in any reasonable situation ... he seems to know which way to go before the ball reaches him'. He was both full-back and centre for Randwick, for whom he played ten grand finals. Glen represented NSW on 25 occasions and played four Tests for Australia. On his retirement in 1987 the press paid him great tribute: 'his easy going friendly nature has endeared him to rugby men throughout the world ... he wouldn't have a rugby enemy'. In 1994–1995 he became backline coach for the Australian Wallabies team. Later he became the technical adviser to the ACT Brumbies and coach of the Australian sevens team (which won a bronze medal at the 1998 Commonwealth Games). Photo: News Limited.

MARK ELLA, OAM

When Randwick defeated Gordon in the 1980 rugby union grand final, the losing coach grumbled it was 'bloody unfair that one team should have all three of them'. One of 'them' was Mark Gordon Ella, perhaps the most celebrated Australian rugby player in history: he was the first of seven Australians inducted into the International Rugby Hall of Fame. Born in La Perouse (NSW) in 1959, the man with marvellous hands and anticipation played five-eighth for Randwick, including eight grand finals. A key member of the Australian Schoolboys' to Britain in 1977–1978, Mark played 23 games for NSW, 26 Tests for Australia of which he was captain in nine. One critic said 'he had a brain moving at shutter speed, quicker than anyone else in the game'. He was 1983 Young Australian of the Year. After retirement he coached the Mediolanum rugby team in Italy. Photo: Fairfax Photo Library/courtesy John Fairfax Holdings.

FRANK IVORY

Frank Ivory was the first Aboriginal man to play representative football in any code. Born in Maryborough (Qld), possibly in 1872, of a Scottish father who established Eidsvold Station, and an Aboriginal mother, Frank junior attended Maryborough Grammar School — an unusual situation for an Aboriginal boy in those genocidal years in Queensland. In 1893 he played rugby union for Queensland in the side that beat New South Wales. In 1894 he again played for his state, once as full-back and once in the centre. The *Sydney Morning Herald* praised him for his 'good handling' and 'safe play'; the *Referee*, the famous sporting newspaper, lauded his 'fine judgement of distance and his effective tackling'. Given the attitudes towards 'people of colour' at the time, it is interesting to note that the Queensland XV had two 'native' players: Ivory, and the captain, who was a Māori. Photo: *Town & Country Journal*.

LLOYD McDERMOTT

Lloyd McDermott had parents with athletic ability. They were also anxious that he have a good education 'to get out of the ruck of all the usual discrimination'. Born near Eidsvold (Qld) in 1939, Lloyd went to the Church of England Grammar School in Brisbane where his talents earned him a scholarship for most of his schooling. There he suffered racial abuse and 'retaliated' by winning the school sprint championships and becoming the best all-round sportsman. He studied law at Queensland University, during which time he played ten rugby union matches on the wing for Queensland against Fiji, France and the All Blacks. In that position he played two Tests for the Wallabies against New Zealand in 1962. To finance a house he played rugby league for Wynnum-Manly in 1964. The NSW Rugby Union has established the Lloyd McDermott Rugby Development Team, a signal honour in recognition of his services. Lloyd was a barrister in Sydney. Photo: Norbert Byrne.

CECIL RAMALLI

At the turn of the 20th century Ramallie Nashie Deen came from Bombay, possibly illegally. Settling in Queensland he changed his name to Nashie Deen Ramalli (without the 'e'). He married Adeline Doyle who was resident at the Aboriginal reserve that was later to become Toomelah at Boggabilla. Their son Cecil played his rugby at Sydney's Hurlstone Agricultural School. He played two Tests against New Zealand. He and John Howard were in the same 1938 second Test side. Cecil not only survived the infamous Fall of Singapore to the Japanese in February 1942 and unduly harsh treatment as a prisoner of war on the Thai-Burma railroad, but he was in Nagasaki, fortunately a few hundred feet underground as a prisoner in a mine, when an atomic bomb obliterated that city. After the war, he became a great coach and did much for junior rugby on Sydney's North Shore. Photo: Peter Ramalli.

ANDREW WALKER (2)

The youngest of thirteen children, Andrew is from the Wiradjuri nation. Born in Bomaderry (NSW) in 1973, he joined Randwick in 1990 as a full-back and winger. His prodigious kicking skills, deft passing, and speed off the mark led to a switch of codes to rugby league in 1992. He switched back to union in 2000 to join the ACT Brumbies. Walker played an astonishing 7 Tests for the Wallabies, 56 super rugby matches, one rugby league Test match for Australia, and 145 first-grade NRL games (scoring 600 points). A series of personal problems saw Andrew play rugby in France, then return to the Queensland Reds. Andrew is now passionately working in the Aboriginal community and continues to play and coach in Ipswich (Qld). Photo: Sean Davey/Fairfax Syndication.

LLOYD WALKER

Some British critics suggested that his name was appropriate for this less than speedy rugby union centre and five-eighth. But what Lloyd lacked in speed of foot he made up for in intelligence, penetration, elusive running, speedy hands and finding holes in opponents' defence. Born in Sydney in 1959, he learned his rugby with the **Ella brothers** at Matraville High School under coach Geoff Mould. His career started with Randwick Colts in 1978 and he was in the senior team the following year. Lloyd played 161 games for Randwick — rated as possibly the best club side in world rugby — including eight grand finals. A great representative player, he had 15 games for New South Wales and 8 Tests for Australia, the last against New Zealand in Auckland in 1989. While playing for Wanderers in Dublin in 1992 he was invited to join the touring Wallabies squad. He retired in 1994. Photo: Fairfax Photo Library/courtesy John Fairfax Holdings.

JIM WILLIAMS

Born in Young (NSW) in 1968, Jim has had a long career in rugby as a national team player, a national sevens rugby player and as a coach in Australia and Ireland. Jim played for West Hartlepool in the UK, for Warringah (NSW), the ACT Brumbies, Munster in Ireland and then 74 games for the Greater Sydney Rams. He coached Munster from 2006 to 2008, then was assistant coach to the Australian national rugby union team. He has been head coach of the Greater Sydney Rams in the national rugby championship since 2015. As a player he had 14 caps for the Wallabies, played in two Bledisloe Cup matches, in one IRB World Cup and in four Rugby Cup Championships. Jim was also in the national sevens side at the Commonweal Games in Kuala Lumpur in 2008. Photo: Fairfax Photo Library/courtesy John Fairfax Holdings.

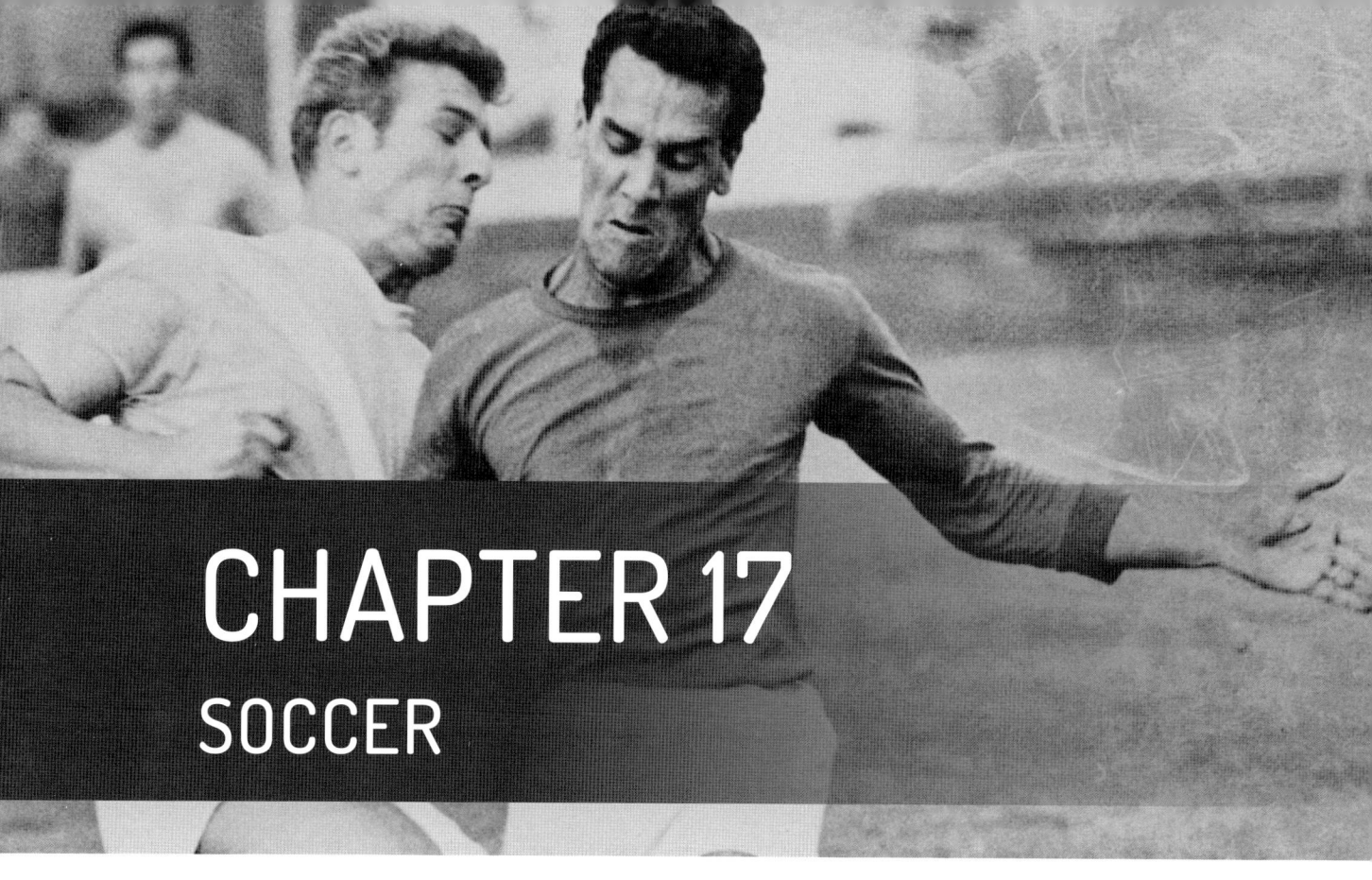

CHAPTER 17
SOCCER

Soccer, as it is often called, may have been around in China 2,000 years ago. But association football, soccer, the round ball game, or just plain 'football' — the world's most popular game as we know it — started in England in about 1863.

Why soccer has not attracted more Aboriginal or Islander people is a puzzle. It is accessible, relatively inexpensive and in **Charlie Perkins**'s experience an arena where ethnic communities have given Aboriginals a warmer welcome than have 'Anglos' in other sports. John Maynard's *The Aboriginal Soccer Tribe* (2011) analyses the subject.

Growing up in the St Francis Home in Adelaide, an assimilation institution, three 'inmates' — **John Moriarty**, **Charles Perkins** and **Gordon Briscoe** — took to soccer. Briscoe played for Preston North End in the English league while Perkins had a short career in England, mainly with an amateur side. Two Nungas from South Australia, Andy Betts and Eddy Cruse, played a few international games against New Zealand and the United States in 1983 and 1984. Until this century, only **Harry Williams** had a strong international career for Australia. One prominent soccer writer has lamented 'this incredible waste of talent'.

Recent era players of note have included Travis Dodd, Kasey Wehrman, Tahj Minniecon and **Jade North**. Tahj had a fine career in under-20 internationals. Travis represented Australia in under-17 and under-19 matches and twice played for Australia. Cloncurry-born Wehrman played for Australia in under-20 and under-23 matches and had 12 games for Australia as a senior. In the women's game, Tanya Oxtoby has been a player of some note and an outstanding coach. **Leanne Edmundson**, **Kayleen Jansen**, **Karen Menzies**, **Bridgette Starr**, **Kyah Simon** and **Lydia Williams** have been outstanding players. Lydia has had 64 caps as at the end of 2017.

Travis Dodd played eight under-17 to under-20 matches for Australia and two senior Test games. He was captain of the highly successful Adelaide team in the A-League.
Photo: Stefan Moore/Fairfax Syndication

Kasey Wehrman had 26 under-23 caps for Australia, played in 12 senior internationals, was an Olympic representative and had eight years in Norwegian soccer.
Photo: Ryan Osland/Fairfax Syndication

Kyah Simon has played a total of 130 senior games for Cenral Coast Mariners, Sydney FC and for the Boston Breakers (WPSL Elite, USA), and had 76 caps for Australia as a striker.
Photo: Cole Bennetts/Fairfax Syndication

David Williams played 234 senior games for the Queensland Roar, Brondby (Denmark), North Queensland Fury, Melbourne City and Haladas (Hungary). He has 37 junior caps and two senior caps for Australia as a striker.
Photo: Steve Christo/Fairfax Syndication

GORDON BRISCOE, AO

Born at The Bungalow institution in Alice Springs in 1938, Gordon Briscoe was removed first to Mulgoa (NSW) and then to St Francis Anglican Home in South Australia. Invited by the state under-18 team coach to play his team, the St Francis boys — including **Charles Perkins**, **John Moriarty**, Vince Copley and Gordon — beat the representative side 12–0. That quartet joined Port Thistle, with Gordon making the state's intermediate team. Gordon played both soccer and Australian football for Port Lincoln and then, with **Charles Perkins**, was in the Adelaide Croatia team that won the Ampol Cup. In England he played for Preston North End, in B and C divisions, with several first-division appearances. He helped establish the Aboriginal Medical Service in Sydney, was assistant director to Fred Hollows in the national trachoma program and then completed a Bachelors, Masters and PhD at the Australian National University. Photo: Rod Macrae/Fairfax Syndication.

LEANNE EDMUNDSON

Leanne Edmundson (now Metcalfe) spent most of her life playing championship quality indoor and outdoor soccer. Born in 1970 in Sydney, Leanne's first representation for New South Wales was in the under-15s when her team won the national title. Later came selection for the New South Wales open team and inclusion in the 1987 Australian under-18 side which made the semi-finals in the Dallas Cup in Texas. In 1988 she was in the all-age New South Wales side in a Perth carnival, whereupon she was picked for a national side that played the United States. In 1995 she played for Blacktown City Super League which is the top echelon of women's soccer. In the indoor game Leanne played for the New South Wales open team in the successful side in the 1992 national titles. She played against the visiting Canadian Indians in 1991 and was selected for the tour to Canada the following year. She also toured Canada with the national under-21 side. A shattered ankle ended her career in 1995. Photo: Leanne Edmundson.

FELICITY HUNTINGTON

A Torres Strait Islander, Felicity Huntington was born in Lae, Papua New Guinea in 1968. As a junior she played a great deal of age-representation outdoor soccer for New South Wales as well as touring New Zealand with a high schools team. She switched to indoor soccer, futsal, in 1985. In 1990 she played in the International Aboriginal Cup against the Canadian Indians both here and in Canada. She was selected for Australia's international team which toured Brazil in 1993. Reverting to the outdoor game, Felicity played sweeper for Blacktown City in the Super League in 1995 and 1996. In 1996 she retired from outdoor soccer but still plays futsal for Rooty Hill in the national competition run by the Australian Indoor Soccer Association. Felicity served with the NSW Anti-Discrimination Board. Photo: Felicity Huntington.

KAYLEEN JANSSEN

Indoor and outdoor soccer are two very different sports and it is uncommon for someone to be skilled in both. Indoor soccer, or futsal, is played five a side, with a heavier ball and in a very limited space. Kayleen Janssen has been in both versions of the game. Born in Brisbane in 1968 she was in the Australian indoor soccer squad in 1988. Her outdoor soccer career began for Queensland in 1986 and she was a regular state player from 1989 to 1995. By the end of 1995 Kayleen had represented Australia on 23 occasions, including a tour of Papua-New Guinea in 1994; she has a record of 14 official international caps. Kayleen, a midfielder, was in the Australian side that contested the World Cup in Sweden in 1995. (Australia bowed out of the strong group comprising China, the USA and Denmark.) Photo: *Queensland Times*.

KAREN MENZIES

Karen was born in Sydney in 1962. She spent her first 17 years in that city, then moved to Newcastle where she played both indoor and outdoor soccer. As indoor soccer for women was not graded as a major sport in the 1980s, she turned to the very different outdoor version in which she excelled. She had an exceptionally long career playing for Northern New South Wales from 1977 to 1991 and was chosen for Australia in three Oceania Cups — in 1983, 1986 and 1989 — for a total of seven international caps. Karen has coached the first division and reserve Newcastle regional teams and in 1995 was assistant coach to the national team that played in the World Cup in Denmark. (**Kayleen Janssen** was a member of that side.) Karen made her career in the public service. Photo: Karen Menzies.

JOHN MORIARTY, AM

John graduated from Flinders University a few years after his kinsman **Charles Perkins**. Like **Wally McArthur**, he was born in the Northern Territory, at Borroloola on the McArthur River in 1938, and moved to a succession of assimilation homes. It was at St Francis's Home in Adelaide that he and fellow inmates **Briscoe**, **McArthur** and **Perkins** turned to sport. John began his soccer career in South Australia with Port Thistle, Port Adelaide, Croatia, International United and Juventus. He then moved on to Prague in New South Wales. He played 17 games for South Australia and was the first Aboriginal player to be chosen for Australia on a tour to Asia, which regrettably was cancelled. After a long public service career he became a successful owner of the Balarinji design company, initially famous for decorating the Qantas 747 jumbo with Aboriginal motifs. In 2000 he was honoured for his political advocacy on behalf of Aboriginal and Torres Strait Islanders and his contribution to Aboriginal culture. Photo: *Advertiser*.

JADE NORTH

Born at Taree (NSW) in 1982, Jade North began his soccer career at the age of 6. After a spell in Queensland soccer he was awarded an AIS scholarship. Honours have followed at an astonishing rate. He played in the finals of the under-17 World Championships, had 17 appearances for the Qantas Joeys, six for the Young Socceroos, 20 for the Australian under-23 side and by the end of 2008 had played 22 games for the national Socceroos. Chosen for the 2004 Athens Olympics, he was selected as one of the over-age (over 23) players in the Beijing Olympics. With great speed, agility and air play, he has been in five national soccer grand final winning teams: Olympic Sharks (2001, 2002), Perth Glory (2003, 2004) and the Newcastle Jets in 2008, the team he captained to victory. He and Travis Dodd captained A-League sides in 2008. Photo: Tim Clayton/Fairfax Syndication.

CHARLES PERKINS, AO

A major figure in Aboriginal and Islander affairs from the early 1960s, Charles was born at the Old Telegraph Station, Alice Springs in 1936. At St Francis's Home in Adelaide he developed an interest in soccer, the sport which gave him his start in life. Playing at an away match in Oxford, he was inspired to gain a university qualification. It was soccer that paid his way through Sydney University and gave him the confidence needed to fight for Aboriginal and Islander advancement, whether through pressure group organisations, freedom rides in New South Wales (to help break the colour bar in social amenities) in the 1960s, as permanent Secretary of the [then] federal Department of Aboriginal Affairs and as Deputy Chairman of ATSIC. Charles played for Budapest and Croatia (both SA), Pan-Hellenic (NSW), and Bishop Auckland (UK). He played a number of games for South Australia and was involved in Aboriginal sport and soccer administration. Photo: *Australian Soccer Weekly*.

JADE NORTH

Born at Taree (NSW) in 1982, Jade North began his soccer career at the age of 6. After a spell in Queensland soccer he was awarded an AIS scholarship. Honours have followed at an astonishing rate. He played in the finals of the under-17 World Championships, had 17 appearances for the Qantas Joeys, six for the Young Socceroos, 20 for the Australian under-23 side and by the end of 2008 had played 22 games for the national Socceroos. Chosen for the 2004 Athens Olympics, he was selected as one of the over-age (over 23) players in the Beijing Olympics. With great speed, agility and air play, he has been in five national soccer grand final winning teams: Olympic Sharks (2001, 2002), Perth Glory (2003, 2004) and the Newcastle Jets in 2008, the team he captained to victory. He and Travis Dodd captained A-League sides in 2008. Photo: Tim Clayton/Fairfax Syndication.

CHARLES PERKINS, AO

A major figure in Aboriginal and Islander affairs from the early 1960s, Charles was born at the Old Telegraph Station, Alice Springs in 1936. At St Francis's Home in Adelaide he developed an interest in soccer, the sport which gave him his start in life. Playing at an away match in Oxford, he was inspired to gain a university qualification. It was soccer that paid his way through Sydney University and gave him the confidence needed to fight for Aboriginal and Islander advancement, whether through pressure group organisations, freedom rides in New South Wales (to help break the colour bar in social amenities) in the 1960s, as permanent Secretary of the [then] federal Department of Aboriginal Affairs and as Deputy Chairman of ATSIC. Charles played for Budapest and Croatia (both SA), Pan-Hellenic (NSW), and Bishop Auckland (UK). He played a number of games for South Australia and was involved in Aboriginal sport and soccer administration. Photo: *Australian Soccer Weekly*.

BRIDGETTE STARR

Bridgette always wanted to be a soccer star, and she certainly achieved that. Born in Tamworth (NSW) in 1975, Bridgette was in the Australian youth team that won the 1993 Dana Cup in Denmark and she was in the Australian youth team tour in New Zealand 1994. That was a good year for Bridgette: she made her debut for Australia playing in a one-off test match against Japan, one she regarded as one of the biggest of her life. She was a member of the Australian team that won two Oceania football nations cups (1994 in Papua New Guinea, and in 1998). She played in the 1999 FIFA Women's World Cup and was in the Sydney Olympic Games where Australian drew one match and lost two. Bridgette played in several series in the United States. Her regular team was the Sapphires. Photo: Australian Women's Soccer Association.

HARRY WILLIAMS

Harry was the first Aboriginal soccer star to take the field for Australia. Born in Sydney in 1951, he began his sporting life at the age of 9 with the St George Police Boys' Club. He rose through the ranks of St George Budapest and in 1970 was picked for the national side that undertook a world tour. He was a brilliant left back, with tremendous acceleration. Local pundits felt he would have been a sensation in European soccer, at home among them as people and at home with their style of play. In the mid-1980s he was still running professionally. He played for St George and for Canberra City between 1970 and 1980, and in that period — despite serious illness — he gained seventeen representative caps for Australia and played in six World Cup matches. Photo: News Limited.

LYDIA WILLIAMS

Regarded as one of the best female goalkeepers in the world, Lydia was born in Katanning (WA) in 1988. Her father, who was a tribal elder in the Kalgoorlie region, worked and preached in remote Aboriginal communities. A move to Canberra (ACT), enabled Lydia to pursue her two passions: zoology and soccer. She is now a qualified zoo-keeper and has kept goal for Australia on 64 occasions. Lydia has played a further 140 first-grade matches for Canberra United, Melbourne City, Pitea IF (Sweden), Western New York Flash (USA), Houston Dash (USA), and the Seattle Reign (USA). An outspoken proponent for better pay for women players, Williams is a character who provides guidance and leadership from behind for her teams. Photo: Jeffrey Chan/Fairfax Syndication.

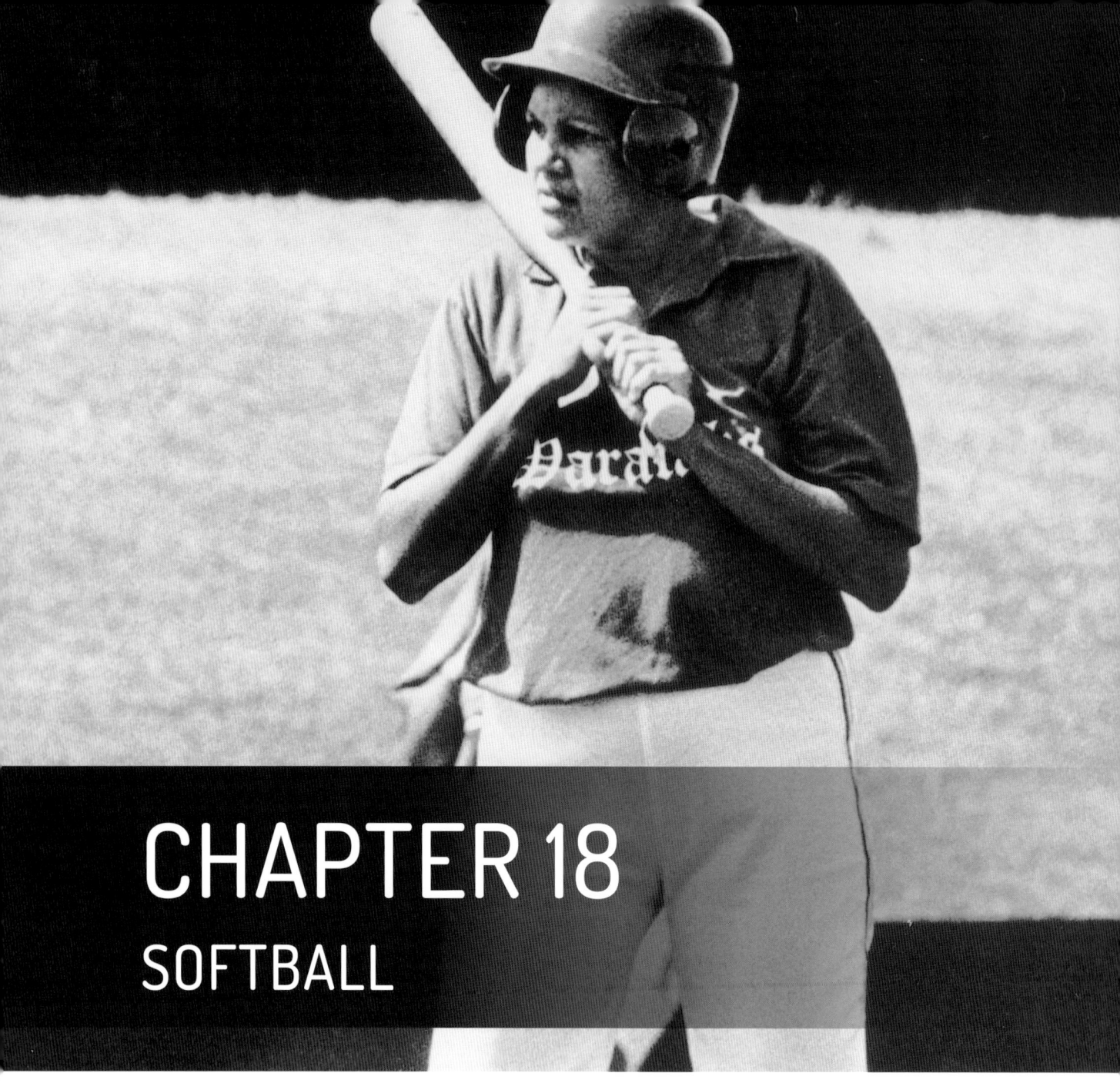

CHAPTER 18
SOFTBALL

Invented in the United States in 1887 — and once known as kitten ball, pumpkin ball and diamond ball — softball derives from its parent sport, baseball. The game was introduced into Australia in 1939. It requires less space, a bigger ball, and is a faster game, with 9-a-side, it is played essentially by New Zealand, Australia, China, the United States, Japan and several European countries.

Australia has come a long way in the sport, winning bronze in the women's event at three Olympiads (Atlanta, Sydney and Beijing) and a silver at Athens. Australian women have won the world championship twice — in 1965 and 1998. Aussie Spirit, as the women's team is known, is one of the country's most successful sporting teams. The men's team, the Aussie Steelers, was ranked fourth in the world in 2017.

JEFF GOOLAGONG

Playing in the Australian Capital Territory, Jeff was twice a world championship player. As a member of the ACT team, he was in their winning side in 2001, 2003, 2006–2009, and 2012 in the **Australian** Open men's championship. In 2012, Jeff was awarded best player in the John Reid Shield grand final. At the 2006 International Softball Congress Tournament, Jeff was selected in the All World Second Team as an outfielder. In 2008 he was in the Australian team that defeated New Zealand to win the Pacific International Series. His most significant achievement was in 2009 at the XIIth ISF men's world championship when the Aussie Steelers became world champions. In a fine career, Jeff played 109 games for Australia. Jeff is a nephew of **Evonne Goolagong-Cawley**. Photo: Softball Australia.

DONNA HUNTER

Donna is one of a quintet of outstanding all-rounders from the Northern Territory. She joins **Rose Damaso**, **Louisa Collins**, **Karmi Dunn** and **Nova Peris** as a member of an all-sport, all-star cast. Born in Darwin in 1957, Donna was named Player of the Decade (the 1970s) in Territory softball. She was a regular representative of both Darwin and the Territory in the national competitions. Donna played A-grade hockey and senior netball and won best and fairest in all three of her chosen sports. Donna also turned her skills to basketball and was a key member of the Aboriginal women's basketball team that toured New Zealand in 1975. Her sporting distinction is not so much that she played four different sports but that she played all four simultaneously in a season. Donna had a long career with the ATSIC office in Darwin. Photo: *NT News*.

SHANE KING

Shane lists his long-term goal as 'seeing men's softball overtaking the women's game'. Born in Mt Isa (Qld) in 1967, he may well achieve that goal single-handed. His first club team was in Mt Isa in 1987. He played for several Canadian clubs from 1992 to 1993, then for Queensland under-age and open teams as a short stop and utility man for seven years. In 1992 and 1996 he played eleven games for Australia in the World Men's Open in Manila and Michigan respectively. He has co-captained Australia in these events and was captain of the national team that played in the World Men's Open in South Africa in 2001. He was named a member of All-World teams in the International Softball Congress competition. He is an accredited coach of both men's and women's teams. For good measure, he has played touch and under-15 rugby league for North Queensland. Photo: Shane King.

JOANNE LESIPUTTY

Joanne has the distinction of being a dual Australian representative: in softball and indoor cricket. For good measure, she was a champion basketballer and netballer. Born in Murwillumbah (NSW) in 1966, Joanne was selected for Australia in the 2nd Youth Girls World Championships in the United States in 1985. There she was voted most valuable player in the national side. She was elevated to the national senior team for the South Pacific Classic in Melbourne in 1985, played in that event in New Zealand in 1986, in the 1989 series against New Zealand, for the Bicentennial Challenge in 1988, and the Intercontinental Cup held in Italy in 1989. Joanne also played indoor cricket for New South Wales for three seasons and for Australia in 1989. If that were not enough, she was captain of the ACT under-18 basketball team in 1984 and played netball for the all-Aboriginal team which toured the Cook Islands in 1987. Photo: Joanne Lesiputty.

SHANE KING

Shane lists his long-term goal as 'seeing men's softball overtaking the women's game'. Born in Mt Isa (Qld) in 1967, he may well achieve that goal single-handed. His first club team was in Mt Isa in 1987. He played for several Canadian clubs from 1992 to 1993, then for Queensland under-age and open teams as a short stop and utility man for seven years. In 1992 and 1996 he played eleven games for Australia in the World Men's Open in Manila and Michigan respectively. He has co-captained Australia in these events and was captain of the national team that played in the World Men's Open in South Africa in 2001. He was named a member of All-World teams in the International Softball Congress competition. He is an accredited coach of both men's and women's teams. For good measure, he has played touch and under-15 rugby league for North Queensland. Photo: Shane King.

JOANNE LESIPUTTY

Joanne has the distinction of being a dual Australian representative: in softball and indoor cricket. For good measure, she was a champion basketballer and netballer. Born in Murwillumbah (NSW) in 1966, Joanne was selected for Australia in the 2nd Youth Girls World Championships in the United States in 1985. There she was voted most valuable player in the national side. She was elevated to the national senior team for the South Pacific Classic in Melbourne in 1985, played in that event in New Zealand in 1986, in the 1989 series against New Zealand, for the Bicentennial Challenge in 1988, and the Intercontinental Cup held in Italy in 1989. Joanne also played indoor cricket for New South Wales for three seasons and for Australia in 1989. If that were not enough, she was captain of the ACT under-18 basketball team in 1984 and played netball for the all-Aboriginal team which toured the Cook Islands in 1987. Photo: Joanne Lesiputty.

KELLY MCKELLAR-NATHAN

Kelly was born in Brisbane in 1973 and began playing softball at 7. With lightning speed, natural talent and a great deal of determination, Kelly was a member of the Australian under-19 team in 1991. She made her international open debut in 1992, but was then dropped from the Queensland senior team the same year. Opportunity came with a three-year scholarship to Oklahoma City University. Returning a much stronger player, her strong switch hitting propelled her into the national senior team which had an historic victory over the United States in the Superball Tournament. Kelly was most valuable player in Queensland's victory over New South Wales in the 1998 grand final. Kelly played over 100 internationals for Australia, 32 of them in 1999. A sport and recreation adviser, her goal is to be a role model for Aboriginal and Islander players. Photo: Softball Australia.

STACEY PORTER

Stacey was born in Tamworth (NSW) in 1982. She played for New South Wales in Australian national competitions and won several national championships as a member of the junior and senior teams. Stacey was in the University of Hawaii team from 2001 to 2003, set several records and was named in the All-American team. She plays professional softball in Japan. Stacey played in the 2004 Athens Olympics, winning a silver medal and the 2008 Beijing Olympics where she won a bronze. She also won a gold medal at the world championships. At the 2009 World Cup of Softball, Australia won the silver. Stacey captained the national side at the 2010 world championships in Venezuela, and was in the national team in 2011. In 2012 she played in test series against the Japan women's national softball team in Canberra. Photo: Sam Donkin/Softball Australia

CHAPTER 19
SQUASH

Squash evolved from an English game called 'rackets'. It developed at Harrow School in England with boys hitting a squeezable ball against a wall rather than over a net. It was an upper-class activity and it accompanied British officials and soldiers to the Asian colonies in the days of the Empire. The famous Khan dynasty in what is today's Pakistan started out as 'ball boys' and cleaners, playing after hours. They went on to rule the squash world for decades. Hashim Khan was the 'daddy' of them all, and his cousins included the legendary Jahangir Khan, Jahingir's father Rosham, and brother Tosam.

Australia has produced outstanding players, with men like Geoff Hunt, Cam Nancarrow and Chris Dittmar at the top of the world. In the women's game, Heather McKay won 16 consecutive British Opens from 1962 to 1977 and was rated not only the best player in history but possibly Australia's greatest sports achiever.

There are only three Aboriginal players of note in squash: **Steve Bowditch**, **Adam Schreiber** and Paul Bushel.

STEVE BOWDITCH

Steve Mangirri Bowditch is the son of a well-known newspaper editor and a descendant of the Central Australian Arabuna tribe. Born in Darwin in 1955, Steve had an outstanding career in international squash. He represented the Northern Territory and the Australian Junior team in 1973, the Australian professional team in 1978 and captained that team in 1981. His victories included the NSW Junior title; the Victorian, Koln, Jenfeld, Danish, Austrian, Biarritz, Indonesian, Jardines and Cleveland Opens; the World Individual Championship, Sweden, 1981 and the US Open Pro Softball title in 1985. He achieved a ranking of no. 2 junior in Australia in 1973, no. 9 in the world in 1981 and no. 2 in US squash in 1986. Australia's greatest squash champion Geoff Hunt regards Bowditch as the 'most talented racquet skills player ever'. Champion Jonah Barrington described Bowditch being at his best 'when he is totally uninhibited ... when he is free, he plays gloriously'. Photo: Steve Bowditch.

ADAM SCHREIBER

Adam Schreiber and **Steve Bowditch** are the two Aboriginal men who have achieved top honours in this sport. Adam was born in Sydney in 1968. He had an outstanding career as a junior: he was in the Australian under-19 tour to New Zealand, represented Australia in the World Junior Titles in 1986 and won the NSW Junior Open title every year from 1982 to 1987. Adam won the South Pacific Open in 1981 and 1983, and a further five international events between 1986 and 1990. His best ranking as a junior was fourth in the world in 1986; he achieved number one ranking in New South Wales, seventh in Australia, and 25th in the world in 1990. Photo: Bill Schreiber.

CHAPTER 20
TENNIS

Apart from the magnificent **Evonne Goolagong-Cawley and Ashleigh Barty** nearly a half-century later, there has been little achievement. Lee Madden was a most promising junior tennis player who won a New South Wales North Coast Open and competed for a while on the European circuit. **Evonne Goolagong-Cawley**'s brother Ian was good enough to win a tennis scholarship to a Texas university and to play in the satellite tours in America and Europe for two years. He joined his sister in the mixed doubles at Wimbledon in 1982. Again there was and is an access problem: while practically every country town could boast one usable tennis court, we have yet to see a tennis court in any specifically Aboriginal community. Evonne has established a foundation, but like many other sports, there is no noticeable drive by Tennis Australia to recruit young Aboriginal players.

Lee Madden won a NSW North Coast Open and played tennis in the European circuit for a while. Photo: *Abnews*

ASHLEIGH BARTY

In recent times Ashleigh Barty, a cricketer and tennis player, has reached the top rungs of women's tennis. In 2017 she was awarded the John Newcombe Medal for the Most Outstanding Australian Player of the Year and was ranked 17th in the world. Born in Ipswich (Qld) in 1996 to a Ngarigo father and an English mother, Ashleigh became a professional at 15. Her greatest achievement as a junior was winning the Wimbledon Girls' title in 2011. In 2014 she took a break from tennis, switched to cricket in 2015, earning a contract with the Brisbane Heat for the inaugural Women's Big Bash League. In 2016 she returned to tennis and by 2017 Ashleigh had won one WTA and four ITF titles, earning over a million dollars in prizemoney. She has had notable success in doubles and mixed doubles events. Photo: Australian Sports Commission Image Library.

EVONNE GOOLAGONG-CAWLEY, AC, AO, MBE

Born in Griffith (NSW) in 1951, of Wiradjuri descent, and raised in Barellan, Evonne Goolagong-Cawley is possibly the most distinguished Aboriginal sportsperson. Critics and opponents loved her for both the joy and genius with which she competed. London's Rex Bellamy wrote of her: 'wonderfully gifted … with a swift grace of balanced movement, an instinctive tactical brain, a flexible repertoire of strokes, and an equable temperament'. She won seventeen state titles, three Australian Hardcourt championships (1970–1972), the Australian singles four times (1974–1976, 1978), the French Open in 1971, the Italian in 1973 and the South African in 1977. Evonne won three Virginia Slims events and crowned a great career with two Wimbledon Singles titles — beating Margaret Court in 1971 as Ms Goolagong and Chris Evert-Lloyd in 1980 as Mrs Cawley. Her only 'failure' was in the United States singles title, an event in which she was runner-up on four occasions. The centre court at the new International Tennis Centre at Homebush, Sydney is named The Evonne Goolagong Court. Photo: Ern McQuillan Jr.

CHAPTER 21
TOUCH FOOTBALL/OZTAG

Touch, which is also known as touch football, is clearly the fastest growing sport in Australia and international competition is burgeoning. A variant of rugby league, tackling has been replaced by touching. It is a thrilling sport that allows people of all ages to participate. It is one of few sports that allows for mixed gender teams in competition. Touch football has some 700,000 registered members and an additional 500,000 children participating in school programs and related activities.

Stephen Prince, brother of **Scott Prince**, played touch football for Australia from 2013 to 2015.

Oztag is now a popular variant. It is played eight-a-side on a somewhat smaller rugby field. Players wear shorts with a velcro patch that holds a small piece of cloth, called a tag. When an opponent pulls off the tag of the player holding the ball, he or she has to release it. Like touch and the other rugby codes. The object is to score tries. The Australian team is called, unsurprisingly, the Tagaroos.

Oztag has burgeoned as a sport for Aboriginal and Islander players — so much so that there are now separate Indigenous Oztag teams that compete in the World Cup (2012 and 2015), and the Oceania Cup (2012 and 2014). Fifteen team competed in the 2015 World Cup in Mooloolaba (Qld), and an even bigger contingent went to the 2018 Coffs Harbour (NSW) cup.

Australian representatives include **Cliff Lyons**, Jason Hardy, and Jeff Hardy (who runs the South East Sydney and Indigenous Oztag organisations with his wife Anne). A host of NRL players have played for the Indigenous team: **Cliff Lyons**, John Simon, Craig Simon, Mark Simon, Rod Silva, **Nathan Blacklock**, Darryl Trindall, **Andrew Walker (2)**, Dennis Moran, Beau Mundine, Will Robinson, and Jeff Hardy.

Current Wallaby rugby sevens sensation Maurice Longbottom has played Oztag for both the Australian and the Indigenous teams. Tiarna Mason, the current NSW under-20 400 m girls champion, has also been a member of both teams.

BO DE LA CRUZ

The charismatic dual internationalist was born in Darwin (NT) in 1981 and raised there. Like four other Territory women in this Hall, she excelled at several sports simultaneously. Bo began playing touch football at 12. Selected for the Australian under-18s in 1998, Bo won the most valuable player award at the national titles in 2000. The following year, de la Cruz joined the open team and later was vice-captain of the team that won the 2003 and 2007 World Cup titles. Not resting on her laurels, Bo switched codes to rugby sevens in 2008. She was a vital member of the triumphant 2009 World Cup team, and the 2011 and 2012 IRB Challenge Cups. Bo helps run the Palmerston Girls Academy in Darwin. Both Bo and **Shane Frederiksen** have All Stars teams named after them. Photo: Marco Del Grande/Fairfax Syndication.

SHANE FREDERIKSEN

Shane's playing style is exciting, unpredictable and undisciplined in the sense of being unmachine-like, often flamboyant. Born in 1966 in Townsville (Qld), Shane has reached the highest pinnacles of the fast-growing sport of touch (originally known as touch football). His playing career began in 1993 in the National Championships, which later became the National Touch League. His first of many State of Origin matches for New South Wales was in 1995. Shane has played in two Trans-Tasman Tests, in 1997 and 1998, followed by the highest pinnacle of the sport, representing Australia in the World Cup Mixed in 1995 and the World Cup Men's in 1999. The Australian Touch Association rates him as 'brilliant beyond what one expects of brilliance', often 'freakish' and 'one of the better players in the world'. Photo: Peter Topp, Australian Touch Association.

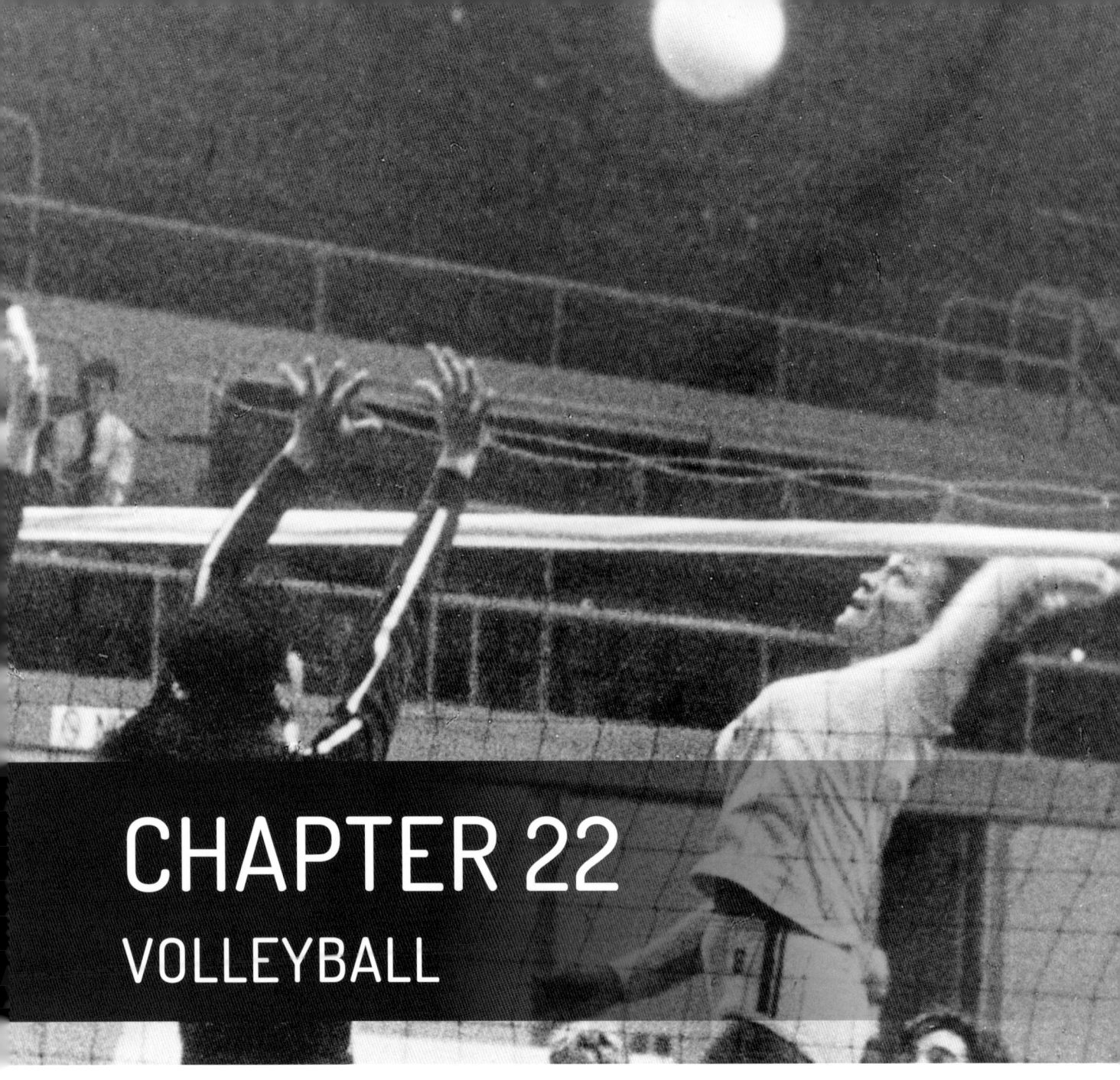

CHAPTER 22
VOLLEYBALL

In 1895, an American physical educationist created a new game called *mintonette* as an indoor pastime, one less rough than basketball. With a net 6 ft 6 in (1.98 m) high, a match consisted of nine innings, with three serves for each team in each inning. This was the game that was to became known, and admired, as volleyball.

The **Tutton** brothers created a special record when all three played in the national volleyball side (of six) in the 1983 Asian Championships. Again, it is surprising that Aboriginal and Torres Strait Islanders have not tuned to this accessible sport in greater numbers but not as surprising as the apparent Aboriginal lack of interest in outdoor soccer, at least by men.

Taliqua Clancy played in the Australian beach volleyball team at the Rio Olympics in 2016.

SHARON FIREBRACE

Sent to a home at the age of 6, 'and pushed out at 16', Sharon (*right*) did it all the hard way. Multiple jobs enabled this young woman, born in Echuca (Vic.) in 1953, to complete an Education Diploma and a Bachelor of Education. An excellent swimmer and top school athlete, she represented Victoria and Australia in under-age basketball teams. Sharon's major sport was volleyball, and in that arena she was in Victorian and Australian senior sides in 1968 and 1969. In the latter year she was voted best player in the national side. A business consultant, Sharon was an ATSIC Councillor for the Tumbukka region in Victoria and in 2000 was appointed chair of the national Indigenous Land Corporation. (Her sister Shirley is pictured left.) Photo: Sharon Firebrace.

DELMA SMITH

Delma (centre front) was — like **Louisa Collins**, **Rose Damaso**, **Donna Hunter**, **Karmi Dunn**, **Bo de la Cruz** and **Joanne Lesiputty** — an outstanding all-rounder: field athlete, netballer, basketballer, and volleyballer. Born in Quirindi (NSW) in 1965, her first achievement was to win the Australian junior long jump championship in 1977. In 1987 she toured the Cook Islands with an all-Aboriginal netball team. Team mates included **Joanne Lesiputty** and **Marcia Ella**. In the mid 1980s she became one of Australia's best volleyball players. In the under-21 World Championships in Italy in 1985, she was voted Australia's best player. Later that year she was selected for the senior national side and played in the World Qualifying Championships. A strong woman, Delma was a rare asset: she was a left-handed spiker, considered an advantage in this sport. At the end of her volleyball career, she turned to top basketball in Canberra. Photo: Delma Smith.

THE TUTTON BROTHERS

The most remarkable feat of Aboriginal families in sport has been in volleyball: the Tutton brothers achieved something rare — they formed one half of the national volleyball team in the Asian Championships in 1983. **Steve**, *left*, born in Darwin in 1960, was in the South Australian junior and youth side from 1976 to 1978, the South Australian senior side from 1978 to 1990, and the Australian senior side from 1982 to 1988. Steve captained Australia from 1982 to 1986, and again in 1988. He was manager of the Australian beach volleyball team at the 1996 Olympic Games. Brother **Reg**, *centre*, born in Darwin in 1964, was selected for the Australian junior side in 1982, and was in the senior team in 1983. **Mark**, *right*, is the middle brother, born in Darwin in 1962. He was in the South Australian junior and youth sides from 1978 to 1982, the Australian senior team from 1979 to 1990, touring India, China, Indonesia, Japan, Italy, Iran and Fiji. He played in the World Championships Qualification Tournament in Greece in 1986. Photo: *Advertiser*.

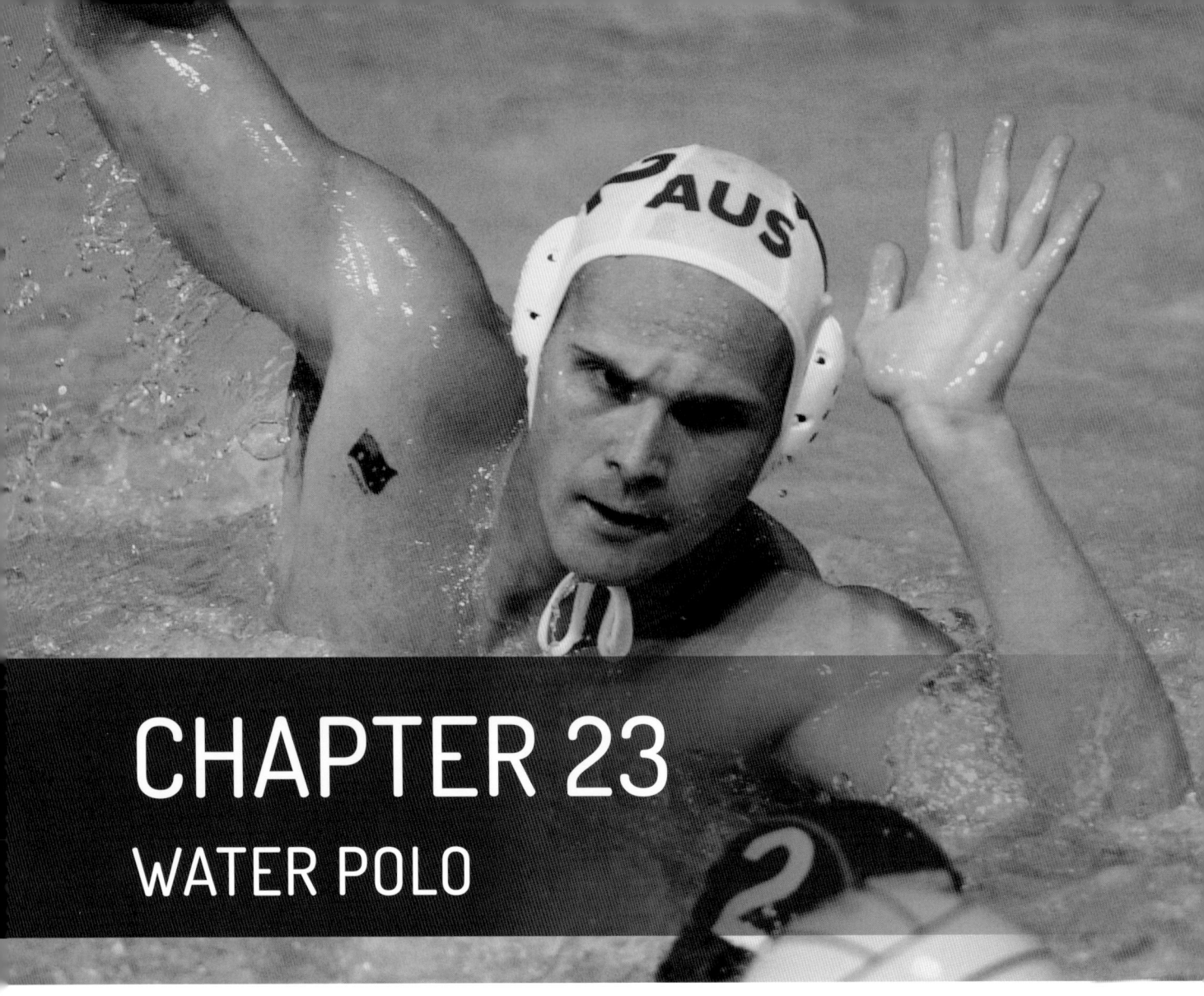

CHAPTER 23
WATER POLO

The sport is said to have originated in Scotland in the late nineteenth century. It was described as 'water handball', 'aquatic football' and even 'water rugby'. An Olympic event, it is played by two teams of seven-a-side, with four quarters of eight minutes each.

The sport can be rough and tough and one particular match is well-cemented into the history books. During the Cold War, Hungary beat the Soviet Union in the final 4–0 at the 1956 Melbourne Olympics, a match known as 'Blood in the Water'.

Known as 'the sharks', the Australian men's team first competed internationally at the 1948 London Olympics, was placed fifth in two Olympic Games, at Los Angeles in 1984 and Barcelona in 1992. Australia has placed fourth in a world championship (Perth 1998).

Few Aboriginal players were prominent before the advent of **Dean Semmens**, Nathan Thomas and Joel Swift. Joel, from Western Australia, made his Olympic debut in the 2016 Rio games. Gavin Clark played for South Australia from 1976 to 1990. Ron May was of championship standard in New South Wales in the 1980s. Other players of some note in the 1990s were Jessica Whaler, Kelly Denner, Ben Denner and Ashley Anderson.

DEAN SEMMENS

Born and raised in Balmain, Sydney in 1979, Dean is of Wiradjuri descent. He began his career with the Australian team in 1997 as a 17-year-old and was a member of the national side for the remarkable period of nine years, a long time in a tough sport. Dean played over 150 games for his country and retired after a series of operations. He captained the Australian junior men's team that won the silver medal in the 1999 World Championships. An injury kept him out of the Sydney 2000 Olympics but he played in the 2004 Athens Olympics where Australia placed ninth. He also played in the World Championships in Barcelona in 2003. Dean also played professionally for Sant Andreu in Spain. Photo: Dean Semmens.

NATHAN THOMAS

Born in August 1972, Nathan calls Sydney home but was born and breed in Tamworth (NSW). He began his extensive career at Tamworth High School and captained the Australian School Boys team to victory in a TransTasman series. Invited to attend the Australian Institute of Sport in 1991, Nathan was then selected to the Australian team in 1993 and was a member of the historic World Cup bronze medal winning team that year. He represented Australia in over 350 games, participating in four world championships, two World Cups, two World Student Games and two Olympic Games (Sydney 2000 and Athens 2004 as captain). He played four seasons with Club Natacio Barcelona in Spain and was the first Australian to be a member of European club title winning team. On retirement Nathan continued playing for Sydney University; he coaches, volunteers and nurtures his daughters as strong competitors. Photo: Barry Smith/Fairfax Syndication.

CHAPTER 24
WOODCHOPPING

Woodchopping has been a serious activity for centuries and in several cultures. Contestants attempt to be the first to cut or saw through a log or other block of wood. There are a number of distinct and differing events: standing block, underhand, tree felling, single saw, double saw, hot saw and so on. Different axes are used for different woods. The venues are usually state fairs and agricultural shows.

Woodchopping began in Tasmania and it is fitting that the Axeman's Hall of Fame is located in that state. **Greg Lovell**'s achievements are described below. His brother Gary was not far behind his achievements having represented Australia in New Zealand and Tasmania for several years. Sport is clearly a family tradition: Greg's son Andrew played Australian football for North Melbourne and West Coast Eagles.

LEO APPO

Leo was born in Tweed Heads (NSW), possibly in 1900. He was a great axeman in a time of severe discrimination. In 1922 he was advised to enter the Royal Easter Show championships as a New Zealander — in the belief that there was less prejudice against that label. Appo won numerous events at Royal Easter Shows in Sydney between 1920 and 1929, as well as a Commonwealth championship in 1928 for the 15 inch (38 cm) log, standing erect, in 60 seconds. He won £40 and his money and gold medal were awarded amid great applause by Lady Stonehaven, the Governor-General's wife. In 1931 the critics ranked him third in Australia. He was described as 'a dark-skinned, beautifully proportioned axeman ... a thoroughly scientific chopper and showman [who] rarely made a mistake'. His 'graceful style, coupled with his all-round ability, made him an attraction wherever he appeared'. Appo held the world record for tree-felling and for the 15 inches underhand event. He was active until 1948. Photo: Royal Agricultural Society of NSW.

GREG LOVELL

There is still a pervasive myth that there are no Aboriginals left in the island state of Tasmania. Woodchopping as a sport began in Tasmania in 1874 and it is both ironic and fitting that an Aboriginal axeman should be the state's undoubted hero figure. Greg was born in Franklin (Tas.) in 1952. He has held no less than 400 Tasmanian, 45 Australian and 16 world woodchopping titles. In 1980 he achieved an extraordinary feat at the Sydney Royal Easter Show: he broke four world records in one event, winning two world underhand and two world standing block titles. His brother Gary was also a champion axeman and his son, Anthony (Andy), played 121 games of Australian football for Melbourne between 1988 and 1995 and 43 for West Coast Eagles between 1996 and 1998. Photo: Greg Lovell.

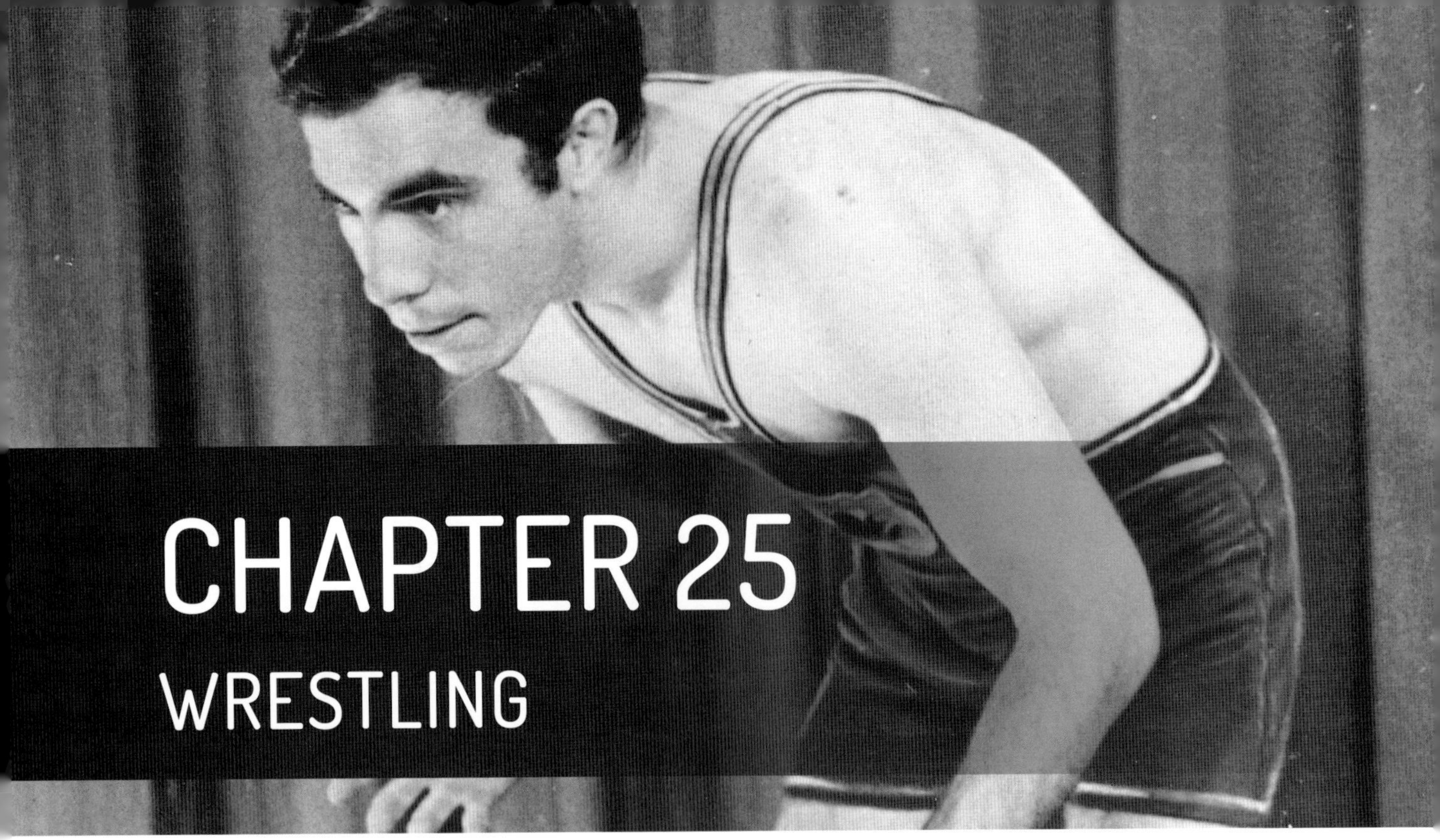

CHAPTER 25
WRESTLING

Wrestling dates back to some 15,000 years ago. Ancient Greek and Roman documents and sculptures inform us of the prominence and importance of this form of combat. Several West African nations developed their own forms of wrestling long before any colonial occupations.

There are several forms of combat wrestling apart from show wrestling as an entertainment: folk wrestling, freestyle wrestling, Turkish oil wrestling, and Greco-Roman wrestling. The latter has been the form used from the start of the modern Olympics in 1896.

Wrestling is not a commonplace activity and recruits tend to come from some gyms, especially the Police Boys' Clubs.

By 2008 there was one Aboriginal wrestler on the national and international scene: **John Kinsella**. As boxing has declined Aboriginal athletes have turned to mixed martial arts, forms of kickboxing and, it would seem, wrestling. **Shane Parker** is now in this Hall and in the next update of members there will doubtless be place for Stevie Kelly, a young lady from Katherine (NT) who has represented Australia at a Commonwealth Games in the 63 kg category. She is also an Australian judo champion.

Stevie Kelly
Photo: Robert Leeson/Newspix

JOHN KINSELLA

Born in Surry Hills (NSW) in 1949, of Wiradjuri and Jawoyn descent, John was until recently the only Aboriginal wrestler of note. Taken by his father to the Police Boys' Club in Leichhardt to learn boxing, he was asked to stand in for the local wrestling champion's missing opponent. There was to be no going back, with John winning the Australian flyweight championship in 1968, 1972 and 1975. Wrestling is lucky if it gets three places out of ten weight divisions in the national contingent. To make the three is a badge of great distinction. John achieved a rare feat: he represented Australia at two Olympic Games — in Mexico in 1968 and Munich in 1972. He also wrestled for Australia at the World Championships in Istanbul in 1974. In between, so to speak, he served in the Australian forces in Vietnam. Photo: John Kinsella.

SHANE PARKER

Shane (*on top*) was raised in the poor and rough outer western suburb of Sydney, Mt Druitt. Weighing only 57 kg, he took up Greco-Roman wrestling, and became the first Aboriginal wrestler to represent Australia at the Commonwealth Games, coming fifth in the 55 kg class at Delhi in 2010. He later fought at the 2014 Glasgow Games in the 57 kg freestyle class. In 2014, Parker switched to the more brutal mixed martial arts (MMA) arena — billed as 'Showtime'. To date he has won three and lost three of his professional bouts. Shane has been a practitioner and teacher of the ancient Aboriginal sport of coreeda — a mix of dance, wrestling, and martial arts — much like the Brazilian capoeira. Photo: Kate Geraghty/Fairfax Syndication.

ADDENDUM I
OLYMPIC AND COMMONWEALTH GAMES REPRESENTATIVES

(A) OLYMPIANS AND PARALYMPIANS (to 2016)

[NOTE: The first Aboriginal /Islander Olympians participated in 1964. Members of the Hall of Fame are listed in **bold** font.]

1.	**Ahmatt, Michael**	1964 Tokyo	basketball
2	**Blair, Adrian**	1964 Tokyo	boxing
3.	**Roberts, Francis (Frank)**	1964 Tokyo	boxing
4.	Carney, Robert	1968 Mexico City	boxing
5.	**Donovan, Joseph (Joe)**	1968 Mexico City	boxing
6.	Kinsella, John	1968 Mexico City	wrestling
		1972 Munich	wrestling
7.	**Barrett, Raymond (Ray)**	1972 Heidelberg	Paralympic athletics
8.	Stevens, Norman	1980 Moscow	boxing
9.	**Morseu, Danny**	1980 Moscow	basketball
		1984 Los Angeles	basketball
10.	Kirby, Peter	1984 New York/Stoke Mandeville	Paralympic athletics
11.	Lawton, Warren	1984 New York/Stoke Mandeville	Paralympic athletics
		1992 Barcelona	Paralympic goalball
		1996 Atlanta	Paralympic goalball
		2000 Sydney	Paralympic goalball
12.	Coombs, Kevin	1960 Rome	Paralympic basketball
		1968 Tel Aviv	Paralympic basketball
		1972 Heidelberg	Paralympic basketball
		1980 Arnhem	Paralympic basketball
		1988 Seoul	Paralympic basketball
13.	Hiles, Darrell	1988 Seoul	boxing
14.	**Burns, Donna**	1992 Barcelona	basketball
15.	**Crawford, Justann**	1992 Barcelona	boxing
16.	**Feifar, Karl**	1992 Barcelona	Paralympic athletics
17.	**Barrell, Tracy Lee**	1992 Barcelona	Paralympic swimming

ADDENDUM I

18.	**Peden, Robert**	1992 Barcelona	boxing
		1996 Atlanta	boxing
19.	**Riley, Samantha**	1992 Barcelona	swimming
		1996 Atlanta	swimming
20.	Freeman, Catherine	1992 Barcelona	athletics
		1996 Atlanta	athletics
		2000 Sydney	athletics
21.	**Choppy, Baedon**	1996 Atlanta	hockey
22.	**Peris, Nova**	1996 Atlanta	hockey
23.	**Swan, James**	1996 Atlanta	boxing
		2000 Sydney	boxing
24.	**Vander Kuyp, Kyle**	1996 Atlanta	athletics
		2000 Sydney	athletics
25.	Collins, Henry	2000 Sydney	boxing
26.	**Geale, Daniel**	2000 Sydney	boxing
27.	**Martin, Anthony**	2000 Sydney	weightlifting
28.	**Starr, Bridgette**	2000 Sydney	soccer
29.	Wehrman, Kasey	2000 Sydney	soccer
30.	**Austin, Ben**	2000 Sydney	Paralympic swimming
		2004 Athens	Paralympic swimming
		2008 Beijing	Paralympic swimming
31.	Rotumah, Tahlia	2008 Beijing	Paralympic athletics
32.	Hore, Bradley	2000 Sydney	boxing
		2004 Athens	boxing
33.	**Johnson, Patrick**	2000 Sydney	athletics
		2004 Athens	athletics
34.	**Thomas, Nathan**	2000 Sydney	water polo
		2004 Athens	water polo
35.	Pittman, James	2004 Athens	boxing
36.	**Semmens, Dean**	2004 Athens	water polo
37.	Butler, Scott	2004 Athens	basketball referee
		2008 Beijing	basketball referee
38.	Little, Anthony	2004 Athens	boxing
		2008 Beijing	boxing
39.	**North, Jade**	2004 Athens	soccer
		2008 Beijing	soccer
40.	**Porter, Stacey**	2004 Athens	softball
		2008 Beijing	softball
41.	**Ross, Joshua (Josh)**	2004 Athens	athletics
		2012 London	athletics
42.	**Abbott, Desmond (Des)**	2008 Beijing	hockey
43.	Luke, Boyd	2008 Beijing	boxing
44.	**Cox, Rohanee**	2008 Beijing	basketball
45.	Fleming, Paul	2008 Beijing	boxing

ADDENDUM I

46.	**Harradine, Benn**	2008 Beijing	athletics
		2012 London	athletics
		2016 Rio	athletics
47.	Clarke, Kayla	2012 London	Paralympic swimming
48.	**Mills, Patrick**	2008 Beijing	basketball
		2012 London	basketball
		2016 Rio	basketball
49.	**Carroll, Joel**	2012 London	hockey
50.	Blake (Isaac), Torita	2012 London	Paralympic athletics
51.	Hammond, Cameron	2012 London	boxing
52.	Hooper, Damien	2012 London	boxing
53.	Beki, Lee	2012 London	athletics
54.	Ross, Jesse	2012 London	boxing
55.	Young, Khalen	2012 London	cycling
56.	Clark, Kayla	2012 London	swimming
57.	**Peris, Brooke**	2016 Rio	hockey
58.	Simon, Kyah	2016 Rio	soccer
59.	**Williams, Lydia**	2016 Rio	soccer
60.	Clancy, Taliqua	2016 Rio	beach volleyball
61.	Swift, Joel	2016 Rio	water polo
62.	Porch, Jon	2016 Rio	rugby sevens
63.	Leilani, Mitchell	2016 Rio	basketball
64.	**Williams, Mariah**	2016 Rio	hockey
65.	**Reid, Amanda**	2012 London	Paralympic swimming
		2016 Rio	Paralympic cycling
66.	Young, Khalen	2012 London	BMX cycling
67.	Smith, Rebecca (Beki)	2012 London	athletics (walking)

(B) COMMONWEALTH GAMES REPRESENTATIVES (TO 2014)

[Note: This table may be incomplete.]

1.	**Austin, Ben**	2002 Manchester	swimming
		2006 Melbourne	swimming
		2010 New Delhi	swimming
2.	Barney, Eddie	1962 Perth	boxing
3.	**Blair, Adrian**	1962 Perth	boxing
4.	Carney, Tom	1978 Edmonton	boxing
5.	**Crawford, Justann**	1994 Victoria	boxing
6.	**Crowther, Robert**	2014 Glasgow	athletics
7.	**Donovan, Joseph** (Joe)	1974 Christchurch	boxing,
8.	Drahm, Shane	1998 Kuala Lumpur	rugby sevens
9.	**Dynevor, Jeff**	1962 Perth	boxing
10.	Edwards, Jim Jr	1962 Perth	boxing
11.	**Freeman, Catherine**	1994 Victoria	athletics

ADDENDUM I

		2002 Manchester	athletics
12.	**Geale**, **Daniel**	2002 Manchester	boxing
13.	Hammond, Cameron	2010 New Delhi	boxing
14.	**Harradine**, **Benn**	2006 Melbourne	athletics
		2010 New Delhi	athletics
		2014 Glasgow	athletics
15.	**Hobson**, **Percy**	1962 Perth	athletics
16.	Hooper, Damien	2010 New Delhi	boxing
17.	Hore, Bradley	2002 Manchester	boxing
		2006 Melbourne	boxing
18.	**Johnson**, **Patrick**	1998 Kuala Lumpur	athletics
		2006 Melbourne	athletics
		2010 New Delhi	athletics
19.	Kelly, Stevie	2014 Glasgow	wrestling
20.	McCann, Shannon	2014 Glasgow	athletics
21.	**Parker**, **Shane**	2010 New Delhi	wrestling
		2014 Glasgow	wrestling
22.	Peden, Robert	1994 Victoria	boxing
23.	**Peris**, **Brooke**	2014 Glasgow	hockey
24.	**Peris**, **Nova**	1990 Auckland	hockey
		1998 Kuala Lumpur	athletics
25.	**Riley**, **Samantha**	1994 Victoria	swimming
26.	Sam, Doug	1982 Brisbane	boxing
27.	**Swan**, **James**	1994 Victoria	boxing
		1998 Kuala Lumpur	boxing
28.	**Vander Kuyp**, **Kyle**	1994 Victoria	athletics
		2006 Melbourne	athletics
29.	Williams, Brendan	1998 Kuala Lumpur	rugby sevens
30.	**Williams**, **Gary**	1978 Edmonton	boxing
31.	**Williams**, **Jim**	1998 Kuala Lumpur	rugby sevens

ADDENDUM II
HALL OF FAME MEMBERS

[Note on British and Australian Honours: KCVO = Knight Commander of the Victorian Royal Order; OBE = Officer of the Most Excellent Order of the British Empire; MBE = Member of the Most Excellent Order of the British Empire; BEM = British Empire Medal; AO = Officer of the Order of Australia; AM = Member of the Order of Australia; OAM = Medal of the Order of Australia.]

[**Indicates membership of Australia's Sports Hall of Fame]

1868 team to England — cricket
Abbott, Desmond (Des) — hockey
Ahmatt, Michael — basketball
Allen, Willie — Australian football, shooting, soccer
Ambrum, George — rugby league
Anderson, Bob — athletics
Anderson, Kyle — darts
Anderson, Sam — cricket
Appo, Bob — lawn bowls
Appo, Leo — woodchopping
Archer, Georgina — vigoro, hockey
Austin, Albert (Pompey) — Australian football, athletics
Austin, Ben, OAM — Paralympic swimming
Austin, Lawrence ('Baby Casius') — boxing
Backo, Sam — rugby league
Badger Creek team — Australian football
Bailey, Soli — surfing
Barney, Charmaine — darts
Barrell, Tracey Lee, OAM — swimming
Barrett, Raymond (Ray) — Paralympic athletics
Barty, Ashleigh — tennis
Beale, Kurtley — rugby union
Beetson, Arthur (Artie), OAM** — rugby league
Bennett, Elliott (Elley) — boxing
Betts, Eddie — Australian football
Black, Lindsay — roughriding
Blacklock, Nathan — rugby league
Blair, Adrian — boxing
Bowditch, Steve Mangiri — squash
Bowen, Matt — rugby league
Bowman, Patrick — athletics
Bracken, George — boxing
Briscoe, Gordon, AO — soccer
Brown, Roger — cricket
Burgoyne, Peter — Australian football
Burgoyne, Shaun — Australian football
Burns, Donna, OAM — Paralympic basketball
Butler, Scott — international basketball referee
Cable, Barry, MBE** — Australian football
Cadell, Johnny — roughriding
Callaghan, Jimmy — showring riding
Campbell, Mabel — cricket
Campbell, Preston — rugby league
Carr, Wally — boxing
Carroll, Joel — hockey
Chalker, May — golf
Chapman, Tommy — boxing
Choppy, Baedon — hockey
Christian, Trevor, AM — boxing, refereeing
Clark, Phynea — hockey
Cochrane, Mal — rugby league

ADDENDUM II

Collins, Louisa — basketball, soccer, hockey
Coombs, Kevin, OAM — Paralympic basketball
Cooper, Lynch — athletics
Cooper, Reuben — Australian football, cricket, soccer
Corowa, Larry, MBE — rugby league
Cowburn, Gary — boxing
Cox, Rohanee — basketball
Crawford, Justann — boxing
Crouch, Edna — cricket
Crouch, Glen (Paddy) — rugby league
Crowther, Robert — athletics
Currie, Anthony (Tony) — rugby league
Cusack, Nicole — netball
Cuzens, Johnny — cricket
Daley, Laurie, AM — rugby league
Damaso, Rose — basketball, netball, softball, hockey
Dancey, Tom — athletics
de la Cruz, Bo — touch football, rugby sevens
Dempsey, William (Billy), MBE — Australian football
Dennis, Steve — boxing
Devine, Bernie — powerlifting
Donovan, Joseph (Joe) — boxing, judging
Duncan, Leslie (Lance) — judo
Dunn, Carmelita (Karmi) — basketball, netball, softball, soccer
Dynevor, Jeffrey (Jeff) — boxing
Edmundson, Leanne — soccer
Edwards, Joanne (Jodi) — powerlifting
Ella, Gary — rugby union, coaching
Ella, Glen — rugby union, coaching
Ella, Marcia, OAM — netball
Ella, Mark, AM** — rugby union, coaching
Ella, Steve — rugby league
Fanning, Katrina — rugby league
Farmer, Graham (Polly), MBE** — Australian football
Farmer, Jeff — Australian football
Feifar, Karl — Paralympic athletics
Ferguson, John ('Chicka') — rugby league

Finnan, Sharon, OAM — netball, coaching
Firebrace, Sharon — volleyball
Fisher, Frank ('Big Shot') — rugby league
Foster (Wilson), Eileen — darts
Franklin (Giteau), Bianca — netball, basketball
Franklin, Lance ('Buddy') — Australian football
Frederiksen, Shane — touch football
Freeman, Catherine (Cathy), OAM** — athletics
Geale, Daniel — boxing
Gibbs, Ron — rugby league
Gilbert, Eddie — cricket
Gillespie, Jason — cricket
Goodes, Adam — Australian football
Goodwin, Leigh-Anne — horseracing
Goolagong-Cawley, Evonne, AC AO, MBE** — tennis
Goolagong, Jeff — softball
Graham, Michael — Australian football
Green, George — rugby league
Hampton, Ivy — darts
Hampton, Kenneth, OAM — athletics
Harradine, Benn — athletics
Hassen, Jack — boxing
Hayden, Alec — roughriding
Hayward, Maley — Australian football, athletics
Henry, Albert (Alec) — cricket, athletics
Hill, Stephen — Australian football
Hinton, Rollo — boxing
Hobson, Percy — athletics
Hodges, Justin — rugby league
Hunter, Donna — softball, hockey, netball, basketball
Huntington, Felicity — soccer
Inglis, Greg — rugby league
Ivory, Frank — rugby union
Jackson, Sydney (Syd) — Australian football
James, Des — Australian football
James, Glenn, OAM — Australian football umpire
Janssen, Kayleen — soccer
Jawai, Nathan — basketball

Jerome, Jeremiah (Jerry) — boxing, athletics
Johnson, Allen (Dick) — rugby league
Johnson, Chris — Australian football
Johnson, Joe — Australian football
Johnson, Lindsay (Lin) — rugby league
Johnson, Patrick — athletics
Jonas, Billy — showring riding
Kantilla, David — Australian football
Kickett, Dale — Australian football
Kickett, Derek — Australian football
Kilmurray, Ted ('Square') — Australian football
King, Ian — cricket, boxing
King, Shane — softball
Kinnear, Robert (Bobby) — athletics
Kinsella, John — wrestling
Kirby, Peter — Paralympic athletics
Krakouer, Jim — Australian football
Krakouer, Phil — Australian football
Lake Tyers team — Australian football
Landy-Ariel (Young), Julie — rugby league, Oztag
Larkin, Steve — hockey
Lawton, Warren — Paralympic goalball, athletics
Lesiputty, Joanne — softball
Lew Fatt, Bennie — basketball, Australian football,
Lew Fatt, Clifford (Gympie) — Australian football
Lew Fatt, Terry — Australian football, basketball
Lewis, Chris — Australian football
Liddiard, David, OAM — rugby league, youth sport
Long, Michael — Australian football
Longbottom, Kevin ('Lummy') — rugby league
Lovell, Greg — woodchopping
Lyons, Cliff — rugby league
Mallee Park Football Club — Australian football
Mansell, Brian — cycling
Marsh, Jack — cricket, athletics

Martin, Anthony — weightlifting
Mason, Andrea — netball, athletics
Matera, Peter — Australian football
Maynard, Merv — horseracing
McAdam, Gilbert — Australian football
McArthur, Wally — rugby league, athletics
McCarthy, Richard (Darby) — horseracing
McDermott, Lloyd — rugby union
McDonald, Norman — Australian football, athletics, boxing
McDonald, Robert (Bobby) — athletics
McGuire, John — cricket, Australian football
McKellar-Nathan, Kelly — softball
McLean, Michael — Australian football, coaching
McLeod, Andrew — Australian football
Meninga, Mal, AM** — rugby league, coaching
Menzies, Karen — soccer
Michael, Stephen — Australian football
Mills, Patrick — basketball
Morgan, Lionel — rugby league
Moriarty, John, AM — soccer
Morrissey, Lorrelle — hockey
Morseu, Danny — basketball
Mullagh, Johnny — cricket
Mullett (Drayton), Cheryl — badminton
Mullett, Sandra — badminton
Mundine, Anthony — boxing, rugby league
Mundine, Anthony (Tony), OAM — boxing, coaching
Musselwhite (Cosier), Michelle — basketball
Narkle, Phil — Australian football
Narwan Football Club — rugby league
New Norcia team — cricket
Nicholls, Sir Douglas, KCVO, OBE — Australian football, athletics
North, Jade — soccer
O'Loughlin, Michael — Australian football
Olive, Bruce — rugby league
Parker, Shane — wrestling
Peachey, David — rugby league
Peden, Robert — boxing

ADDENDUM II

Peris, Nova, OAM — hockey, athletics
Peris, Brooke — hockey
Perkins, Charles, AO — soccer
Pickett, Byron — Australian football
Porter, Stacey — softball
Prince, Scott — rugby league
Ramalli, Cecil — rugby union
Redfern All Blacks team — rugby league
Reed, Chad, AM — motor cycling
Reid (Fowler), Amanda — Paralympic cycling, swimming
Renouf, Steve — rugby league
Reys, Frankie — horseracing
Richards, Randell (Ron) — boxing
Riley, Samantha, OAM — swimming
Rioli, Cyril — Australian football
Rioli, Maurice — Australian football
Roberts, Brian — boxing
Roberts, Francis (Frank) — boxing
Roe, Billy, BEM — Australian football, basketball
Rose, Lionel, MBE** — boxing*
Ross, Joshua (Josh) — athletics
Rovers Football Club — Australian football
Saddler, Ron — rugby league
Sailor, Wendell — rugby league, rugby union
Samuels, Charlie — athletics
Sands, Dave** — boxing
Schreiber, Adam — squash
Scott, Colin — rugby league
Seden, Horrie — darts
Semmens, Dean — water polo
Shearer, Dale — rugby league
Simms, Eric — rugby league
Sing, Matt — rugby league
Sinn, Bobby — boxing
Smith, Delma — volleyball
St Albans, Peter — horseracing
St Mary's Football Club — Australian football
Starr, Bridgette — soccer
Swan, James — boxing
Tahu, Timana — rugby league

Tallis, Gorden — rugby league
Thaiday, Sam — rugby league
Thomas, Faith — cricket
Thomas, Nathan — water polo
Thompson, Hector — boxing
Thurston, Jonathon — rugby league
Tutton, Mark — volleyball
Tutton, Reg — volleyball
Tutton, Steve — volleyball, coaching
Twopenny (Murrumgunrrimin) — cricket
Vander Kuyp, Kyle — athletics
Waite, Billy — showring riding
Walford, Ricky — rugby league
Walker, Andrew (1) — Australian football
Walker, Andrew (2) — rugby union, rugby league
Walker, Lloyd — rugby union
Walker, Shannon — rugby sevens
Wandin, Robert (Bobby) — athletics
Wanganeen, Gavin — Australian football
Watson, Jack ('Sonny Carbine') — roughriding
Wells, Daniel — Australian football
White, Darryl — Australian football
Widders, Dean — rugby league
Williams, Claude — basketball, coaching
Williams, Gary — boxing
Williams, Harry — soccer
Williams, Jesse — American football
Williams, Jim — rugby union, coaching
Williams, Jimmy — roughriding
Williams, Lydia — soccer
Williams, Mariah — hockey
Williams, R S (Bobby) — boxing
Wilson, Fred ('Mulga Fred') — roughriding
Windsor, Harley — ice-skating
Winmar, Neil (Nicky) — Australian football
Wirrpanda, David — Australian football
Young (Anderson), Rebecca (Bec) — rugby league, rugby union

ADDENDUM III
THE ERAS OF ACHIEVEMENT

The eras in which Hall of Fame members achieved their triumphs are not hard and fast. But their biographical details and life experiences allow a reasonable categorisation of the periods in which they lived. Inevitably some eras overlap, for example, child removal practices coincided with the eras of protection-segregation and the beginnings of liberation from oppressive special laws that applied only to Aboriginal and Islander peoples.

The framework
(a) The age of freedom, albeit the genocidal period (**1804–1897**);
(b) The protection-segregation period (**1897–1985 effectively**);
(c) The epoch of stolen children and 'assimilation' (**1839–1988**);
(d) The decades of hope (**1960–1985**);
(e) The time of (relative) liberation (**1986 to the present**).

The Genocidal Age
1868 cricket team
Anderson, Bob — athletics
Austin, Albert (Pompey) — Australian football
Bowman, Patrick — athletics
Cuzens, Johnny — cricket
Ivory, Frank — rugby union
Jerome, Jeremiah (Jerry) — boxing, athletics, shooting
Kinnear, Robert (Bobby) — athletics
Marsh, Jack — cricket, athletics
McDonald, (Robert) Bobby — athletics
Mullagh, Johnny — cricket
New Norcia cricket team
Samuels, Charlie — athletics
St Albans, Peter — horseracing
Twopenny (Murrumgunrrimin) — cricket

The Protection-Segregation Period
Allen, Willie — Australian football
Anderson, Sam — cricket
Appo, Leo — woodchopping
Badger Creek team — Australian football
Bennet, Elliott (Elley) — boxing
Black, Lindsay — roughriding
Blair, Adrian — boxing
Bracken, George — boxing
Cadell, Johnny — roughriding
Campbell, Mabel — cricket
Chapman, Tommy — boxing
Cooper, Lynch — athletics
Cooper, Reuben — Australian football
Crouch, Edna — cricket
Crouch, Glen (Paddy) — rugby league
Dancey, Tom — athletics
Dynevor, Jeff — boxing
Fisher, Frank ('Big Shot') — rugby league
Gilbert, Eddie — cricket
Green, George — rugby league
Hassen, Jack — boxing
Hayden, Alec — roughriding
Hayward, Maley — Australian football
Henry, Albert (Alec) — cricket, athletics
Hinton, Rollo — boxing
Hobson, Percy — athletics
Johnson, Allen (Dick) — rugby league

Johnson, Joe — Australian football
Johnson, Lindsay (Lin) — rugby league
Jonas, Billy — showring riding
Kantilla, David — Australian football
Lake Tyers team — Australian football
McDonald, Norm — Australian football, athletics, boxing
Nicholls, Douglas — Australian football, athletics
Ramalli, Cecil — rugby union
Reys, Frankie — horseracing
Richards, Randall (Ron) — boxing
Roberts, Brian — boxing
Roberts, Francis (Frank) — boxing
Roe, Billy, BEM — basketball, Australian football
Sands, Dave — boxing
Simms, Eric — rugby league
Sinn, Bobby — boxing
St Marys Football Club — Australian football
Waite, Billy — showring riding
Wandin, Robert (Bobby) — athletics
Watson, Jack ('Sonny Carbine') — roughriding
Williams, Jimmy — roughriding
Wilson, Fred ('Mulga Fred') — roughriding

Assimilation and Child Removals

Briscoe, Gordon — soccer
Callaghan, Jimmy — showring riding
Carr, Wally — boxing
Collins, Louisa — basketball, soccer, hockey
Dempsey, William (Billy) — Australian football
Farmer, Graham (Polly) — Australian football
Firebrace, Sharon — volleyball
Hampton, Kenneth (Ken) — athletics
Jackson, Sydney (Syd) — Australian football
Kilmurray, Ted ('Square') — Australian football
McArthur, Wally — rugby league, athletics
Moriarty, John, — soccer
Perkins, Charles — soccer
Redfern All Blacks team — rugby league
Thomas, Faith — cricket

Decades of Hope

Ahmatt, Michael — basketball
Ambrum, George — rugby league
Appo, Bob — lawn bowls
Archer, Georgina — vigoro, hockey umpiring
Austin, Lawrence ('Baby Casius') — boxing
Barrett, Raymond (Ray) — disabled athletics
Beetson, Arthur (Artie) — rugby league, coaching
Bowditch, Steve — squash
Brown, Roger — cricket
Cable, Barry — Australian football
Chalker, May — golf
Christian, Trevor — boxing, judging
Clark, Phynea — hockey
Cochrane, Mal — rugby league
Coombs, Kevin — wheelchair basketball
Corowa, Larry — rugby league
Cowburn, Gary — boxing
Damaso, Rose — basketball, netball, softball, hockey
Dennis, Steve — boxing
Donovan, Joseph (Joe) — boxing, judging
Duncan, Leslie (Lance) — judo
Dunn, Carmelita (Karmi) — basketball, netball, softball, soccer
Edmundson, Leanne — soccer
Edwards, Joanne (Jodi) — powerlifting
Ella, Gary — rugby union
Ella, Glen — rugby union
Ella, Marcia — netball
Ella, Mark — rugby union
Ella, Steve — rugby league
Foster (Wilson), Eileen — darts
Goolagong-Cawley, Evonne — tennis
Graham, Michael — Australian football
Hampton, Ivy — darts
Hunter, Donna — softball, hockey, netball, basketball
Huntington, Felicity — soccer
James, Des — Australian football
James, Glenn — Australian football umpire

Janssen, Kayleen — soccer
King, Ian — cricket
Kinsella, John — wrestling
Krakouer, Jim — Australian football
Krakouer, Phil — Australian football
Larkin, Steve — hockey
Lew Fatt, Bennie — basketball, Australian football
Lew Fatt, Terry — Australian football, basketball
Lew Fatt, Clifford (Gympie) — Australian football
Longbottom, Kevin ('Lummy') — rugby league
Lovell, Greg — woodchopping
Mallee Football Club — Australian football
Mansell, Brian — cycling
Mason, Andrea — netball
Maynard, Merv — horseracing
McCarthy, Richard (Darby) — horseracing
McDermott, Lloyd — rugby union
McGuire, John — cricket, Australian football
Menzies, Karen — soccer
Michael, Stephen — Australian football
Morgan, Lionel — rugby league
Morrissey, Lorelle — hockey
Morseu, Danny — basketball
Mullett, Cheryl (Drayton) — badminton
Mullett, Sandra — badminton
Mundine, Anthony (Tony) — boxing, coaching
Narwan Football Clun — rugby league
Olive, Bruce — rugby league
Rioli, Maurice — Australian football
Rovers Football Club — Australian football
Rose, Lionel — boxing
Saddler, Ron — rugby league
Schreiber, Adam — squash
Scott, Colin — rugby league
Sedden, Horrie — darts
Shearer, Dale — rugby league
Smith, Delma — volleyball
Thompson, Hector — boxing
Tutton, Mark — volleyball
Tutton, Reg — volleyball

Tutton, Steve — volleyball, coaching
Williams, Claude — basketball, coaching, rugby league
Williams, Gary — boxing
Williams, Harry — soccer
Williams, R S (Bobby) — boxing

The Liberated Present

Abbott, Des — hockey
Anderson, Kyle — darts
Austin, Ben — Paralympic swimming
Backo, Sam — rugby league
Bailey, Soli — surfing
Barney, Charmaine — darts
Barrell, Tracey Lee — Paralympic swimming
Barty, Ashleigh — tennis
Beale, Kurtley — rugby union
Betts, Eddie — Australian football
Blacklock, Nathan — rugby league
Bowen, Matt — rugby league
Burgoyne, Peter — Australian football
Burgoyne, Shane — Australian football
Burns, Donna — basketball Paralympics
Butler, Scott — basketball referee
Campbell, Preston — rugby league
Carroll, Joel — hockey
Choppy, Baedon — hockey
Cox, Rohanee — basketball
Crawford, Justann — boxing
Crowther, Robert — athletics
Currie, Anthony (Tony) — rugby league
Cusack, Nicole — netball
Daley, Laurie — rugby league
de la Cruz, Bo — touch football
Devine, Bernie — powerlifting
Fanning, Katrina — rugby league
Farmer, Jeff — Australian football
Feifar, Karl — disabled athletics
Ferguson, John ('Chicka') — rugby league
Finnan, Sharon — netball
Franklin (Giteau), Bianca — netball
Franklin, Lance ('Buddy') — Australian football

ADDENDUM III

Fredericksen, Shane — touch football
Freeman, Catherine (Cathy) — athletics
Geale, Daniel — boxing
Gibbs, Ron — rugby league
Gillespie, Jason — cricket, coaching
Goodes, Adam — Australian football
Goodwin, Leigh-Anne — horseracing
Goolagong, Jeff — softball
Harradine, Benn — athletics
Hill, Stephen — Australian football
Hodges, Justin — rugby league
Inglis, Greg — rugby league
Jawai, Nathan — basketball
Johnson, Chris — Australian football
Johnson, Patrick — athletics
Kickett, Dale — Australian football
Kickett, Derek — Australian football
King, Shane — softball
Kirby, Peter — disabled athletics
Landy-Ariel (Young), Julie — rugby league, Oztag
Lawton, Warren — athletics, goalball, Paralympics
Lesiputty, Joanne — softball
Lewis, Chris — Australian football
Liddiard, David — rugby league
Long, Michael — Australian football
Lyons, Cliff — rugby league
Martin, Anthony — weightlifting
Matera, Peter — Australian football
McAdam, Gilbert — Australian football
McKellar-Nathan, Kelly — softball
McLean, Michael — Australian football
McLeod, Andrew — Australian football
Meninga, Mal — rugby league, coaching
Mills, Patrick — basketball
Mundine, Anthony — boxing, rugby league
Musselwhite, (Cosier), Michelle — basketball
Narkle, Phil — Australian football
North, Jade — soccer
O'Loughlin, Michael — Australian football
Parker, Shane — wrestling
Peachey, David — rugby league

Peden, Robert — boxing
Peris, Nova — hockey, athletics
Peris, Brooke — hockey
Pickett, Byron — Australian football
Porter, Stacey — softball
Prince, Scott — rugby league
Reed, Chad — motorsport
Reid, Amanda (Fowler) — Paralympics, swimming, cycling
Renouf, Steve — rugby league
Riley, Samantha — swimming
Rioli, Cyril — Australian football
Ross, Joshua (Josh) — athletics
Sailor, Wendell — rugby league, rugby union
Semmens, Dean — water polo
Sing, Matt — rugby league
Starr, Bridgette — soccer
Swann, James — boxing
Tahu, Timana — rugby league
Tallis, Gorden — rugby league
Thaiday, Sam — rugby league
Thomas, Nathan — water polo
Thurston, Jonathan — rugby league
Vander Kuyp, Kyle — athletics
Walford, Ricky — rugby league
Walker, Andrew (1) — Australian football
Walker, Andrew (2) — rugby league, rugby union
Walker, Lloyd — rugby union
Walker, Shannon — rugby sevens
Wanganeen, Gavin — Australian football
Wells, Daniel — Australian football
White, Darryl — Australian football
Widders, Dean — rugby league
Williams, Jesse — American football
Williams, Jim — rugby union, coaching
Williams, Lydia — soccer
Williams, Mariah — hockey
Windsor, Harley — ice-skating
Winmar, Neil (Nicky) — Australian football
Wirrpanda, David — Australian football
Young (Anderson), Rebecca (Bec) — rugby league, rugby union

GENERAL INDEX

Aboriginal and Islander, identity of, 4–5, 8–9, 10, 15, 18, 149, 259, 263
Aboriginal and Islander Sports Hall of Fame, 4–5, 6–7, 13, 65–6
Aboriginal and Islander women in sport, 10–13
Aboriginal and Torres Strait Islander Commission (ATSIC), 19
Aboriginal history, teaching of, 20
Aboriginal policies
    assimilation, 2–3, 4, 44
    cattle station wage awards, 223
    control of movement, 16
    'exclusion on demand', 16, 61, 63, 66, 254, 258
    exemption certificates, 43
    genocide/genocidal massacres, 1, 3, 13, 17, 18, 20
    health care, 16–17
    incarceration, 17–18, 20
    intervention, 19, 20
    protection-segregation, 1, 2, 3, 4, 17, 41–2, 254
    racial classification, 3, 42, 43
    removal of children, 2, 3, 4, 20, 44
    see also incarceration rates, missions; settlements; stolen generations; suicide
American football, 22
Anderson, Michael, 257
assimilation homes, 2, 17, 44, 76, 77, 84, 92, 254, 321, 329
see also Aboriginal policies
Australian Football League code of conduct, 64, 120, 257
Australian Institute of Aboriginal and Torres Strait Islander Studies (AIATSIS), 7, 10, 218
Australian Sports Hall of Fame, 5, 62

barriers to participation in sport, 15, 21, 42, 44, 254
Barwick, Diane, 60, 70
boat sports, 13, 21
bodybuilding, 22
Broome, Richard, 6, 95, 140–1, 243

Clark, Chris ('Honky'), 2, 3, 4
Coe, Paul, 140
Community Development Employment Project (CDEP), 17
Commonwealth Games representation, 10, 14–15, 44, 143
Commonwealth Games representatives, 363–6
Corris, Peter, 141
Currey, Carl, 4
Cutts, John, 9
cycling, 13, 22

Davis, Professor Megan, 12
deaths in custody, 19
de Castella, Robert, 13
deafness, 16
disabled sports, 15, 202–3
discrimination 4, 8, 18, 29, 140, 176, 259
    see also racism
distribution of sports, 13–14
Dodson, Mick, 7
Dodson, Pat, 19

Edwards, Ken, 4, 6
Elarde, Patsy, 12
Ellicott, John, 284
Egan, Ted, 4, 5, 115, 224
eras of achievement, 372–5
exhibitions, Hall of Fame, 4, 6–7

GENERAL INDEX

extreme sports, 13
famous teams, 15
Flanagan, Martin, 63–64, 94
Foundation for Aboriginal Affairs, 293

gender *see* women in sport
genocide/genocidal massacres, 1, 3, 13, 17, 18, 20
golf, 13–14, 23
Gorman, Sean, 65
gymnastics, 13, 21

Hall of Fame members, 367–70
    see also selection of Hall of Fame members
Halls of Champions, 5
Harcourt, Rex, 175
Hay, Roy, 6, 61
health, 16–17 *see also* deafness; trachoma
Hine, Dick, 122
honours, Imperial or Australian, 3, 6
Hutchinson, Col, 4

ice-skating, 12, 21, 23–4
incarceration rates, 17–18, 20
inter-racial marriage, 2

Jackomos, Alick, 4
judo, 24

karate, 12
kerentan, 125 *see also* basketball
kickboxing/mixed martial arts, 24
kinship, 14
    families and clans, 14
Klugman, Matthew, 64

lacrosse, 12, 13
lawn bowls, 13, 25

Marngrook, 61 *see also* Australian Football
Maynard, Fred, 227, 236
Maynard, John, 4, *5*, 227, 322
Middleton, David, 4

missions, 2, 5, 125, 253
Mitchell, Ray, 141, 142
Moore, Andrew, 253
motocross, 25
motorcycle racing, 25
Mould, Geoff, 309, 313, 319
Mulvaney, John, 175

National Aboriginal Congress, 19
National Aboriginal Consultative Committee (NACC), 18–19
nomenclature for Aboriginal people, 2, 3, 4, 42
Noonuccal, Oodgeroo (Kath Walker), *177*

Olympic Games representation, 10, 14–15, 44, 143, 355
Olympic Games representatives, 363–6
Osmond, Gary, 64

Page, Ricky, 255
Paralympic Games representation, 10, 15, 44
Paralympic Games representatives, 363–6
participation in sports, 13–14
Peachy, Eunice, 12
political voices, 18–19
powerlifting *see* weightlifting

Racial Discrimination Act 1975, 18
racial vilification, 18, 63–5
    see also sledging, racial
racism, 8, 15, 18, 19, 43, 63
    in Australian Football, 61, 63–5
    in rugby league, 257, 258
    in rugby union, 309
Recognition Statement, 8
Referendum Council, 19
Reynolds, Henry, 1, 20
Roberts, Paul, 62
rowing, 13, 21–2, 25–6
Royal Commission into Aboriginal Deaths in Custody, 19
rugby sevens, 26, 310, 311,

Ryan, Lyndall, 1, 20
Ryan, Maurice, 180s

selection of Hall of Fame members, 4–5
settlements, 2, 5, 43, 125
sexual exploitation, 223
shooting, 13, 26
sledging, racial, 255, 291
South Sea Islanders, 7, 8–9, 15
sport and kinship, 14
sports facilities, lack of, 10, 12, 16, 23, 28
sports, uneven distribution in, 13–14
Stephen, Matthew, 6
stolen generations, 2 *see also* Aboriginal policies
suicide, 16–17
surfing, 13, 26–8
swimming, 28

Tatz, Colin, 4, *6*, 7
Tatz, Paul, 4, *6*
tenpin bowling, 12, 13, 21
Tilbrook, Lois, 62
Torres Strait Islanders, 3, 7, 8–9, 19
trachoma, 16
trampolining, 12, 28
tribal and linguistic affiliation, 9–10

Uluru Statement, The, 19

vigoro, 28
voices to Parliament, 18–19

weightlifting, 12, 28
Whitton, Evan, 259
women in sport, 10–13
word usage for Aboriginal people, 8–9

youth detention centres, 17–18

INDEX
OF ABORIGINAL AND ISLANDER SPORTSPEOPLE

Note: Members of the Hall of Fame in **bold**. Page references to images in *italics*.

1868 Team to England (cricket), 146, 179, 367, 371

Abbott, Desmond (Des), 14, 213, 214, *214*, 215, *220*, 364, 367, 373
Aboriginal All Stars (AFL), 65, 91, 96, 104, 112, 119
Abraham, Winston, 64
Agius, Laura, 13
Agius, Lois, 249
Ahmatt, Michael, 15, 126, 127, *127*, 137, 167, 363, 364, 372
Ahmatt, Michelle, 13, 127
Ahmatt, Shane, 127
Ahwong, Valerie, 13
Allen, Willie, 6, 68, *68*, 367, 371
Ambrum, George, 255, 261, *261*, 290, 367, 372
Ambrum, John, 290
Anderson, Ashley, 354
Anderson, Beau, 14, 195, *195*, 196
Anderson, Bob, 42, 45, *45*, 367, 371
Anderson, Kyle, 14, 195, 197, *197*, 367, 373
Anderson, Sam, 45, 176, 177, 180, *180*, 367, 371
Appo, Bob, 25, 29, *29*, 367, 372
Appo, Leo, 165, 358, *358*, 367, 371
Appo, Lyall, 143, 227, *227*
Archer, Georgina, 12, 30, *30*, 219, 368, 373
Austin, Albert (Pompey), 6, 61, 69, *69*, 368,

Austin, Ben OAM, 28, 204, *204*, 364, 365, 367, 373
Austin, Laurence ('Baby Casius'), 143, 146, *146*, 150, 155, 172, 367, 372
Austin, Maisie, 12, *13*

Backo, Sam, 255, 262, *262*, 263, 367, 373
Badger Creek team (AFL), 60, 66, 70, *70*, 367, 371
Bailey, Soli, 31, *31*, 367, 373
Baldwin, Robert, 126
Ball, Mary, 13, 25, *25*
Barber, Sampson, *177*
Barney, Charmaine, 12, 195, 198, *198*, 199, 367, 373
Barney, Eddie, 15, 148, 157, 365
Barrell, Tracey Lee OAM, 28, 205, *205*, 363, 367, 373
Barrett, Raymond (Ray), 206, *206*, 363, 367, 372
Barty, Ashleigh, 344, 345, *345*, 367, 373
Bates, Isaac (Ike), 25, *25*
Beale, Kurtley, 310, 311, *311*, 367, 373
Beetson, Arthur (Artie) OAM, 4, 6, 20, 138, 157, 255, 261, 263, *263*, 290, 367, 372
Bennell, Melissa, 13
Bennett, Elliot (Elley), 142, 143, 147, *147*, 367, 371
Betts, Andy, 321
Betts, Eddie, 63, 71, *71*, 367, 373
Bindi Jack, 143
Binge, Johnny, 143

378

INDEX OF ABORIGINAL AND ISLANDER SPORTSPEOPLE

Bird, Greg, 256, 258
Bird, Jack, 258
Black Chris, 141
Black Paddy, 141
Black Wand, 141
Black, Lindsay, 225, 230, *230*, 367, 371
Blacklock, Nathan, 257, 264, *264*, 266, 347, 367, 373
Blacklock, Ray, 255, *257,* 264
Blackman, Tony, 196
Blair, Adrian, 15, 143, 148, *148*, 157, 363, 364, 365, 371
Blake (Isaac), Torita, *203*, 365
Blandon, Merv, 141, 151
Bligh, Scott, 309
Bond, Jack, 225
Bonson, John, 134
Bowden, Jack, 15, 151
Bowditch, Steve Mangirri, 341, 342, *342,* 343, 367, 372
Bowen, Matt, 257, 265, *265*, 367, 373
Bowman, Patrick, 42, 46, *46*, 367, 371
Boyd, Luke, 143
Bracken, George, 4, 142, 143, 149, *149,* 150, 153, 155, 367, 372
Briggs, Selwyn, 44
Briscoe, Gordon AO, 322, 324, *324,* 329, 368, 373
Brooke, Graeme, *145*
Brown, Berty, 22
Brown, Ian, 196, *196,* 201
Brown, Roger, 14, 34, 175, 177, 181, *181*, 367, 372
'Bullocky,' 175, *176*
Burgoyne, Peter (Jr), 63, 65, 66, 72, *72*, 73, 367, 373
Burgoyne, Peter (Sr), 72, 73
Burgoyne, Shaun, 63, 65, 66, 72, 73, *73*, 367, 373
Burns, Donna, 207, *207,* 208, 363, 367, 373
Bush, Alison, 13
Bushel, Paul, 342
Butler, Scott, 128, *128,* 364, 367, 373
Bux, Wally, 44

Cable, Barry, MBE, 62, 63, 65, 74, *74,* 106, 107, 138, 190, 367, 372, 379
Cadell, Johnny, 225, 231, *231*, 367, 371
Callaghan, Jimmy (Paul Joseph Coe), 226, 228, 232, *232*, 368, 372
Campbell, Jordie, 27
Campbell, Mabel, 16, 175, 182, *182,* 183, 269, 367, 371
Campbell, Preston, 257, 260, 264, 266, *266*, 367, 373
Campton, Stacey, *244*
Capewell, Nick, 24
Carey, Otis, 28
Carney, Robert, 363
Carney, Tom, 365
Carr, Wally, 143, 150, *150*, 367, 372
Carroll, Joel, 14, 213, 215, *215,* 220, 365, 367, 373
Carroll, Roy, *152, 152*
Chalker, Marion, 13, 32
Chalker, Mark, 23, 32
Chalker, May, 14, 23, 32, *32*, 367, 372
Chambers, Will, 258
Champion, Beverley, 44, 208, 209
Chapman, Tommy, 15, 49, 143, 151, *151,* 160, 367, 371
Cherbourg team (rugby league), 260, *260*
Chisholm, Scott, 64
Choppy, Baedon, 213, 216, *216,* 364, 367, 373
Christian, Dan, 175
Christian, Trevor AM, 152, *152*, 367, 373
Clancy, Taliqua, 350*,* 365
Clark, Bert, 225, *228*
Clark, Gavin, 354
Clark, Phynea, 215, 217, *217,* 219, 367, 372
Clarke, Banjo, 146
Clarke, Kayla, *202,* 365
Clarke, Joe, 126, *126*
Clay, Alfie, 143
Cochrane, Mal, 256, 267, *267*, 367, 372
Cockatoo-Collins, Che, *66*
Cole, King, 179

INDEX OF ABORIGINAL AND ISLANDER SPORTSPEOPLE

Collard, Chris, *24*
Collard, Cyril, 62
Collins, Andrea, 12, *125*
Collins, Henry, 140, 143, 146, 364
Collins, Lilly Jane, 12
Collins, Louisa, 129, *129,* 131, 132, 217, 219, 336, 352, 368
Combardello Billy (Billy Thompson), 5, 42, 46
Combo, George, 46
Combo, Melissa, 13
Cooley, Peter, 27
Coombs, Kevin OAM, 15, 208, *208,* 210, 363, 368, 372
Cooper, Lynch, 42, 43, 44, 47, *47,* 82, 138, 368, 371
Cooper, Reuben, 6, 26, 68, 75, *75,* 368, 371
Corowa, Larry MBE, 255, 268, *268,* 368, 372
Costello, King, 225
Cowburn, Gary, 143, 149, 153, *153,* 155, 368, 372
Cox, Rohanee, 12, 130, *130,* 364, 368, 373
Craigie, Owen, 257, 264
Crawford, Justann, 34, 143, 154, *154,* 363, 365, 368, 373
Crouch, Edna, 6, 175, *182,* 183, *183,* 269, 271, 368, 371
Crouch, Glen (Paddy), 182, 183, 253, 269, *269,* 368, 371
Crouch, Glen (Jr), 183
Crouch, Thelma, 13, 183, 269
Crouchy, Walter, 224
Crow, Jim, 146, 179
Crowther, Robert, 44, 48, *48,* 365, 368, 373
Cruse, Eddy, 321
Cummings, Percy, 62
Currie, Anthony (Tony), 254, 255, 259, 270, *270,* 368, 373
Currie, Arthur ('Stokel', 'Stoker'), 254, 259, 270
Cusack, Nicole, 12, 245, *245,* 247, 368, 373
Cuzens, Johnny, 69, 146, 175, *179,* 184, *184,* 191, 368, 371

Daby, Dottie, 214
Daby, Joe, 213, 215
Daisy, Frank, *255*
Daisy, Vern, *255,* 293
Daley, Laurie AM, 20, 257, 271, *271,* 273, 368, 373
Damaso, Rose, 131, *131,* 132, 138, 217, 219, 336, 352, 368, 372
Dancey, Tom, 42, 43, 49, *49,* 151, 368, 371
Dann, Kenny, 27
Davis, Leon, 65
Davis, Nathan, 256
Davis, Ray, 22
Dawney, Belinda, 12
de la Cruz, Bo, 12, 26, 258, 348, *348,* 352, 368, 373
Dempsey, William (Billy) MBE, 65, 76, *76,* 107, 368, 372
Denner, Ben, 354
Denner, Kelly, 354
Dennis, Steve, 143, 145, 155, *155,* 172, 368, 372
Deshong, Jack, 141, 143
Devine, Bernie, 28, 251, *251,* 368, 373
Devonshire, Brian, 28
Dhurrkay, Gary, 64
Dickinson, Gavin, 27
Dickson, Leonie, 13
Dillon, Bobbi, 13
Dinah, Beaufort, *142*
Dixon, Brian, *126*
Doctor, Rowley, 226, *228,* 232, 240
Dodd, Tommy, 225
Dodd, Travis, 321, *322,* 329
Donaldson, Jack, 44
Donnelly, Tiger, 160
Donohue, Quentin, 143
Donovan, Joseph (Joe), 143, 156, *156,* 174, 363, 365, 368, 372
Drahm, Shane, 309, 365
Duggan, Tim, 126
Duncan, Dean, 24
Duncan, Glen, 24
Duncan, Leslie (Lance), 24, 33, *33,* 368, 372

INDEX OF ABORIGINAL AND ISLANDER SPORTSPEOPLE

Dunn, **Carmelita** (**Karmi**), 131, 132, *132*, 336, 352, 368, 372

Dynevor, **Jeffrey** (**Jeff**), 15, 143, 148, 157, *157*, 164, 365, 368, 371

Edmundson, **Leanne**, 12, 322, 324, *324*, 368, 372

Edwards, Jim Jr, 148, 365

Edwards, **Joanne** (**Jodi**), 12, 28, 252, *252*, 368, 372

Edwards, Shane, 65

Elarde, Patsy, 12

Ella, **Gary**, 4, 138, 309, 312, *312*, 368, 372

Ella, **Glen**, 138, 309, 312, 313, *313*, 368, 372

Ella, **Marcia** OAM, 12, 14, 246, *246*, 249, 352, 368, 372

Ella, **Mark** AM, 4, 138, 177, 309, 312, 313, 314, *314*, 368, 372

Ella, **Steve**, 14, 256, 272, *272*, 368, 372

Elms, Terry, 13, *213*, 217, 219

Ewan, Tim, 44

Fanning, **Katrina**, 4, 13, 254, 273, *273*, 368, 373

Farmer, **Graham** (**Polly**) MBE, 20, 62, 65, 74, 77, *77*, 92, 99, 106, 107, 157, 255, 368, 372

Farmer, **Jeff**, 78, *78*, 368, 373

Feifar, **Karl**, 44, 208, 209, *209*, 363, 368, 373

Fejo-Frith, Helen, 12

Ferguson, Andrew, 27

Ferguson, Blake 258

Ferguson, Eric, 255, *257*

Ferguson, **John** ('**Chicka**'), 256, 257, 274, *274*, 368, 373

Finnan, **Sharon** OAM, 12, 247, *247*, 368, 373

Firebrace, **Sharon**, 351, *351*, 368, 372

Fisher, Frank (Sr) (horse sports), 224

Fisher, Frank ('Big Shot') (rugby league), 14, 224, 254, 259, 275, *275*, 368, 371

Fleming, Paul, 143, 365

Foster (**Wilson**), **Eileen**, 12, 14, 195, 198, 199, *199*, 200, 368, 372

Franklin (**Giteau**), **Bianca**, 12, 14, 79, 248, *248*, 368, 373

Franklin, **Lance** (**Buddy**), 14, 65, 79, *79*, 83, 90, 91, 110, 118, 368, 373

Franks, Leslie, 224

Fraser, Donald, *226*

Fraser, Ritchie, 225, 230

Frederiksen, **Shane**, 348, 349, *349*, 368, 374

Freeman, **Catherine** (**Cathy**) OAM, 11, 14, 44, 50, *50*, 254, 259, 275, 364, 366, 368, 374

Fuller, Harry, 227

Gabelish, Aretha, 13

Gabelish, Toni, 13

Gagai, Dane, 258

Gardiner, Scott, 23, *23*

Geale, **Daniel**, 34, 143, 158, *158*, 364, 366, 368, 374

Gentle, Simon, 225

Gibbs, **Ron**, 256, 276, *276*, 368, 374

Gibson, Lowanna, 24

Gidgup, Darren, 24

Gigg, Ross, 255

Gilbert, **Eddie**, 6, 14, 15, 20, 157, 175-177, 181, 185, *185*, 188, 189, 254, 278, 368, 371

Gillespie, **Jason**, 14, 138, 175, 177, 178, 181, 186, *186*, 368, 374

Goodes, **Adam**, 65, 80, *80*, 109, 368, 374

Goodwin, **Leigh-Anne**, 12, 227, 233, *233*, 368, 374

Goolagong-Cawley, **Evonne** AC, AO, MBE, 4, 11, 14, 20, 157, 255, 335, 344, 346, *346*, 368, 372

Goolagong, Ian, 344

Goolagong, **Jeff**, 14, 335, *335*, 368, 374

Gordon, Ashley, 257

Graham, Colin, 62, 143

Graham, **Michael**, 63, 65, 81, *81*, 115, 368, 372

Graham, Wade, 258

Grant, David, 255

Green, Charlie, 43

Green, **George**, 9, 253, 277, *277*, 281, 368, 371

Grogan, Harry, *140*

Hall, Brett, 26, *26*

INDEX OF ABORIGINAL AND ISLANDER SPORTSPEOPLE

Hamm, Treanha, 13
Hammond, Cameron, 143, 365, 366
Hampton, Ivy, 12, 14, 195, 199, 200, *200*, 368, 372
Hampton, Kenneth (Ken) OAM, 44, 51, *51*, 368, 372
Hansen, Stuey, 22
Hardy, Jason, 347
Hardy, Jeff, 257, *259*
Harp, Clarissa, 13
Harradine, Benn, 44, 52, *52*, 365, 366, 368, 374
Hassen, Jack, 142, 143, 159, *159*, 368, 371
Hawkins, Harry, 224
Hayden, Alec, 14, 225, 234, *234*, 242, 368, 371
Hayes, Harry, 144, *144*
Hayward, Bill, 62, *67*, 82
Hayward, Eric, 62, *67*, 82
Hayward, Maley, 62, 82, *82*, 368, 371
Henry, Albert (Alec), 14, 42, 175, 176, 187, *187*, 188, 368, 371
Hiles, Darrell, 363
Hill, Bradley, 83
Hill, Stephen, 83, *83*, 368, 374
Hinton, Rollo, 15, 143, 151, 160, *160*, 368, 371
Hobson, Percy, 44, 53, *53*, 367, 368, 371
Hocking, Eddie, 81
Hodges, Justin, 255, 256, 276, 278, *278*, 368, 374
Hoffman, Josh, 256
Homer, Nancy, 12
Hood, Stewart, 95
Hookey, Lee, 257
Hooper, Damien, 143, 365, 366
Hooper, Gilbert, 143
Hore, Bradley, 364, 366
Howard, John, 308, 309, *310*, 317
Hubbard, Jim, 224
Hunt, Jacob, 28
Hunter, Donna, 12, 131, 336, *336*, 352, 368, 372
Huntington, Felicity, 12, 235, *325*, 368, 372

Indigenous All-Stars (rugby league), 257
Indigenous Dreamtime team (rugby league), 258
Indigenous Women's All-Stars (rugby league), 258
Inglis, Greg, 255, 256, 266, 279, *279*, 368, 374
Ivory, Frank, 308, 315, *315*, 368, 371

Jackson, Eddie ('Gentleman Ted'), 62, *66*
Jackson, Peter ('Cocoa'), 15
Jackson, Sydney (Syd), 4, 62, 63, 65, 84, *84*, 107, 368, 372
James, Des, 63, 85, *85*, 86, 368, 372
James, Glenn OAM, 63, 65, 85, 86, *86*, 368, 372
James, Ryan, 256, 258
James, 'Shady', 62
Janssen, Kayleen, 12, 326, *326*, 327, 368, 373
Jawai, Nathan, 126, 133, *133*, 368, 374
Jerome, Jeremiah (Jerry), 6, 20, 26, 141, 143, 151, 161, *161*, 224, 369, 374
Jetta, Leroy, 118
Jetta, Lewis, 118
Johncock, Graham, 65
Johns, Marlon, 196, 201
Johnson, Allen (Dick), 254, 280, *280*, 281, 369, 371
Johnson, Bert, 62, 63, *66*, 81
Johnson, Chris, 65, 87, *87*, 369, 374
Johnson, Joe, 61, 88, *88*, 369, 372
Johnson, Lindsay (Lin), 254, 280, 281, *281*, 369, 372
Johnson, Mitchell, 65
Johnson, Patrick, 44, 54, *54*, 364, 366, 369, 374
Johnson, Percy, 62
Jonas, William (Billy), 235, *235*, 369, 372
Jones, Bonnie, 249
Jose, Debbie, 13

Kantilla, David, 20, 65, 81, 89, *89*, 115, 369, 372
Kapeen, George, *141*, 142
Karpany, Tanya, 28
Keeler, Doris, 249
Kelly, Damien, 309
Kelly, Glen, 143
Kelly, Joseph, 213
Kelly, Kevin, 143

INDEX OF ABORIGINAL AND ISLANDER SPORTSPEOPLE

Kelly, Stevie, 360, *360*
Kickett, Dale, 79, 90, *90,* 91, 369, 374
Kickett, Derek, 79, 90, 91, *91*, 111, *120*, 369, 374
Kilmurray, Ted ('Square'), 65, 76, 77, 92, *92,* 107, 369, 372
King, Ian, 14, 138, 175, 176, 177, 178, 188, *188*, 369, 373
King, Shane, 337, *337*, 369, 374
Kingsmill, Fred, 5, 42, 46
Kinnear, Robert (Bobby), 42, 55, *55*, 369, 371
Kinsella, John, 255, 360, 361, *361*, 363, 369, 373
Kirby, Peter, 44, 208, 210, *210*, 363, 369, 374
Knight, Percy, 255
Knox, Les, 177
Koonibba Football Club (AFL), 114
Krakouer, Jim, 63–64, 65, 93, *93,* 94, 369, 373
Krakouer, Phil, 71, 93, 94, *94*, 369, 373

Lake Tyers Football Club (AFL), 66, 95, *95*, 369, 372
Landy-Ariel (Young), Julie, 282, *282*, 369, 374
Landy-Ariel, Nick, *24,* 282
Larkin, Fred, 218
Larkin, Irene, 218
Larkin, Steve, 215, 218, *218*, 369, 373
Lawton, Warren, 211, *211*, 363, 369, 374
Lea, Barry, 309
Leglise, Pat, 143
Leilani, Mitchell, 365
Lesiputty, Joanne, 12, 273, 338, *338,* 352, 369, 374
Lew Fatt, Bennie, 96, 115, 134, *134*, 369, 373
Lew Fatt, Clifford (Gympie), 96, *96,* 115, 126, 369, 373
Lew Fatt, Terry, 97, *97*, 115, 369, 373
Lew Fatt, Walter, 96
Lewis, Cameron, 98
Lewis, Chris, 63, 65, 98, *98*, 369, 374
Lewis, Clayton, 98
Lewis, Irwin, 98

Liddiard, David OAM, 283, *283*, 369, 374
Little, Anthony, 143*,* 364
Lloyd McDermott Rugby Development Team, 310
Logue, Kathleen, 12
Long, Michael, 64, 65, 87, 99, *99,* 103, 111, 115, 120, 369, 374
Longbottom, Kevin ('Lummy'), 255, 284, *284,* 290, 369, 373
Longbottom, Maurice, 358
Lovell, Anthony (Andy), 63, 359
Lovell, Gary, 357, 359
Lovell, Greg, 34, 63, 357, 359, *359*, 370
Lovett, Ted, 62
Lowien, Nicole, 23
Luke, Boyd*,* 364
Lyons, Cliff, 256, 285, *285,* 347, 369, 374

Madden, Lee, 344
Mailman, Wally, 225, *229*
Mainhard, Michael, 175, 177
Mainsbridge, Michelle, 199
Major, Greg, 196
Mallee Park Football Club, 66, 73, 100, *100*, 369, 373
Mansell, Brian, 22, 34, *34*, 369, 373
'Manuello,' 42
Marsh, Jack, 14, 42, 175, 176, 188, 189, *189*, 369, 371
Martin, Anthony, 35, *35,* 364, 369
Mason, Andrea, 12, 51, 249, *249*, 369, 373
Mason, Tiarna, 347
Matera, Peter, 64, 65, 101, *101*, 369, 374
Matera, Phillip, 64, 101
Matera, Wally, 64, 101
May, Ron, 354
Maynard, John 4, *5,* 227, 321
Maynard, Merv, 227, 236, *236*, 369, 373
Maynard, Neil, 63
Maynard, Ritchie, 63
McAdam, Gilbert, 4, 81, 102, *102*, 369, 374
McAdam, Greg, 81, 102

INDEX OF ABORIGINAL AND ISLANDER SPORTSPEOPLE

McArthur, Wally, 44, 51, 254, 286, *286*, 328, 369, 372
McCann, Shannon, 44, 368
McCarthy, Richard (Darby), 6, 49, 227, 237, *237*, 369, 373
McDermott, Lloyd, 4, 6, 157, 308, 309, 316, *316*, 369, 373
McDonald, Norman, 44, 62, 65, 66, 103, *103*, 369, 372
McDonald, Robert (Bobby), 43, 56, *56*, 369, 371
McDowell-White, William, 126
McGrady, Ewan, *256*, 267
McGrath, Ashley, 65
McGuiness, Kevin, 257
McGuire, John, 177, 190, *190*, 369, 373
McKellar-Nathan, Kelly, 12, 339, 369, 374
McKenna, Chris, 257
McLean, Michael, 65, 104, *104*, 369, 374
McLeod, Andrew, 63, 65, 73, 81, 105, *105*, 369, 374
Meninga, Mal AM, 9, 20, 29, 255, 287, *287*, 369, 374
Meninga, Norm, 29
Menzies, Karen, 12, 138, 321, 327, *327*, 369, 373
Michael, Stephen, 65, 76, 106, *106*, 369, 373
Mills, Patrick (Patty), 126, 135, *135*, 365, 369, 374
Minniecon, Tahj, 321
Molony, Russell, 28
Moran, Dennis, 347
Moran, Lance, 259
Moree Boomerangs (rugby league), 254
Morey, Sony, *63*, 81
Morgan, Ambrose, 258
Morgan, Bradley, 288
Morgan, Lionel, 157, 255, 261, 288, *288*, 369, 373
Moriarty, John AM, 51, 61, 321, 323, 328, *328*, 369, 372
Morissey, Jack, 235
Morrissey, Lorelle, 213, 217, 219, *219*, 369, 373

Morseu, Danny, 126, 133, 136, *136*, 138, 363, 369, 373
'Mosquito,' 146
Muir, Charlie, *42*, 44
Muir, Kane, 126
Muir, Robert, 62, 63
Mullagh, Johnny, 175, 179, 184, 191, *191*, 369, 371
Mullett (Drayton), Cheryl, 122, 123, *123*, 124, 137, 255, 369, 373
Mullett, David, 224
Mullett, Linda, 122
Mullett, Pauline, 13, 122
Mullett, Phillip, 122, 124
Mullett, Russell, 122, 124
Mullett, Sandra, 122, 123, 124, *124*, 137, 369, 373
Mundine, Anthony, 14, 143, 158, 162, *162*, 256, 257, 369, 373
Mundine, Beau, 347
Mundine, Tony OAM, 14, 143, 150, 162, 163, *163*, 269, 373
Murphy, Mahalia, 310
Murray, Jim, *43*, 44
Murray, Mick, 22
Musselwhite (Cosier), Michelle, 12, 137, *137*, 369, 374
Mussing, Walter, *9*, 254

Nagas, Ken, 257
Narkle, Dempsey, 107
Narkle, Keith, 107
Narkle, Phil, 64, 107, *107*, 369, 374
Narwan Football Club (rugby league), 289, *289*, 369, 373
Nelson, George, 44
New Norcia team (cricket), 192, *192*, 369, 371
Nicholls, Sir Douglas KCVO, OBE, KSTJ, 18, 43, 62, 103, 108, *108*, 121, 175, 369, 372
Nielsen, Dane, 256
Norford, Debbie, 12
North, Jade, 321, 329, *329*, 364, 369, 374

INDEX OF ABORIGINAL AND ISLANDER SPORTSPEOPLE

NSW Schools Aboriginal XI (cricket), 178, *178*

O'Loughlin, **Michael**, 65, 81, 91, 109, *109*, 369, 374

Olive, **Bruce**, 255, 290, *290*, 369

Oxenham, Steven, 24

Oxtoby, Tanya, 321

Page, Robbie, 28

Parker, **Shane**, 360, 362, *362*, 366, 369

Patrick, Marjorie, 208

Pattel, Neil, *145*

Peachey, **David**, 257, 291, *291*, 369, 374

Peachey, Tyrone, 258

Peachy, Eunice, 12

Peardon, Derek, 62, 63

Peats, Nathan, 256, 258

Peden, **Robert**, 143, 157, 164, *164*, 364, 366, 369, 374

Pepper, Phillip, 22

Peris, **Nova OAM**, 4, 14, 44, 213, 215, 217, 219, 220, 221, *221*, 336, 364, 366, 370, 374

Peris, **Brooke**, 14, 213, 215, 217, 219, 229, *220*, 365, 370, 374

Perkins, **Charles AO**, 4, 51, 176, 199, 259, 286, 321, 323, 328, 330, *330*, 370

Perry, Dale, 24

Phillips, Harry ('Wild Harry'), 224, *225*

Pickett, **Byron**, 65, 66, 79, 91, 110, *110*, 370, 374

Pitt, Eric, 255, 290

Pittman, James, 143, 364

Porch, Jon, 365

Porter, **Stacey**, 12, 340, *340*, 364, 370, 374

Preece, Cilla, 13

Prince, **Scott**, 257, 285, 292, *292*, 347, 370, 374

Prince, Stephen, 347

Ramalli, **Cecil** (**Cec**), 308, 309, 317, *317*, 370, 372

Redfern All-Blacks team (rugby league), 25, 254, 258, 259, *293*, 306, 370, 372

Reed, **Chad AM**, 21, 36, *36*, 370, 374

Reid (**Fowler**), **Amanda**, 22, 28, 212, *212*, 365, 370, 374

Reilly, Elkin, 62

Renouf, Charlie, 294

Renouf, **Steve**, 257, 278, 294, *294*, 370, 374

Reys, **Frankie**, 227, 238, *238*, 370, 372

Richards, Dale, *27*, 28

Richards, Max (Maxie), 15, 160

Richards, **Randall** (**Ron**), 6, 15, 141, 142, 143, 150, 151, 165, *165*, 170, 372

Rigney, Roger, 63, *65*, 81

Riley, **Samantha OAM**, 11, 20, 28, 37, *37*, 364, 366, 370, 373

Rioli, **Cyril**, 111, *111*, 370, 374

Rioli, **Maurice**, 65, 106, 111, 112, *112*, 115, 370, 373

Ritchie, Dennis, 15, *144*

Roberts, Alby, 15, 141, 143, 151

Roberts, Albert, 178

Roberts, **Brian**, 166, *166*, 370, 372

Roberts, **Francis** (**Frank**), 143, 148, 166, 167, *167*, 363, 370, 372

Roberts, James, 256

Robinson, Eric, 255, 290

Robinson, Will, 347

Roe, **Billy BEM**, 113, *113*, 115, 126, 138, 370, 372

Rose, **Lionel MBE**, 95, 122, 137, 142, 143, 144, 149, 168, *168*, 255, 370, 373

Rose, Norman, *229*

Ross, David, 309

Ross, Jesse, 143, 365

Ross, **Joshua** (**Josh**), 42, 44, 54, 57, *57*, 364, 370, 374

Rotumah, Tahlia, *203*, 364

Rovers Football Club (AFL), 114, *114*, 370, 373

Rowan, Barry, 196

Rowe, Paul, *22*

Russell, Ben, 23

Ryan, Jackie, 143, 160

Saddler, **Ron**, 255, 261, 295, *295*, 370, 373

Sailor, **Wendell**, 257, 296, *296*, 310, 370, 374

Sainsbury, Mark ('Sanga'), 28

Salvatori, Craig, 257, *257*

Sam, Doug, 366

INDEX OF ABORIGINAL AND ISLANDER SPORTSPEOPLE

Samuels, Billy, 141
Samuels, Charlie (**Sambo Combo**), 6, 42, 46, 58, *58*, 371, 370
Sands, Alfie, 142, 143, 145, *145,* 169
Sands, Clem, 169
Sands, Dave, 20, 142, 143, 145, 150, 169, *169,* 261, 370, 372
Sands, George, 169
Sands, Percy, 169
Sands, Russell Jr, *144*
Sands, Russell Sr, 149, 169, 170
Sarmardin, Cliff, 143
Saunders, Keith, *143*
Schreiber, Adam, 341, 343, *343*, 370, 373
Scott, Colin, 255, 297, *297*, 370, 373
Seden, Horrie, 195, 201, *201*, 370, 373
Semmens, Dean, 354, 355, *355,* 364, 370, 374
Sewter, Tania, 12
Shearer, Dale, 255, 298, *298*, 370, 373
Shiney (Shinal), 1
Silva, Rod, 257, 347
Simms, Eric, 255, 261, 284, 299, *299*, 370, 372
Simon, Craig, 347
Simon, John, *254,* 257, 347
Simon, Kyah, 321, *322,* 365
Simon, Mark, 347
Simon, Taleena, 310
Sing, Matt, 257, 300, *300*, 370, 374
Sinn, Bobby (**Robert Wills**), 143, 170, *170,* 370, 372
Smith, Delma, 273, 352, *352*, 370, 373
Smith, Rebecca (Beki), 365
Smith, Troy, 24
Smith, Wayne, 23
Soward, Jamie, 258, *258*
St Albans, Peter, 9, 227, 239, *239*, 370, 371
St Mary's Football Club (AFL), 63, 72, 89, 96, 97, 99, 112, 113, 115, *115*, 370, 372
Stanton, Tanisha, 310
Starr, Bridgette, 12, 321, 331, *331*, 365, 370, 374
Stevens, Norman, 143, 363
Stewart, Bruce (Larpa), 14, 255, *309,* 310

Stokes, Vanessa, 12
Suey, Nicole, 12
'Sundown,' 179
Swan, James, 143, 171, *171,* 364, 366, 370, 374
Swift, Joel, 354*,* 365

Tahu, Timana, 257, 296, 301, *301,* 310, 370, 374
Tallis, Gorden, 257, 302, *302*, 370, 374
Taylor, Ash, 256, 258
Thaiday, Sam, 255, 303, *303*, 370, 374
Thomas (**Coulthard**), **Faith**, 4, 14, 175, 176, 193, *193*, 370, 372
Thomas, Brian, 24
Thomas, Lardie, 22
Thomas, Lindsay, 65
Thomas, Nathan, 354, 356, *356,* 364, 370, 374
Thomas, William, 22
Thompson, Hector, 143, 146, 155, 172, *172,* 370, 373
Thurston, Jonathan, 256, 258, 278, 279, 304, *304*, 370, 373
Tindall, Billy, 225
Tranquille, Paul, 253, 281
Trindall, Darrell, 257, 347
Tucker, Priscilla, 13
Turner, Kyle, 256
Tutton, Mark, 353, *353*, 370, 373
Tutton, Reg, 353, *353*, 370, 373
Tutton, Steve, 353, *353*, 370, 373
Tweed Heads All-Blacks, 254, 259, 270, 288
Twopenny (**Murrumgunrrimin**), 175, 179, 194, *194*, 370, 371

Ugle, Henry, 22
Ugle, Troy, 64
Vander Kuyp, Kyle, 44, 59, *59,* 364, 366, 370, 374
Vickery, Erin, 12
Vigona, Benny, 115

Waite, Billy, 224, 240, *240*, 370, 372
Walford, Ricky, 256, 305, *305*, 370, 374

Walker, **Andrew** (AFL), 65, 116, *116*, 370, 374
Walker, **Andrew** (rugby), 257, 296, 310, 318, *318,* 347, 370, 374
Walker, Cody, 256
Walker, Kath (Oodgeroo Noonuccal), *177*
Walker, **Lloyd**, 309, 319, *319*, 370, 374
Walker, Margot, 249
Walker, **Shannon**, 26, 38, *38*, 370, 374
Wandin, Jimmy ('Juby'), 62, *63*
Wandin, **Robert** (**Bobby**), 60, *60*, 370, 372
Wanganeen, **Gavin**, 63, 65, 81, 87, 117, *117*, 370, 374
Warlosz, Letitia, 13
Watson, **Jack** ('**Sonny Carbine**'), 225, 241, *241*, 370, 372
Wehrman, Kasey, 321, *322,* 364
Wells, **Daniel**, 65, 118, *118*, 370, 374
Wesser, Rhys, *257,* 256
West, Darryl, 63
West, Jim ('Big Jim'), 143, *144*
West, Priscilla, 13
Whaler, Jessica, 354
White, **Darryl**, 65, 119, *119,* 126, 370, 374
Whittle, Timothy, 22
Wickey, Terry, 255
Widders, **Dean**, 258, 306, *306*, 370, 374
Williams, Brendan, 309, 366
Williams, **Claude**, 138, *138,* 370, 373
Williams, David, *322*
Williams, **Gary**, 143, 173, *173,* 270, 363
Williams, **Harry**, 321, 322, *322*, 370, 373
Williams, **Jesse**, 22, 39, *39*, 370, 374
Williams, **Jim** (rugby union), 26, 320, 366, 370, 374
Williams, **Jimmy** (roughriding), 14, 26, 225, 227, 234, 242, *242,* 370, 372
Williams, **Lydia**, 12, 321, 333, *333,* 365, 370, 374
Williams, **Mariah**, 213, 222, *222*, 365, 370, 374
Williams, **R S** (**Bobby**), 5, 42, 46, 174, *174,* 370, 373
Williamson, Harena, 12, 195, *195*

Willoughby, Keith, 114
Wilson, **Fred** ('**Mulga Fred**'), 6, 225, 243, *243*, 370, 372
Wilson, Wilbur, 63, *64*, 81, 249
Winch, Scott, 27
Windsor, **Harley**, 21, 24, 40, *40*, 370, 374
Wing, Craig, 257
Winmar, **Neil** (**Nicky**), *7,* 64, 65, 107, 119, 120, *120*, 370, 374
Wirrpanda, **David**, 65, 121, *121*, 370, 374
Wright, Catherine, 24
Wright, Mark, 255

Yeh, Kevin Yow, 255, 290
Young, Emma, 282
Young (**Anderson**), **Rebecca** (**Bec**), 282, 307, *307*, 310, 370, 374
Young, Khalen*,* 365